Lecture Notes in Computer Science 4906

Commenced Publication in 1973
Founding and Former Series Editors:
Gerhard Goos, Juris Hartmanis, and Jan van Leeuwen

Michael Cebulla (Ed.)

Object-Oriented Technology

ECOOP 2007 Workshop Reader

ECOOP 2007 Workshops
Berlin, Germany, July 30-31, 2007
Final Reports

 Springer

Volume Editor

Michael Cebulla
Technische Universität Berlin
Fakultät IV - Elektrotechnik und Informatik
Franklinstr. 28/29, 10587 Berlin, Germany
E-mail: mce@cs.tu-berlin.de

Library of Congress Control Number: 2008920684

CR Subject Classification (1998): D.1, D.2, D.3, F.3, C.2, K.4, J.1

LNCS Sublibrary: SL 2 – Programming and Software Engineering

ISSN   0302-9743
ISBN-10   3-540-78194-3 Springer Berlin Heidelberg New York
ISBN-13   978-3-540-78194-3 Springer Berlin Heidelberg New York

Springer is a part of Springer Science+Business Media

springer.com

© Springer-Verlag Berlin Heidelberg 2008
Printed in Germany

Typesetting: Camera-ready by author, data conversion by Scientific Publishing Services, Chennai, India
Printed on acid-free paper   SPIN: 12228454   06/3180   5 4 3 2 1 0

Preface

This volume contains the reports from the workshops held at the 21st European Conference on Object-Oriented Programming – ECOOP 2007 – at Technische Universität Berlin. Nineteen workshops were held in the course of this conference on July 30 and July 31, 2007, covering a large spectrum of hot research topics. As in previous editions of ECOOP, numerous scientists from academia and industry took the chance to present innovative and topical ideas in an environment offering optimal conditions for exciting discussions and fruitful interactions.

The Workshop Reader which contains the reports from the workshops has been a substantial part of the ECOOP conference for more than 10 years. During the pre-conference phase the workshop organizers are invited to author a report about their workshops where they have the opportunity to describe the state of the art, the discussions and the trends in the fields of their workshop. In addition some of the organizational aspects may be discussed.

This volume collects 19 reports from high-quality workshops whose topics were related to selected aspects in the field of object-oriented programming and technology. Following the example of previous workshop readers we introduced some notions in order to establish thematic clusters. These notions are (1) Programming Languages, (2) Aspects, (3) Formal Techniques, Roles, Components, (4) Software Engineering, and (5) Applications.

Three months after the conference we are now able to present the reports which describe the state of the art, the discussions and the relevant trends in the research fields addressed by the workshops. In sum, each of these reports thus contributes to a panoptic overview of the current tendencies in the lively field of object-oriented programming and technology. Readers from academia and industry who want to be informed about the current developments in this research area thus can highly profit from this volume.

This Workshop Reader of ECOOP 2007 is the result of the cooperation of a large group of people, which includes the workshop organizers, the co-authors of the reports and the participants who contributed to the workshops with their presentations and statements. Further, I wish to thank the Workshop Chairs Peter Pepper and Arnd Poetzsch-Heffter and the members of the Workshop Selection Committee. I am also indebted to Doris Fähndrich for her support.

November 2007   Michael Cebulla

Organization

Workshop Selection Committee

Peter Pepper (Co-chair)   Technische Universität Berlin, Germany
Arnd Poetzsch-Heffter
   (Co-chair)   Technische Universität Kaiserslautern,
                Germany
Uwe Aßmann   Technische Universität Dresden, Germany
Lodewijk Bergmans   University of Twente, Netherlands
Nick Mitchell   IBM T.J. Watson Research Center, USA
Mario Südholt   Ecole des Mines, Nantes/INRIA, France
Jan Vitek   Purdue University, USA

Sponsoring Institutions

Organization

In cooperation with

Supported by

 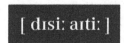 

Table of Contents

Formal Techniques, Roles, Components

Software Engineering

Applications

Lisp

Report on the 4th European Lisp Workshop at ECOOP 2007

Christophe Rhodes[1], Pascal Costanza[2], Theo D'Hondt[2], Arthur Lemmens[3], and Hans Hübner[4]

[1] Goldsmiths College, University of London, UK
[2] Vrije Universiteit Brussel, Belgium
[3] Amsterdam, Netherlands
[4] Berlin, Germany

Abstract. This report covers the activities of the 4th European Lisp and Scheme Workshop. We introduce the motivation for a workshop focussing on languages in the Lisp family, and mention relevant organisational aspects. We summarize the presentations and discussions, including Alexander Repenning's keynote talk, and provide pointers to related work and events.

1 Introduction

Lisp is one of the oldest computer languages still in use today. In the decades of its existence, Lisp has been a fruitful basis for language design experiments as well as the preferred implementation language for applications in diverse fields.

The structure of Lisp makes it easy to extend the language or even to implement entirely new dialects without starting from scratch. Common Lisp, with the Common Lisp Object System (CLOS), was the first object-oriented programming language to receive an ANSI standard and retains the most complete and advanced object system of any programming language, while influencing many other object-oriented programming languages that followed.

It is clear that Lisp is gaining momentum: there is a steadily growing interest in Lisp itself, with numerous user groups in existence worldwide, and in Lisp's metaprogramming notions which are being transferred to other languages, as for example in Aspect-Oriented Programming, support for Domain-Specific Languages, and so on.

The theme of the workshop held at ECOOP 2007 was intentionally broad, aimed at encouraging lively discussion between researchers proposing new approaches and practitioners reporting on their experience with the strengths and limitations of current Lisp technologies, with the intent to address the near-future evolution of Lisp-based languages and Object-Oriented techniques in research, industry and education.

M. Cebulla (Ed.): ECOOP 2007 Workshop Reader, LNCS 4906, pp. 1–6, 2008.
© Springer-Verlag Berlin Heidelberg 2008

2   Organisation

This section describes the organisational aspects of the workshop. The submitted papers and workshop slides can be found at the workshop's website: http://lisp-ecoop07.bknr.net/

2.1   Organisers

Pascal Costanza
pc@p-cos.net

Theo D'Hondt
tjdhondt@vub.ac.be

Arthur Lemmens
alemmens@xs4all.nl

Christophe Rhodes
c.rhodes@gold.ac.uk

Hans Hübner
hans.huebner@gmail.com

2.2   Call for Participation

> ... *please* don't assume Lisp is only useful for Animation and Graphics, AI, Bioinformatics, B2B and E-Commerce, Data Mining, EDA/Semiconductor applications, Expert Systems, Finance, Intelligent Agents, Knowledge Management, Mechanical CAD, Modeling and Simulation, Natural Language, Optimization, Research, Risk Analysis, Scheduling, Telecom, and Web Authoring just because these are the only things they happened to list.
>
> – Kent Pitman [1]

Potential attendees were invited to contribute a long paper (10 pages) presenting scientific or empirical results about Lisp- and Scheme-based uses or new approaches for software engineering purposes; a short essay (5 pages) defending a position about where research and practice based on Lisp should be heading in the near future; or a proposal for a breakout group describing an agenda for discussion.

Suggested topics for presented papers included: new language features or abstractions; experience reports or case studies; protocol metaprogramming and libraries; educational approaches; software evolution; development aids; persistent systems; dynamic optimization; implementation techniques; innovative applications; hardware support for lisp systems; macro-, reflective-, meta- and/or rule-based development approaches; and aspect-oriented, domain-oriented and generative programming.

2.3   Format

The workshop was held on the first day of ECOOP 2007; after a welcome, Alexander Repenning's keynote talk on Antiobjects was followed by presentations of the accepted paper contributions (described in Section 3); the workshop continued with a demonstration of current development in ContextL and Context-Oriented Programming, and concluded with an open discussion session.

3   Presentations

There were five accepted papers for presentation at the workshop, along with the invited keynote talk from Alexander Repenning and the demonstration of ContextL by Pascal Costanza and Robert Hirschfeld.

Antiobjects: Mapping Game AI to Massively Parallel Architectures using Collaborative Diffusion
Alexander Repenning, University of Colorado

Modern game consoles offer enormous computational power at very low cost but are difficult to program in a way to make full use of their parallel architectures. The notion of antiobjects is a computational metaphor useful to conceptualize and solve hard problems by swapping computational foreground and background. Similar to optical illusions based on potential confusion of background versus foreground perceptions, antiobjects are the inverse of what we perceive to be the computational objects.

If we implement, as part of a Pacman game, a ghost, we are tempted to think of the necessary behavior associated with the ghost object; if we simulate the behavior of an air bubble in a water glass we are tempted to think of how the bubble object should behave; if we build a soccer simulation we are tempted to think of how the soccer player objects should interact with the ball and other player objects. Antiobjects turn traditional object oriented thinking on its head. In the case of Pacman we put the main computation into the maze; to simulate the behavior of an air bubble we put the main computation into the water; to create a collaborative soccer game we put the main computation into the soccer field.

Putting computation into antiobjects, *e.g.* the maze, the water, and the soccer field, can substantially simplify hard problems in Artificial Intelligence and simulations. Moreover, the mapping of computation from a small number of objects to a much larger number of typically homogenous antiobjects can by employed to parallelize computation in ways that it can be executed on parallel architectures such as GPUs and multicore CPUs with very little overhead. A number of games implemented in AgentCubes which, in turn, is implemented in Lisp, will be presented.

Are functional languages a good way to represent productive meta-models?
Sebastién Mosser, CNRS, I3S Lab, Université Nice

Following Model Driven Development guidelines, developers will define meta-models, models and then implement transformations between models. Existing tools based on models require highly specific skills and knowledge from developers, and use Domain Specific Language (DSL) as the entry point for final users. Is it possible to describe DSL-based meta-models using functional programming concepts and languages? Can we do fast Model Driven Development using such techniques?

Dynamic data models: an application of MOP-based persistence in Common Lisp
Pierre Thierry, Thierry Technologies
Simon E.B. Thierry, LSIIT, Strasbourg, France

The data model of an application, the nature and format of data stored across executions, is typically a very rigid part of its early specification, even when prototyping, and changing it after code that relies on it was written can prove quite expensive and error-prone. Code and data in a running Lisp image can be dynamically modified. A MOP-based persistence library can bring this dynamicity to the data model. This enables to extend the easy prototyping way of development to the storage of data and helps avoiding interruptions of service. This article presents the conditions to do this portably and transparently.

CLOS discriminating functions and user-defined specializers
Christophe Rhodes, Goldsmiths College

We discuss the interrelationships of ANSI-standardized Common Lisp, the de facto standard AMOP, and the possibility for users to extend the mop:specializer metaobject class. We provide two simple examples, a specializer on a disjunction of classes and a simple pattern-matching specializer, noting the extent to which they can be accomodated with the standard mechanisms, detailing the work done to support that in a contemporary implementation of the CLOS MOP [2] in Steel Bank Common Lisp [3], and discussing the open problems and scope for resolving them.

Specialization Oriented Programming
Jim Newton, Cadence Design Systems

This paper presents an implementation of a generalization of OOP called SOP (Specialization Oriented Programming). Numerous examples are provided of how the system is used both at the meta programming level as well as the application level. The SOP system presented here implemented in Skill, a lisp interpreter product of Cadence Design Systems. The design of the infrastructure is understandable to those familiar with Common Lisp and CLOS (Common Lisp Object System), and have a high level understanding of the CLOS MOP (metaobject protocol [2]). Although the system's main applications are in Electronic Design Automation (EDA), no understanding of EDA is necessary to understand the concepts presented here.

Thread and Interrupt Safe Method Dispatch in PCL

Nikodemus Siivola, Steel Bank Studio Ltd

Efficient Method Dispatch in PCL [4] describes some of the strategies used in the original Portable Common Loops implementation of Common Lisp Object System and MOP. We informally discuss the modifications done in the Steel Bank Common Lisp version of PCL [5] to provide thread and interrupt safe method dispatch.

Recent Developments in ContextL and Context-oriented Programming

Pascal Costanza, Vrije Universiteit Brussel, Belgium
Robert Hirschfeld, HPI, Univerität Potsdam, Germany

There is an increased need for context-aware applications that can dynamically adjust their behavior to the context of their use. Two years ago, we introduced ContextL, our first programming language extension that explicitly supports Context-oriented Programming (COP). In COP, programs consist of partial class and method definitions that can be selected and combined at runtime as needed. Employing runtime adaptations to class and method definitions, COP does not only allow expressing context-aware behavior, but encourages continually adjusting behavior of programs according to their context.

With contemporary mainstream programming languages, the only way to introduce context-dependent behavior into a program is either by inserting if statements wherever necessary, violating one of the fundamental principles of object-oriented programming, namely to avoid explicit conditionals for achieving polymorphic behavior, or else by using design patterns to factor out the context-dependent behavior. Both approaches lead to unnecessarily complicated code that is hard to comprehend and even harder to maintain.

With COP on the other hand, we can modularize behavioral variations of a software system into layers. Layers are composed into or out of the system depending on the context apparent during program execution. We extend this idea by the notion of dynamically scoped layer activation, resulting in a viable approach to the expression of context-dependent behavior.

Since then, we have carried out a number of successful application and language extension experiments which show that the basic building blocks (layers and scoped activation) remain stable cornerstones in context-aware systems. Among others, we have implemented multiple context-dependent views on the same object, coordination of screen updates, discerning of phone calls based on the context of both callers and callees, and selecting context-dependent billing schemes. ContextL has also already been integrated into Lisp on Lines, a Web framework that is used in commercial applications. In other settings, we have developed ContextS for Smalltalk/Squeak, and context-oriented extensions of AmbientTalk. We have also taken first steps towards supporting the design and the requirements engineering phases to address the specific needs of context-aware applications.

4 Discussion

The papers by Rhodes and Newton were closely related and in many ways complementary: Rhodes describes the technical infrastructure necessary for a contemporary Common Lisp implementation to support user-defined specialization methods for generic functions, while Newton gave an experience report of developing and using a particular form of such specializers in a system of industrial interest, along with a description of the protocols used. It is hoped that a joint publication exploiting this complementarity will be forthcoming.

5 Related Events

There is an increasing scope for meetings organized around the broad theme of Computer Science and Lisp technology. In particular, the *International Lisp Conference* was held in April 2007 in Cambridge, UK[1], while 2008 will see the *European Common Lisp Meeting* held in Istanbul (along with a co-located symposium); meanwhile, Lisp user groups continue to thrive throughout the world, with frequent meetings of varying levels of formality.

References

1. Pitman, K.: Re: More lisp (2001),
   http://interviews.slashdot.org/comments.pl?sid=23357&cid=2543265
2. Kiczales, G., des Rivières, J., Bobrow, D.G.: The Art of the Metaobject Protocol. MIT Press, Cambridge (1991)
3. Newman, W.H., et al.: SBCL User Manual (2000), http://www.sbcl.org/manual/
4. Kiczales, G., Rodriguez, L.: Efficient method dispatch in PCL. In: Proceedings of the 1990 ACM conference on LISP and Functionl Programming (1992)
5. Siivola, N., et al.: SBCL Internals Manual (2005),
   http://www.sbcl.org/sbcl-internals/

---

[1] http://www.international-lisp-conference.org/2007/

Dynamic Languages and Applications
Report on the Workshop Dyla'07 at ECOOP 2007

Alexandre Bergel[1], Wolfgang De Meuter[2], Stéphane Ducasse[3],
Oscar Nierstrasz[4], and Roel Wuyts[5]

[1] Hasso-Plattner-Institut, Germany
Alexandre.Bergel@hpi.uni-potsdam.de
[2] Vrije Universiteit Brussel, Belgium
wdmeuter@vub.ac.be
[3] University of Savoie, France
stephane.ducasse@univ-savoie.fr
[4] University of Bern, Switzerland
oscar@iam.unibe.ch
[5] IMEC & Université Libre de Bruxelles, Belgium
roel.wuyts@ulb.ac.be

Abstract. Following last two years' workshop on dynamic languages at
the ECOOP conference, the Dyla 2007 workshop was a successful and
popular event. As its name implies, the workshop's focus was on dynamic
languages and their applications. Topics and discussions at the workshop
included macro expansion mechanisms, extension of the method lookup
algorithm, language interpretation, reflexivity and languages for mobile
ad hoc networks.

The main goal of this workshop was to bring together different dynamic language communities and favouring cross communities interaction. Dyla 2007 was organised as a full day meeting, partly devoted to
presentation of submitted position papers and partly devoted to tool
demonstration. All accepted papers can be downloaded from the workshop's web site.

In this report, we provide an overview of the presentations and a
summary of discussions.

1 Workshop Description and Objective

The advent of Java and C# has been a major breakthrough in the adoption
of some important object-oriented language characteristics. It turned academic
features like interfaces, garbage-collection and meta-programming into technologies generally accepted by industry. But the massive adoption of these languages
now also gives rise to a growing awareness of their limitations. On the one hand,
researchers and practitioners feel themselves wrestling with the static type systems, the overly complex abstract grammars, the simplistic concurrency pro-
visions, the very limited reflection capabilities and the absence of higher-order
language constructs such as delegation, closures and continuations. On the other

M. Cebulla (Ed.): ECOOP 2007 Workshop Reader, LNCS 4906, pp. 7–12, 2008.

hand, dynamic languages like Ruby and Python are getting ever more popular. Therefore, it is time for academia to move on and to help pushing such languages into the mainstream. On the one hand, this requires us to look back and pick up what is out there in existing dynamic languages (such as Lisp, Scheme, Smalltalk, Self,...) to be recovered for the future. On the other hand, it requires us to further explore the power of future dynamic language constructs in the context of new challenging fields such as aspect-orientation, pervasive computing, mobile code, context-aware computing, etc.

The goal of this workshop is to act as a forum where we can discuss new advances in the design, implementation and application of object-oriented languages that radically diverge from the statically typed class-based reflectionless doctrine. The goal of the workshop is to discuss new as well as older "forgotten" languages and features in this context. Topics of interest include, but are certainly not limited to:

- agents, actors, active object, distribution, concurrency and mobility
- delegation, prototypes, mixins
- first-class closures, continuations, environments
- reflection and meta-programming
- (dynamic) aspects for dynamic languages
- higher-order objects & messages
- ... other exotic dynamic features which you would categorize as OO
- multi-paradigm & static/dynamic-marriages
- (concurrent/distributed/mobile/aspect) virtual machines
- optimisation of dynamic languages
- automated reasoning about dynamic languages
- "regular" syntactic schemes (cf. S-expressions, Smalltalk, Self)
- Smalltalk, Python, Ruby, Scheme, Lisp, Self, ABCL, Prolog, ...
- ... any topic relevant in applying and/or supporting dynamic languages.

In addition to the organisers, the program committee of the workshop included:

- Johan Brichau (Universit catholique de Louvain, Belgium)
- Pascal Costanza (Vrije Universiteit Brussel, Belgium)
- Erik Ernst (University of Aarhus, Denmark)
- Robert Hirschfeld (Hasso-Plattner-Institut, University of Potsdam, Germany)
- Matthew Flatt (University of Utah, USA)
- Dave Thomas (Bedarra Research Labs, Canada)
- Laurence Tratt (King's College London, UK)

2   Content

This section describes the organisation aspects of the workshop. The accepted papers and workshop slides can be found on the workshop's website[1].

---
[1] dyla2007.unibe.ch

Contrasting compile-time meta-programming in Metalua and Converge – Fabien Fleutot and Laurence Tratt

> Powerful, safe macro systems allow programs to be programatically constructed by the user at compile-time. Such systems have traditionally been largely confined to LISP-like languages and their successors. In this paper we describe and compare two modern, dynamically typed languages Converge and Metalua, which both have macro-like systems. We show how, in different ways, they build upon traditional macro systems to explore new ways of constructing programs.

This presentation raised several questions regarding differences with other macro mechanism such as the one of Lisp-like languages. Also some issues regarding hygienic were successfully addressed by the presenter.

Relevant references related to this work are:

- The Converge programming language[2] [5]
- Metalua[3]

Collective Behavior – Adrian Kuhn

> When modelling a system, often there are properties and operations related to a group of objects rather than to a single object only. For example, given a person object with an income property, the average income applies to a group of persons as a whole rather than to a single person. In this paper we propose to extend programming languages with the notion of collective behavior. Collective behavior associates custom behavior with collection instances, based on the type of its elements. However, collective behavior is modeled as part of the element's rather than the collection's class. We present a proof-of-concept implementation of collective behavior using Smalltalk, and validate the usefulness of collective behavior considering a real-life case study: 20% of the case-studys domain logic is subject to collective behavior.

The need for an accurate comparison with C++ templates was a good point raised by the audience. This will be addressed in future work, which also cover a formal description of the semantics.

How to not write Virtual Machines for Dynamic Languages – Carl Friedrich Bolz and Armin Rigo

> Typical modern dynamic languages have a growing number of implementations. We explore the reasons for this situation, and the limitations it imposes on open source or academic communities that lack the resources

---

[2] convergepl.org/
[3] metalua.luaforge.net

to fine-tune and maintain them all. It is sometimes proposed that implementing dynamic languages on top of a standardized general-purpose object-oriented virtual machine (like Java or .NET) would help reduce this burden. We propose a complementary alternative to writing custom virtual machine (VMs) by hand, validated by the PyPy project: flexibly generating VMs from a high-level "specification", inserting features and low-level details automatically – including good just-in-time compilers tuned to the dynamic language at hand. We believe this to be ultimately a better investment of efforts than the development of more and more advanced general-purpose object oriented VMs. In this paper we compare these two approaches in detail.

This presentation was preceded with a very convincing demonstration. A small interpret for a reverse polish notation calculator has been implemented. Very aggressive optimisations resulted in an highly optimised generated compiler for this calculator. Discussions were mainly about VM performance, especially when compared with Hotspot. Implementing Java on top of PyPy in order to assess VM performance was suggested. More information about PyPy is available online[4].

On the Interaction of Method Lookup and Scope with Inheritance and Nesting – Gilad Bracha

Languages that support both inheritance and nesting of declarations define method lookup to first climb up the inheritance hierarchy and then recurse up the lexical hierarchy. We discuss weaknesses of this approach, present alternatives, and illustrate a preferred semantics as implemented in Newspeak, a new language in the Smalltalk family.

Pros and cons for having explicit *self* and *outer* sends in presence of virtual classes were presented. Several questions were raised from the large audience. Some of them covered the need of virtual classes in presence of closure. Gilad's answer was that each completes the other.

The Reflectivity: Sub-Method Reflection and more – Marcus Denker

Reflection has proved to be a powerful feature to support the design of development environments and to extend languages. However, the granularity of structural reflection stops at the method level. This is a problem since without sub-method reflection developers have to duplicate efforts, for example to introduce transparently pluggable type-checkers or fine-grained profilers.

This demo presents the Reflectivity, a Smalltalk system that improves support for reflection in two ways: it provides an efficient implementation of sub-method structural reflection and a simplified and generalized model of partial behavioral reflection. We present examples that use the new reflective features and discuss possible future work.

---

[4] codespeak.net/pypy/dist/pypy/doc/news.html and pypy.org

A number of questions were raised concerning the memory overhead. This appears to be largely due to the architecture of VMs, which are bytecode based. AST compression is part of the future work.

Some work related to this presentation[5] are *Sub-Method Reflection* [2], *Unanticipated Partial Behavioral Reflection* [4] and *Higher Abstractions for Dynamic Analysis* [3].

AmbientTalk/2: Object-oriented Event-driven Programming in Mobile Ad hoc Networks – Elisa Gonzalez

The recent progress of wireless networks technologies and mobile hardware technologies has led to the emergence of a new generation of applications. These applications are deployed on mobile devices equipped with wireless infrastructure which collaborate spontaneously with other devices in the environment forming mobile ad hoc networks. Distributed programming in such setting is substantially complicated by the intermittent connectivity of the devices in the network and the lack of any centralized coordination facility. Any application designed for mobile ad hoc networks has to deal with these new hardware phenomena. Because the effects engendered by such phenomena often pervade the entire application, an appropriate computational model should be developed that eases distributed programming in a mobile network by taking these phenomena into account from the ground up. In the previous ECOOP edition, we presented and demonstrated AmbientTalk, a distributed object-oriented programming language specially designed for mobile ad hoc networks. This demonstration showcases AmbientTalk/2, the latest incarnation of the AmbientTalk programming language which supplants its predecessor while preserving its fundamental characteristics. The language is still a so-called ambient-oriented programming language which allow objects to abstract over transient network failures. This demo will highlight the new design choices in AmbientTalk/2 and the rationale behind them. The most important ones are the adoption of an event-driven concurrency model that provides AmbientTalk/2 with finer grained distribution abstractions making it highly suitable for composing service objects across a mobile network, and the integration of leasing techniques for distributed memory management.

The demo is conceived as a hands-on experience in using the main features of the language where we show and discuss the following:

- The development of an ambient application from ground up that illustrates the simplicity and expressive power of AmbientTalk/2.
- While developing the application, participants become gradually acquainted with AmbientTalk/2's concurrency and distribution object models as well as the dedicated language constructs to deal with partial failures, service discovery and distributed memory management.

---

[5] `scg.unibe.ch/Research/Reflectivity/`

- We demonstrate how ambient applications actually behave in a real-life context by showing the execution of a small yet representative application on several portable devices such as laptops and smart phones.

AmbientTalk/2 is available at `prog.vub.ac.be/amop` with documentation and examples.

This very convincing demonstration used a personal digital assistant to communicate to a laptop using a wireless communication protocol. AmbientTalk [1] proves to be more expressive than traditional programming languages, especially about error recovery.

3   Conclusion

Most of the presentations and discussions of Dyla'07 present extensions of traditional dynamic languages. For example Metalua augments lua with an expressive macro mechanism, Converge is a Python dialect, Newspeak a Smalltalk dialect, and AmbientTalk a Self-like language. Comments and encouragement expressed by the audience asserted that dynamic languages constitute a viable research area. Efforts for experimentation and prototyping are greatly reduced in presence of a dynamic type system.

Dyla'07 lived up to its expectations, with high-quality presentations and demonstrations. Discussion were lively and stimulating.

Acknowledgments

We wish to thank Michael Cebulla and Jan Szumiec for their precious support. We also wish to thank all the participants.

References

1. Dedecker, J., Van Cutsem, T., Mostinckx, S., De Meuter, W., D'Hondt, T.: Ambient-oriented programming in ambienttalk. In: Thomas, D. (ed.) ECOOP 2006. LNCS, vol. 4067, Springer, Heidelberg (2006)
2. Denker, M., Ducasse, S., Lienhard, A., Marschall, P.: Sub-method reflection. Journal of Object Technology 6(9), 231–251 (2007)
3. Denker, M., Greevy, O., Lanza, M.: Higher abstractions for dynamic analysis. In: PCODA 2006. 2nd International Workshop on Program Comprehension through Dynamic Analysis, pp. 32–38 (2006)
4. Röthlisberger, D., Denker, M., Tanter, É.: Unanticipated partial behavioral reflection: Adapting applications at runtime. Journal of Computer Languages, Systems and Structures (to appear)
5. Tratt, L.: The Converge programming language. Technical Report TR-05-01, Department of Computer Science, King's College London (February 2005)

Multiparadigm Programming in Object-Oriented Languages: Current Research

Report on the Workshop MPOOL'07 at ECOOP 2007

Kei Davis[1] and Jörg Striegnitz[2]

[1] Los Alamos National Laboratory, Los Alamos, NM 87545, USA,
kei.davis@lanl.gov
http://www.ccs3.lanl.gov/~kei.html
[2] University Of Applied Sciences Regensburg
93053 Regensburg, Germany
joerg.striegnitz@informatik.fh-regensburg.de
http://homepages.fh-regensburg.de/~stj39817/people/striegnitz.html

Abstract. While OO has become ubiquitously employed for design, implementation, and even conceptualization, many practitioners recognize the concomitant need for other programming paradigms according to problem domain. Nevertheless, the choice of a programming paradigm is strongly influenced by the supporting programming language facilities. In turn, choice of programming language is usually highly constrained by practical considerations. We seek answers to the question of how to address the need for other programming paradigms, or even domain specific languages, in the general context of OO languages.

It is clear that this field is yet nascent: novel, disparate approaches and techniques are still being discovered or invented, and this very novelty adds a significant element of intellectual entertainment. This article describes the cross section of research efforts reported at the workshop on Multiparadigm Programming in Object-Oriented Languages held at the 2007 European Conference on Object-Oriented Programming.

Keywords: Object-oriented, multiparadigm, programming.

1 Introduction

While OO has become ubiquitously employed for design, implementation, and even conceptualization, many practitioners recognize the concomitant need for other programming paradigms according to problem domain. We seek answers to the question of how to address the need for other programming paradigms—or even domain specific languages—in the general context of OO languages.

Can OO programming languages effectively support other programming paradigms or the embedding of other languages? The answer seems to be affirmative, at least for some paradigms. For example, significant progress has been made for the case of functional programming in C++. Additionally, several efforts have been made to integrate support for other paradigms as a front-end for OO languages (the Pizza language, extending Java, is a well-known example).

M. Cebulla (Ed.): ECOOP 2007 Workshop Reader, LNCS 4906, pp. 13–26, 2008.

The object-oriented paradigm is in fact well suited to implementation of, and extension to include, other programming paradigms. Our previous years' MPOOL workshops at ECOOP'01, ECOOP'02, OOPSLA'03, ECOOP'04, and OOPSLA'05, and the DP-COOL workshop (Declarative Programming in the Context of Object-Oriented Languages) at PLI'03, bore out our hypothesis that there are many such efforts extant, including theoretical treatments, language implementations, practical (application) implementations, even long-extant (Budd) and new (Van Roy) textbooks on multiparadigm programming, though these texts are not specific to the embedding of other paradigms in an OO language.

In the past the calls for participation have generated sufficient response that a mild deselection process was required to maintain relevance, focus, and quality. This process was performed by the organizers who are recognized experts in the field. At the workshop about half of the time was used for presentation, the other half for discussion, and these discussions tend additionally to continue through breaks and lunch time. This topic seems to attract those interested in personally sharing and debating ideas, making the events enjoyable to organizers and the other participants alike. This year we had presenters not just from academia, but also government laboratories, the public sector, and private industry.

The home page for MPOOL'07, including the archive of papers and presentations, is `http://homepages.fh-regensburg.de/~mpool/mpool07/programme.html`.

2 Presentations

Here we provide synopses of the contributions.

2.1 An Overview of the Ciao Multiparadigm Language and Program Development Environment and Its Design Philosophy (Manuel Hermenegildo and the Ciao Development Team)

Ciao [7,5,1,3,6] is a modern, multiparadigm programming language with an advanced programming environment. Some of the fundamental aspects of the Ciao design, such as its multiparadigm nature and its extensibility, are based on the observation that a single set of basic, well-chosen features (a language kernel) can effectively support several programming paradigms and styles [7,5]. This approach is, of course, not exclusive to Ciao, but in Ciao the facilities that enable building from a simple kernel are very explicitly available (and their use encouraged) from the system programmer level to the application programmer level.

In fact, it is the extensibility of the kernel language that allows Ciao to be a truly multiparadigm programming system incorporating many of the best features of a number of programming paradigms. In particular, the system supports:

- *Functional Programming:* a set of packages allows defining functions, including higher-order (function abstractions and applications), and lazy evaluation (optionally). The same functional syntax can be used for both functions and predicates.

- *Logic Programming:* a set of packages provides support for full ISO-Prolog. However, using a different set of packages in a given module or class brings in instead pure logic programming without Prolog's impure features so that, e.g., a declarative I/O library can be loaded on top instead of the Prolog I/O. In addition to the usual depth-first, left-to-right execution regime of Prolog again by loading different packages several other computation rules are available such as breadth-first, iterative deepening, Andorra model, etc. (and tabling is currently being added). Higher-order logic programming with predicate abstractions is also supported.
- *Constraint Programming:* several constraint solvers and classes of constraints using these solvers are supported including clpq, clpr, and finite domains. The constraint languages and solvers are also extensible at the user level via attributed variables and/or Constraint Handling Rules (CHR) [4,9].
- *Object-Oriented Programming:* object-oriented programming is provided by the O'Ciao *class* and *object* packages [7]. These packages provide capabilities for class definition, object instantiation, encapsulation and replication of state, inheritance, interfaces, etc. These object-oriented features are also natural extensions of the underlying module system, extending its capabilities.
- *Concurrency, parallelism, and distributed execution:* other packages bring in concurrent, distributed, and parallel execution capabilities [2]. A notion of "active objects" also allows compiling objects so that they are ultimately mapped to a standalone process, which is transparently accessed by the rest of an application. In addition to characteristics that are specific to certain programming paradigms, many other additional features are available through libraries such as, e.g., feature terms (records), persistence, answer set programming, WWW programming, etc. Again, all of these can be activated or deactivated on a per-module or class basis.

In addition to characteristics that are specific to certain programming paradigms, many other additional features are available through libraries such as, e.g., feature terms (records), persistence, answer set programming, WWW programming, etc.

1. F. Bueno, D. Cabeza, M. Carro, M. Hermenegildo, P. López-García and G. Puebla (Eds.). The Ciao System. Ref. Manual (v1.13). Technical report, C. S. School (UPM), 2006. Available at http://www.ciaohome.org.
2. D. Cabeza and M. Hermenegildo. Distributed Concurrent Constraint Execution in the CIAO System. In Proc. of the 1995 COMPULOG-NET Workshop on Parallelism and Implementation Technologies, Utrecht, NL, September 1995. U. Utrecht / T.U. Madrid. Available from http://www.cliplab.org/.
3. The Ciao Development Team. The Ciao Multiparadigm Language and Program Development En vironment, November 2006. The ALP Newsletter 19(3). The Association for Logic Programming. Available from http://www.logicprogramming.org/newsletter/nov06/index.html.

4. Thom Frühwirth. Theory and practice of constraint handling rules. Journal of Logic Programming, Special Issue on Constraint Logic Programming, 37(1-3), October 1998.
5. M. Hermenegildo, F. Bueno, D. Cabeza, M. Carro, M. García de la Banda, P. López-García and G. Puebla. The CIAO Multi-Dialect Compiler and System: An Experimentation Workbench for Future (C)LP Systems. In Parallelism and Implementation of Logic and Constraint Logic Programming, pages 65-85. Nova Science, Commack, NY, USA, April 1999.
6. M. Hermenegildo and The Ciao Development Team. Why Ciao? - An Overview of the Ciao System's Design Philosophy. Technical Report CLIP7/ 2006.0, Technical University of Madrid (UPM), School of Computer Science, UPM, December 2006. Available from: http://cliplab.org/papers/ ciao-philosophy-note-tr.pdf.
7. M. Hermenegildo and The CLIP Group. Some Methodological Issues in the Design of CIAO - A Generic, Parallel, Concurrent Constraint System. In Principles and Practice of Constraint Programming, number 874 in LNCS, pages 123-133. Springer-Verlag, May 1994.
8. A. Pineda and F. Bueno. The O'Ciao Approach to Object Oriented Logic Programming. In Colloquium on Implementation of Constraint and LOgic Programming Systems (ICLP associated workshop), Copenhagen, July 2002.
9. Tom Schrijvers. Analyses, Optimizations and Extensions of Constraint Handling Rules. PhD thesis, K.U.Leuven, Belgium, June 2005.

2.2   A Multiparadigmatic Study of the Object-Oriented Design Patterns (Philippe Narbel)

The understanding of programming paradigms has not been fully established yet, though many mainstream languages, e.g. C++, Java, ML, offer more than one paradigm. This paper addresses this understanding problem through a programming experiment: considering the classic object-oriented programming (OOP) design patterns as described in the GoF book [1], we systematically look at them from the viewpoint of other paradigms, in particular the generic modular and the functional paradigms. The main results of this experiment are: (1) Many OO design pattern intents are meaningful in a more general setting than OOP, and as such they are good candidates for exploring paradigms; (2) Many OO design patterns have counterparts in generic modular programming, but with different properties, in particular with respect to dynamic/static behavior and type safety; (3) Some OOP design patterns can be implemented by using basic functional programming, justifying the idea that functional programming can also be seen as a simplified OOP having its place in a OO language; (4) Some OOP design patterns seem definitely associated with the OOP paradigm, stressing the intrinsic properties of this paradigm.

1. E. Gamma, R. Helm, R. Jonhnson, and J. Vlissides. Design Patterns. Addison-Wesley, 1995.

2.3   Implementing Self-adaptability in Context-Aware Systems (Boris Mejias and Jorge Vallejos)

Context-awareness is the property that defines the ability of a computing system to dynamically adapt to its context of use [1]. Systems that feature this property should be able to monitor their context, to reason about the changes in this context and to perform a corresponding adaptation. Programming these three activities can become cumbersome as they are tangled and scattered all over in the system programs.

We propose to model context-aware systems using feedback loops [2]. A feedback loop is an element of system theory that has been previously proposed for modelling self-managing systems. A context-aware system modelled as a feedback loop ensures that the activities of monitoring, reasoning and adapting to the context are modularised in independent components. In this work, we take advantage of such modularisation to explore different programming paradigms for each component of the loop. We believe that this model can be applied to other kind of applications where the use of different programming paradigms in one system is a straight forward solution.

1. Group, I.A., Ambient intelligence: from vision to reality (2003)
2. Van Roy, P., Self management and the future of software design. In: Formal Aspects of Component Software (FACS'06). (2006)

2.4   Type Erasure in C++: The Glue between Object-Oriented and Generic Programming (Thomas Becker)

C++ is a multi-paradigm language. The two main paradigms in C++ are object-oriented programming and generic programming. Many real-world C++ software projects use these two paradigms side by side. This creates considerable tension due to the fact that object-oriented programming is largely based on the judicious choice of types and hierarchies, while generic programming tends to cause an abundance of unrelated types. We show how type erasure can reconcile these conflicting tendencies. We present iterator type erasure as a concrete example that we have implemented and that is being used in production code at Zephyr Associates, Inc..

2.5   Runtime Polymorphic Generic Programming-Mixing Objects and Concepts in ConceptC++ (Mat Marcus, Jaakko Järvi and Sean Parent)

A long-held goal of software engineering has been the ability to treat software libraries as reusable components that can be composed with program-specific code to produce applications. The object-oriented programming paradigm offers mechanisms to write libraries that are open for extension, but it tends to impose intrusive interface requirements on the types that will be supplied to the library. The generic programming paradigm has seen much success in C++, partly due to the fact that libraries remain open to extension without imposing the need to intrusively inherit from particular abstract base classes. However, the static polymorphism that is a staple of programming with templates and overloads in C++, limits generic programming's applicability in application domains where more dynamic polymorphism is required. In this paper we present the **poly<>** library, a part of Adobe System's open source library ASL, that combines the object-oriented and generic programming paradigms to provide non-intrusive, transparent, value-based, runtime-polymorphism. Usage, impact on design, and implementation techniques are discussed.

2.6   Multi-language Library Development—From Haskell Type Classes to C++ Concepts (Marcin Zalewski, Andreas Priesnitz, Cezar Ionescu, Nicola Botta and Sibylle Schupp)

We define a mapping from generic Haskell specifications to C++ with concepts, a recent extension to C++, that can ultimately be automated. More specifically, we provide a translation from Haskell multi-parameter type classes with functional dependencies to **ConceptC++**. Our translation consists of three major parts: the division of Haskell class variables into **ConceptC++** concept parameters and associated types, the corresponding division of superclasses in the context of a type class, and the linearization of Haskell ASTs to the concrete syntax of **ConceptC++**. We also discuss cases in which there is no single correct translation from classes with functional dependencies to concepts. Our translation handles these cases in a reasonable way and is well-defined for the cases most common in practice. The translation is motivated by an ongoing project for distributed adaptive finite volume methods, in which software components are modeled in Haskell and implemented in C++.

2.7   Towards Equal Rights for Higher-Kinded Types (Adriaan Moors, Frank Piessens and Martin Odersky)

Abstract. Generics are a very popular feature of contemporary OO languages, such as Java, C# or Scala. Their support for genericity is lacking, however. The problem is that they only support abstracting over proper types, and not over generic types. This limitation makes it impossible to, e.g., define a precise interface for Iterable, a core abstraction in Scala's collection API. We implemented "type constructor polymorphism" in Scala 2.5, which solves this problem at the root, thus greatly reducing the duplication of type signatures and code.

2.8   Integrating Java and Prolog Using Java 5.0 Generics and Annotations (Maurizio Cimadamore and Mirko Viroli)

Although object-oriented languages are nowadays the mainstream for application development, several research contexts suggest that a multi-paradigm approach is worth pursuing. In particular, a declarative, logic-based paradigm could fruitfully add functionalities related to intelligence, adaptivity, and conciseness in expressing algorithms. In this paper we present a framework for enhancing interoperability between Java and Prolog, based on the tuProlog open-source Prolog engine for Java. Smoother language-interoperability is achieved through two stacked layers: (i) an API layer for automated mapping of Java types into Prolog types (and vice versa) and seamless exploitation of the Generic Collections Framework; and (ii) an annotation layer, that aims at truly extending Java programming with the ability of specifying Prolog-based declarative implementations of Java methods, relying on Java annotations.

2.9 Amalgamating the Session Types and the Object Oriented Programming Paradigms (Sophia Drossopoulou, Mariangiola Dezani-Ciancaglini and Mario Coppo)

We suggest an amalgamation of the session type and the object oriented paradigm whereby sessions are amalgamated with methods; where threads consist of the execution of session bodies on objects and communicate with each other through asynchronously sending/receiving objects on channels; where the choice on how to respond to a session request is based on the name of the request and the class of the object receiving the request; where the choice on how to continue a session is made on the basis of the class of the object sent/received; and where sessions are not first class, but can be delegated to other sessions. We demonstrate our ideas through a small language, STOOP, and an example. We formalize a smaller calculus, Feather^{STOOP}, and give a formal definition, and prove subject reduction and progress. The latter property is notoriously difficult and sometimes impossible to achieve in sessions languages, however it holds in Feather^{STOOP}.

2.10 A Static Framework for Scalable Emulation of Evaluation Semantics (Andreas P. Priesnitz)

Abstract. The power of a programming language depends to a significant extent on its semantics of expression evaluation. It is therefore rewarding and popular to emulate nonexistent evaluation features by library constructs. For instance, one can emulate the functional programming idiom of a (partially) unbound function in an imperative language by providing special functor types. Their instances are created anonymously and represent late bindings if used as function arguments. This approach is of limited scalability to further emulations in this style, because each function implementation has to account for any possible combination of such special argument types. We propose a library-based framework that systematically supports the emulation of evaluation semantics without increasing the complexity order of function implementations. C++ as implementation language allows applying these constructs statically and therefore to avoid performance penalties at run time.

2.11 Improving Large Vector Operations with C++ Expression Template and ATLAS (L. Plagne and F. Hülsemann)

Abstract. This paper describes a short and simple way of improving the performance of vector operations (e.g. $X = aY + bZ + \ldots$) applied to large vectors.

The principle is to take advantage of high performance vector copy operation provided by the ATLAS library [1] used as a kernel for a C++ Expression Template (ET) mechanism. The proposed ET implementation that involves a simple blocking technique, leads to significant performance increase compared to existing implementations (up to 50%) and extends the ATLAS scope.

1. Whaley, R.C., Petitet, A. Minimizing development and maintenance costs in supporting persistently optimized BLAS. Software: Practice and Experience 35(2) (February 2005) 101-121.

ATLAS web page: http://math-atlas.sourceforge.net.

2.12 Lazy Data Types in C++ Template Metaprograms (Adam Sipos, Norbert Pataki, and Zoltán Porkoláb)

C++ is a multiparadigm language. It supports among others the generative paradigm by enabling the creation of programs executed in compile-time. This is called template metaprogramming (TMP), and is based on the language's flexible generic construct, the template.

As the implementation of compile-time recursion and conditional statements is possible, TMP is Turing-complete. Accordingly, in theory the expressive power of TMP is equivalent to that of today's programming languages. On the other hand, TMP is not yet a widely used programming style, so the boundaries of its practical applicability are yet to be determined. TMP has already been successfully applied in a number of important fields: expression templates (optimizing calculations in compile-time [9]), compile-time code adaptation, implementation of active libraries [6], and others.

Compile-time algorithms naturally require compile-time data structures. As regular runtime data types handle objects, these TMP structures store types. Among the most important are typelist[2], and the Boost::MPL library's containers (list, vector, and others)[4].

Due to the similarities between TMP and functional programming (FP), metaprogramming is indeed many times regarded as a pure functional language. The common properties include referential transparency (metaprograms have no side effects) and the lack of variables, loops, and assignments. In our opinion, the similarities require a more thorough examination, as the metaprogramming realm could benefit from the introduction and library implementation of more functional techniques.

At the same time, it would not be the first time, for C++ to utilize functional language-like behavior. Functional C++ (FC++) [8] is a library introducing functional programming tools to C++, including currying, higher-order functions, and lazy data types. FC++, however, is a runtime library, and our aim is to utilize functional programming techniques in compile-time.

One of the main reasons for our research is the introduction of compile-time lazy data types. Note that the aforementioned typelist and Boost::MPL containers are finite structures, holding a limited number of types at the same time.

Contrarily, lazy data types are finite structures representing an infinite number of elements, e.g. all natural numbers. A common example for the usage of lazy lists is the implementation of the Eratosthenes sieve algorithm producing arbitrarily many primes.

In order to demonstrate the connection between TMP and FP, and the possiblity of lazy data types, we have impemented a simplified version of the Clean [5] functional language's logic. Clean programs are represented by an expression graph in the compiler. This graph is constantly rewritten in runtime based on the user program code.

Our implementation relies on pattern matching using template partial specializations. For demonstration purposes we have also implemented the prime sieve with a functional-like programming logic. In the future we intend to refine the syntax with preprocessor macros, to reach an embededd Clean-like syntax.

1. Abrahams, D., Gurtovoy, A.: C++ template metaprogramming, Concepts, Tools, and Techniques from Boost and Beyond. Addison-Wesley, Boston (2004)
2. Alexandrescu, A.: Modern C++ Design: Generic Programming and Design Patterns Applied. Addison-Wesley, Boston (2001)
3. ANSI/ISO C++ Committee. Programming Languages—C++ ISO/IEC 14882: 1998(E). American National Standards Institute (1998)
4. Boost Metaprogramming library,
   http://www.boost.org/libs/mpl/doc/index.html
5. Brus, T.H., et al.: CLEAN: A language for functional graph rewriting. In: Kahn, G. (ed.) FPCA 1987. LNCS, vol. 274, pp. 364–384. Springer, Heidelberg (1987)
6. Czarnecki, K., et al.: Generative Programmind and Active Libraries. Springer, Heidelberg (2000)
7. Karlsson, B.: Beyond the C++ Standard Library, A Introduction to Boost. Addison-Wesley, Boston (2005)
8. McNamara, B., Smaragdakis, Y.: Functional programming in C++. In: Proceedings of the fifth ACM SIGPLAN International Conference on Functional Programming, pp. 118–129 (2000)
9. Veldhuizen, T.: Expression Templates. C++ Report 7(5), 26–31 (1995)

3   Authors Index

Ádám Sipos
Faculty of Informatics
Eötvös Loránd University
shp@inf.elte.hu

Thomas Becker
Zephyr Associates, Inc.
mpool@thbecker.net

Nicola Botta
Potsdam Institute for Climate Impact Research
botta@pik-potsdam.de

Mario Coppo
Dipartimento di Informatica
Université di Torino

Maurizio Cimadamore
DEIS, Cesena
Université degli Studi di Bologna
maurizio.cimadamore@unibo.it

Mariangiola Dezani-Ciancaglini
Dipartimento di Informatica
Université di Torino

Sophia Drossopoulou
Department of Computing
Imperial College London

Manuel Hermenegildo
Facultad de Informática
Universidad Politécnica de Madrid
herme@fi.upm.es

F. Hülsemann
Electricité De France R & D
Clamart France
frank.hulsemann@edf.fr

Cezar Ionescu
Potsdam Institute for Climate Impact Research
ionescu@pik-potsdam.de

Jaakko Järvi
Texas A & M University
jarvi@cs.tamu.edu

Mat Marcus
Adobe Systems Inc.
mmarcus@adobe.com

Boris Mejás
Université catholique de Louvain
boris.mejias@uclouvain.be

Adriaan Moors
Katholieke Universiteit Leuven
adriaan@cs.kuleuven.be

Philippe Narbel
LaBRI, University of Bordeaux
narbel@labri.fr

Martin Odersky
Ecole Polytechnique Federale de Lausanne
martin.odersky@epfl.ch

Sean Parent
Adobe Systems Inc.
sparent@adobe.com

Norbert Pataki
Faculty of Informatics
Eötvös Loránd University
patakino@elte.hu

Frank Piessens
Katholieke Universiteit Leuven
frank@cs.kuleuven.be

L. Plagne
Electricité De France R & D
Clamart France
laurent.plagne@edf.fr

Zoltán Porkoláb
Faculty of Informatics
Eötvös Loránd University
gsd@elte.hu

Andreas Priesnitz
Dept. of Computer Science and Engineering
Chalmers University of Technology
priesnit@cs.chalmers.se
Sibylle Schupp
Chalmers University of Technology
schupp@cs.chalmers.se

Ádám Sipos
Faculty of Informatics
Eötvös Loránd University
shp@inf.elte.hu

Jorge Vallejos
Vrije Universiteit Brussel
jvallejo@vub.ac.be

Mirko Viroli
DEIS, Cesena

Université degli Studi di Bologna
mirko.viroli@unibo.it

Marcin Zalewski
Chalmers University of Technology
zalewski@cs.chalmers.se

4   The Organizers

Kei Davis, co-chair, Ph.D. Computing Science (Glasgow), M.Sc. Computation (Oxford), is a research scientist at Los Alamos National Laboratory, U.S.A. He has conducted research in object-oriented and functional language technology for natural language processing, large system design and implementation, scripting, signal processing, parallel discrete-event simulation, and parallel/high performance scientific computing.

Dr. Kei Davis
Advanced Computing Laboratory, CCS-1
Los Alamos National Laboratory
Los Alamos, NM 87545, USA
kei.davis@lanl.gov
http://www.c3.lanl.gov/~kei

Jörg Striegnitz, co-chair, received his Diploma and Ph.D. in Computer Science from University of Technology at Aachen, Germany. He is now working as a professor for theoretical computer science and programming languages at the University Of Applied Sciences in Regensburg, Germany. His research work includes the integration of programming languages by means of partial evaluation, the application of multiparadigm programming to real world problems, the optimization of programs, and parallel/high performance scientific computing. He authored the FACT! and the EML C++ libraries, that allow for functional programming style with C++.

Prof. Jörg Striegnitz
University Of Applied Sciences Regensburg
93053 Regensburg, Germany
joerg.striegnitz@informtik.fh-regensburg.de
http://homepages.fh-regensburg.de/ stj39817/people/striegnitz.html

Timothy Budd is an Associate Professor of Computer Science at Oregon State University. He is the author of over a dozen books dealing with programming languages and Object-Oriented programming. His 1995 book "Multiparadigm Programming in Leda" laid the foundations for the field of Multiparadigm Programming. He has also presented tutorials on Multiparadigm Programming at previous OOPSLA conferences.

Prof. Timothy Budd
School of Electrical Engineering and Computer Science

Oregon State University
Corvallis, OR 97331-5501, USA

Jaakko Järvi is an assistant professor in the Department of Computer Science
at Texas A&M University. He has a Ph.D. in Computer Science from the University of Turku, Finland. His research interests include generic programming,
programming languages, and software construction in general. He actively participates in the C++ standards committee and is a contributing member of the
C++ Boost community, where his previous work has included template libraries
that bring functional programming features to C++.

Dr. Jaakko Järvi
Department of Computer Science
Texas A&M University
College Station, TX 77843-3112, USA
Email: jarvi@cs.tamu.edu
http://faculty.cs.tamu.edu/jarvi

Zoltán Horváth OC Co-chair of ECOOP 2001, Member of AITO, Designer of
programming language concepts connecting distributed functional programming
with OO programming.

Prof. Zoltán Horváth, PhD, habil.
Department of Programming Languages and Compilers
Faculty of Informatics
University Eötvös Loránd of Sciences, Budapest, Hungary
hz@inf.elte.hu
http://people.inf.elte.hu/hz

Herbert Kuchen received his Diploma, Ph.D., and Habilitation in computer
science from the University of Technology at Aachen, Germany. He is now working as a professor for computer science at the University of Münster, Germany.
He is interested in algorithmic skeletons for parallel programming and in the
integration of programming paradigms, in particular in the combination of functional, logic, and object oriented programming, and he has been on many program committees of corresponding conferences. Recently, he developed a C++
skeleton library.

Prof. Herbert Kuchen
University of Münster
Leonardo Campus 3
48149 Münster, Germany
kuchen@uni-muenster.de

Peter Van Roy's research interests are in programming language design and
implementation, system building, distributed computing, human-computer
interfaces, constraint programming, and computer science education. He has

numerous publications at international level in all these areas. He developed Aquarius Prolog, the first Prolog compiler to generate code competitive in performance with C compilers. He is codeveloper of Wild_Life, an implementation of the logic-functional language LIFE. He is codesigner of the distribution model of the Mozart Programming System, an advanced platform for transparent distributed programming that is robust and efficient, and is based on the multi-paradigm language Oz. He holds one patent in graphic design and developed the commercial Macintosh application FractaSketch based on this patent. He is coauthor of "Concepts, Techniques, and Models of Computer Programming," a comprehensive textbook that uses a novel concepts-based approach to place all major programming paradigms in a uniform framework that is both practical and theoretically sound.

Van Roy has an M.S. and Ph.D. from the University of California, Berkeley (1984 and 1990), and a French "Habilitation a Diriger des Recherches" from the Universite Paris VII Denis Diderot (1996). Since 1996 he is professor at the Catholic University of Louvain in Louvain-la-Neuve, Belgium. He is partner or principal investigator for numerous projects, is a member of the Mozart Consortium, and leads a team of ten researchers.

Prof. Peter Van Roy
Catholic University of Louvain
Department of Computing Science and Engineering
B-1348 Louvain-la-Neuve, Belgium
pvr@info.ucl.ac.be
http://www.info.ucl.ac.be/people/cvvanroy.html

Equation-Based Object-Oriented Languages and Tools
Report on the Workshop EOOLT 2007 at ECOOP 2007

Peter Fritzson[1], David Broman[1], François Cellier[2],
and Christoph Nytsch-Geusen[3]

[1] Linköping University, Sweden
{davbr,petfr}@ida.liu.se
[2] ETH Zurich, Switzerland
fcellier@inf.ethz.ch
[3] Fraunhofer FIRST, Germany
christoph.nytsch@first.fraunhofer.de

Abstract. EOOLT'2007 was the first edition of the ECOOP-EOOLT workshop. The workshop is intended to bring researchers associated with different equation-based object-oriented (EOO) modeling languages and different application areas making use of such languages together. The aim of the workshop is to explore common grounds and derive software design principles that may make future EOO modeling languages more robust, more versatile, and more widely accepted among the various stakeholders. At EOOLT'2007, nineteen researchers with diverse backgrounds and needs came together to present and discuss fourteen different concept papers grouped into the four topic areas of integrated system modeling approaches; hybrid modeling and variable structure systems; modeling languages, specification, and language comparison; and tools and methods.

1 Objectives and Call for Papers

Computer aided modeling and simulation of complex systems, using components from multiple application domains, such as electrical, mechanical, hydraulic, control, etc., have in recent years witnessed a significant growth of interest. In the last decade, novel equation-based object-oriented (EOO) modeling languages, (e.g., Modelica, gPROMS, and VHDL-AMS) based on acausal modeling using equations have appeared. Using such languages, it has become possible to model complex systems covering multiple application domains at a high level of abstraction through reusable model components.

The interest in EOO languages and tools is rapidly growing in the industry because of their increasing importance in modeling, simulation, and specification of complex systems. There exist several different EOO language communities today that grew out of different application areas (multi-body system dynamics, electronic circuit simulation, chemical process engineering). The members of these disparate communities rarely talk to each other in spite of the similarities of their modeling and simulation needs.

M. Cebulla (Ed.): ECOOP 2007 Workshop Reader, LNCS 4906, pp. 27–39, 2008.

The workshop is concerned with, but not limited to, the following themes:

- Acausality and its role in model reusability.
- Component systems for EOO languages.
- Database lookup and knowledge invocation.
- Discrete-event and hybrid modeling using EOO languages.
- Embedded systems.
- EOO language constructs in support of simulation, optimization, diagnostics, and system identification.
- EOO mathematical modeling vs. UML modeling.
- Equation-based languages supporting DAEs and/or PDEs.
- Formal semantics of EOO related languages.
- Multi-resolution / multi-scale modeling using EOO languages.
- Numerical coupling of EOO simulators and other simulation tools.
- Parallel execution of EOO models.
- Performance issues.
- Programming / modeling environments.
- Real-time simulation using EOO languages.
- Reflection and meta-programming.
- Reuse of models in EOO languages.
- Table lookup and interpolation.
- Type systems and early static checking.
- Verification.

The EOOLT workshop series aims at bringing these different communities together to discuss their common needs and goals as well as the algorithms and tools that best support them.

The workshop is intended to become recurrent since this is an important and growing area of research and technology development.

The EOOLT Workshop addresses the current state of the art of EOO modeling languages as well as open issues that currently still limit the expression power and usefulness of such languages through a set of full-length presentations, short position papers, and forum discussions.

Papers and contributions are welcome that offer presentations and discussions of existing languages and tools, their capabilities and limitations; reports on practical experience; demonstrations of languages, tools, ideas, and concepts; positions related to relevant questions; and discussion topics.

Despite the short deadlines and the fact that this is a new not very established workshop series, there was a good response to the call-for-papers. Thirteen papers and one presentation were accepted to the workshop program. All papers were subject to reviews by the program committee.

The workshop program started with a welcome and introduction to the area of equation-based object-oriented languages, followed by paper presentations and discussion sessions after presentations of each set of related papers. EOOLT'2007 was hosted by the Technical University of Berlin, in conjunction with the ECOOP'2007 conference.

2 Organizers

Peter A. Fritzson received his M.Sc. in engineering 1975 and Ph.D. in computer science 1984, both from Linköping University. He is Professor and Director of the Programming Environment Laboratory (Pelab), at the Department of Computer and Information Science, Linköping University, Sweden. Peter Fritzson is vice chairman of the Modelica Association, an organization he helped to establish, and during 1999-2007 served as chairman of the Scandinavian Simulation Society, and secretary of the European simulation organization, EuroSim. His main area of interest is software engineering, especially languages, programming and debugging tools and environments; during recent years with special emphasis on modeling and simulation, and is currently leading the OpenModelica modeling and simulation open source tool effort. Professor Fritzson has authored or co-authored more than 180 technical publications, including 13 books/proceedings. In 1994 he published a textbook "Principles of Object-Oriented Modeling and Simulation with Modelica", 939 pages, Wiley-IEEE Press. He has served as chair of a number of international conferences and workskops, and took the initiative to start the AADEBUG and EOOLT workshop series.

Prof. Dr.-Ing. Peter Fritzson
Programming Environment Laboratory (PELAB)
Linköping University
SE-581 83 Linköping
Sweden
Phone: +46(13)281484
Fax: +46(13)285899
Mobile: +46(708)281484
Email: petfr@ida.liu.se
URL: http://www.ida.liu.se/labs/pelab/

François E. Cellier received his BS degree in electrical engineering in 1972, his MS degree in automatic control in 1973, and his PhD degree in technical sciences in 1979, all from the Swiss Federal Institute of Technology (ETH) Zurich. Dr. Cellier worked at the University of Arizona as professor of Electrical and Computer Engineering from 1984 until 2005. He recently returned to his home country of Switzerland where he assumed a position with ETH Zurich. Dr. Cellier's main scientific interests concern modeling and simulation methodologies, and the design of advanced software systems for simulation, computer aided modeling, and computer-aided design. Dr. Cellier has authored or co-authored more than 200 technical publications, and he has edited several books. He published a textbook on Continuous System Modeling in 1991 and a second textbook on Continuous System Simulation in 2006, both with Springer-Verlag, New York. He served as general chair or program chair of many international conferences, and served recently as president of the Society for Modeling and Simulation International.

Prof. Dr. François E. Cellier
Institute of Computational Science

CAB G82.1
ETH Zürich
CH-8092 Zürich
Switzerland
Phone: +41(44)632-7474
Fax: +41(44)632-1374
Mobile: +41(79)416-7546
Email: fcellier@inf.ethz.ch
URL: http://www.inf.ethz.ch/~fcellier/

Christoph Nytsch-Geusen received his PhD in Engineering at Technology University of Berlin in 2001. Since 2001 he is responsible for the development of simulation methods and simulation tools for complex technical systems at Fraunhofer FIRST. These research activities are focused on object oriented modeling, model compilers, simulation runtime systems, simulator coupling and the integration of simulation tools in the design process of technical systems. He was the leader of a joint project of six Fraunhofer Institutes (2004–2007), within the Modelica-based simulation tool MOSILAB was developed. At University of Arts Berlin he holds a chair in "Building Services Engineering" since 2007, where his research activities are focused on modeling and simulation of complex energy supply systems for single buildings and whole districts.

Prof. Dr.-Ing. Christoph Nytsch-Geusen
Fraunhofer Institute for Computer Architecture and Software Technology
D-12489 Berlin, Germany
Phone +49 (0) 30/6392-1919
Telefax: +49 (0) 30/6392-1805
Email: christoph.nytsch@first.fraunhofer.de
Internet: http://www.first.fraunhofer.de

David Broman is currently pursuing his PhD in computer science at Linköping University, Sweden, where he also received his M.Sc. degree in 2001. Before he started his PhD work, he worked as a software engineer and technical project manager for a security company in Stockholm. David's current research interest is focusing on language semantics and type systems of equation-based object-oriented languages. He is a member of the Modelica Association and has been active in the Modelica design group since 2005.

David Broman
Department of Computer and Information Science
Linköping University
SE-581 83 Linköping
Sweden
Phone: +46(0)13-285724
Fax: +46(0)13-285899
Mobile: +46(0)707-909075
URL: http://www.ida.liu.se/~davbr/

3 Participants

The number of participants of this first EOOLT workshop was 19, of which 18 were physically present and one connected by electronic web conferencing; 17 are present in the table below.

Name	Affiliation	Country	Email
Bernhard Bachmann	University of Applied Sciences, Bielefeld	Germany	bernhard.bachmann@fh-bielefeld.de
Felix Breitenecker	Vienna University of Technology	Austria	felix.breitenecker@tuwien.ac.at
David Broman	Linköping University	Sweden	davbr@ida.liu.se
François E. Cellier	ETH	Switzerland	fcellier@inf.ethz.ch
Peter Fritzson	Linköping University	Sweden	petfr@ida.liu.se
Ramine Nikoukhah	Inria	France	ramine.nikoukhah@inria.fr
Henrik Nilsson	University of Nottingham	UK	nhn@cs.nott.ac.uk
Christoph Nytsch-Geusen	University of Fine Arts, Berlin,	Gerrmany	christoph.nytsch@first.fraunhofer.de
Adrian Pop	Linköping University	Sweden	adrpo@ida.liu.se
Olaf Enge-Rosenblatt	Fraunhofer Institute for Integrated Circuits	Germany	olaf.enge@eas.iis.fraunhofer.de
Miguel A. Rubio	UNED	Spain	marubio@dia.uned.es
Carl-Johan Sjöstedt	Royal Institute of Technology	Sweden	carlj@md.kth.se
Günther Zauner	Vienna University of Technology	Austria	guenther.zauner@drahtwarenhandlung.at
Dirk Zimmer	ETH	Switzerland	dzimmer@inf.ethz.ch
Johan Åkesson	Lund University	Sweden	jakesson@control.lth.se
Michael Cebulla	TU Berlin	Germany	mce@cs.tu-berlin.de
Gilad Bracha	Cadence	U.S.A.	gilad@bracha.org

4 Contributions

All papers are published electronically by Linköping University Electronic Press and available in the electronic proceedings at http://www.ep.liu.se/ecp/024/.

All presentations (together with the papers) are also available at the EOOLT'2007 web site: http://www.ida.liu.se/labs/pelab/conf/eoolt07/.

The workshop sessions are briefly described below. Each session started with paper presentations, followed by a discussion related to the topic of that particular session. Some discussion also took place during the paper presentations.

4.1 Integrated System Modeling Approaches

This session grouped paper that especially emphasized integrated modeling tools for complex systems and integrated modeling environments aimed towards the whole development process. Session chair: Peter Fritzson.

In "The use of the UML within the modeling process of Modelica models," Christoph Nytsch-Geusen presented work on an integration of a subset of UML and Modelica called UML^H. The UML class diagrams, state chart diagrams, and collaboration diagrams are integrated in an extended subset of Modelica including special UML^H, graphical annotations, and language extensions for statechart support. An example model and simulation of a Pool-Billiard game using this approach was shown.

In "Towards Unified System Modeling with the ModelicaML UML Profile," Adrian Pop, David Akhvlediani, and Peter Fritzson presented the new ModelicaML UML profile, based on both SysML and Modelica, with (currently incomplete) implementation in Eclipse based on the Eclipse Modeling Framework EMF. This integrates the graphical software modeling of UML with Modelica modeling of physical systems, thus giving a rather complete integrated approach for full software-hardware complex system development.

In "Developing Dependable Automotive Embedded Systems using the EAST-ADL," Carl-Johan Sjöstedt, De-Jiu Chen, Phillipe Cuenot, Patrick Frey, Rolf Johansson, Henrik Lönn, David Servat and Martin Törngren presented the EAST-ADL modeling language (Embedded Automotive Systems – Architectural Description Language), which is structured in five levels: vehicle, analysis, design, implementation, and operation. Since EAST-ADL is partly implemented as a UML2 profile, an attempt to model a small electrical circuit using SysML parametric diagrams was presented. Difficulties were observed because of the absence of flow variables in SysML. The solution of using flow-split is rather cumbersome.

During the following discussion some questions were raised. For example, why not use the SysML profile instead of UML^H? The explanation is that UML^H was developed much earlier than SysML, partly based on the Smile system and later the MOSI-LAB effort. The second talk also presented an integration approach between Modelica and UML, now based on SysML and Eclipse. There was a question regarding the difference between UML and Modelica connection diagrams. Why do you have both? The UML-style is less compact but better known to software developers, the Modelica-style is common among engineers and usually more compact.

Regarding the third talk, there were some questions – why is EAST-ADL needed, since we have Modelica, VHDL-AMS, SysML etc. EAST-ADL is more specific to the automotive sector, but there are similar efforts and library developments, e.g., for automotive modeling based on Modelica. The EAST-ADL implementation is currently an UML profile.

There was a general discussion regarding continued work in the area, because of the parallel efforts, e.g., Modelica and SysML, as to which approach is more fruitful, standardizing or providing translations between the formalisms. One problem concerns the fuzzy semantics of many modeling languages, especially UML/SysML, which need to be made more precise. There is also a trend with increasing importance to have integrated system development approaches for whole systems including both software and hardware.

It was also remarked that too early standardization and efforts at adoption might be harmful. Instead, focus should be on the hard technical problems, try to solve those, and exchange experiences and results between the different groups.

4.2 Hybrid Modeling and Variable Structure Systems

As apparent from the title, the talks in this session concern two topics: hybrid continuous-time and discrete-time modeling and simulation, and variable structure systems where the structure and number of equations can change at run-time. Session chair was Bernhard Bachmann.

In "Hybrid dynamics in Modelica: Should all events be considered synchronous," Ramine Nikoukhah compared the event semantics of Modelica and Scicos and argued that the Modelica semantics is ambiguous, leading to distinct interpretations by different implementations (e.g., Dymola and Scicos) as to whether certain events are synchronous or not. It is argued that it is better for events to be considered synchronous only if they can be traced back (e.g., through equations) to the same event source, and that this leads to a more efficient and simpler implementation.

In "Extensions to Modelica for efficient code generation and separate compilation," Ramine Nikoukhah complemented the topic of the previous presentation by presenting a consistent way of separate compilation of (Modelica) models as black boxes, which then would have event inputs and event outputs as well as regular inputs and outputs. This would make it possible to connect separately compiled Modelica models, e.g., to models implemented in other formalisms, such as Scicos, Simulink or plain C code.

The next two talks concerned the topic of modeling and simulation of variable structured systems (structural dynamics), i.e., systems where objects can be introduced, removed, and connected/disconnected at run-time. MOSILAB has previously developed a solution to the modeling of structural dynamics by a language extension to Modelica supporting UML state charts.

In "Enhancing Modelica towards variable structure systems," Dirk Zimmer presented ideas and ongoing work on a new Modelica-like modeling language, called Sol, where several restrictions in standard Modelica have been removed and new features added, in particular being able to handle variable structured systems. Sol is intended as a research language to explore ideas, with an interpretive implementation. A model of a machine with a flywheel is sketched in the Sol language.

In "Functional Hybrid Modeling from an Object-Oriented Perspective," Henrik Nilsson, John Peterson, and Paul Hudak presented ideas for how to combine functional programming and modeling to create more powerful modeling languages for hybrid systems. In earlier work, they created a framework for causal hybrid modeling called Functional Reactive Programming (FRP). The goal now is to generalize this towards equation-based modeling (Functional Hybrid Modeling, FHM), in particular to create a declarative language that supports highly structurally dynamic models, based on the power of functional programming concepts combined with run-time code generation. The concept of first class signal relations is introduced. Ideas are sketched for an equation-based language (called Hydra), and a broken pendulum example model is shown. The work is still in an early stage.

In the following discussion, a number of issues were raised. One point is that there is concern for increased model complexity if we remove the Modelica rule that the number of variables must equal the number of equations, as in the first talk for discrete-time variables. Partial answer: these are essentially proposals for intermediate language constructs for hybrid system modeling. They allow to introduce the valuable feature of separate compilation of models/blocks, e.g., in conjunction with Modelica.

Regarding the Sol language, there were some questions about the implementation strategy. Why are programs coded in Sol being interpreted rather than compiled? Motivation: the approach makes it easy to handle structural variation at run-time, i.e., to create/exchange/destruct components on the fly. Sol is designed as a research tool only. The language serves as a proof-of-concept tool, and its implementation must be considered a prototype environment only. Will this approach not limit the tool to dealing with toy problems only? Could just-in-time code generation be used instead of interpretation? Right now, the language is being interpreted, and the flattened system of equations is updated at run-time.

The talk on functional hybrid modeling introduced many interesting ideas. It focused on relations of signals. At a structural change, use a switching function to add or remove signal relation functions in a collection. Hierarchical modeling is done through signal relations. Classes are nice but not needed for hierarchical modeling. One question: why not use constraints? Answer: functions are essential. Relations describe Modelica equations. Another question: functional programming is not widely used, what should be done about that? Answer: this is primarily aimed at a semantic language for dynamic modeling environments.

4.3 Modeling Languages, Specification, and Language Comparison

This session contained presentations and discussions on modeling languages, tools, and comparisons, as well as the topic of more precise specifications of modeling language semantics. Session chair was Christoph Nytsch-Geusen.

In "Important characteristics of VHDL-AMS and Modelica with respect to model exchange," Olaf Enge-Rosenblatt, Joachim Haase, and Christoph Clauß presented a modeling language comparison between the IEEE-standardized language VHDL-AMS and the language Modelica to describe analog and mixed-signal systems. The underlying modeling approaches were compared. Further, the potential to transform models written in one language into models of the other language was discussed.

In "Modeling Structural Dynamics Systems in Modelica/Dymola, Modelica /Mosilab, and AnyLogic", Günther Zauner, Daniel Leitner, and Felix Breitenecker presented a tool comparison between the three state-of-the-art DAE simulation environments Dymola, Mosilab, and AnyLogic regarding the possibilities of coupling of different state spaces. For this purpose, the three modeling approaches "parallel model setup," "serial model setup," and "combined model setup" were discussed. The analogies and discrepancies between these approaches were discussed by use of the classical constrained pendulum example as defined in the ARGESIM comparison C7.

In "Abstract Syntax Can Make the Definition of Modelica Less Abstract," David Broman and Peter Fritzson discussed different aspects of formulating a Modelica language specification. They proposed a "middle-way" strategy, which can make the specification both clearer and easier to reason about. For this purpose, a proposal was formulated, whereby the current informally specified Modelica semantics are complemented with several grammars, specifying intermediate representations of abstract syntax.

In "Physical Modelling with ModelVision, a DAE Simulator with Features for Hybrid Automata," Günther Zauner, Yuri Senichenkov, and Yuri Kolesov presented the modeling capabilities of the hybrid simulator ModelVision. The simulation technology of this simulation tool is based on hybrid state charts, which makes parallel, serial, and conditional combination of continuous models possible, described by DAEs as mathematical equations. State models themselves can be instantiated and replaced as objects during the simulation experiment for modeling and simulating structural dynamic systems. The talk was given by Felix Breitenecker in proxy for the authors.

Regarding the first presentation, one question was regarding VHDL-AMS models: are they compatible between different tools? Is the objective a full model translation tool between VHDL-AMS and Modelica? The answer: not really at this stage, this would be too difficult, and modeling language semantics are still too imprecise.

The second presentation compared three different tools using a constrained pendulum example. The question arose, how these tools can be fairly compared with each other? For example, Modelica allows DAEs, and its implementations usually support index reduction, but AnyLogic currently does not support either index reduction or event handling, which is a serious limitation. Another question raised in the context of MOSILAB that supports UML state charts: are such asynchronous UML state charts really desirable since they prevent the modeler from being able to prove the absence of deadlocks in models? Would it not be more fruitful to work with synchronous model approaches like the Modelica StateGraph library?

The third talk presented ideas how to make model language specifications more precise by combining informal specification, abstract syntax, and additional grammar fragments. One question concerned itself with the kind of grammars used: are they context free or context dependent? Answer: they are context dependent, since certain meta variables range over names and identifiers.

The presentation on the ModelVision tool was an interesting example of a long-term tool development effort in Russia going on in parallel to the mainstream developments, and now supporting many advanced features such as hybrid simulation and index reduction.

In general, it was concluded that more precise language semantics definitions are needed to make progress in model exchange between different modeling languages. The third talk presented some ideas how to make progress in this direction. However, much work is needed before models can be translated automatically, and in many cases there are low-level properties that make automatic model exchange really hard to attain.

4.4 Tools and Methods

The tools and methods session presented three papers of different aspects of modeling and simulation tools. Session chair was Peter Fritzson.

In "An Approach to the Calibration of Modelica Models," Miguel A. Rubio, Alfonso Urquía, and Sebastian Dormido presented a new Modelica library GAP*l*Lib based on genetic algorithms used for identification of unknown model parameter values from measurement data. An application of estimating parameters in a fuel cell model was presented.

In "Dynamic Optimization of Modelica Models – Language Extensions and Tools," Johan Åkesson presented work on extending the Modelica language also for optimization, with a language extension called Optimica. This superimposes four aspects on a model: information about Modelica variables, specification of a grid, definition of a cost function, and specification of constraints. Its use in formulating and solving a start-up problem for a plate reactor system was also presented.

In the paper "Robust Initialization of Differential Algebraic Equation," Bernhard Bachmann, Peter Aronsson, and Peter Fritzson presented a more robust method for initialization of DAE systems based on initialial equation systems. The method allows the initial equation systems to be overdetermined, solved by least square minimization, which gives additional flexibility in specifying initial conditions locally in each component model without concerns for possible problems with overdetermined initial equation systems. Currently, initial equations usually have to be specified in the top level application model to avoid problems with overdetermined systems. An application with a 3-phase electrical system with Park transformations was presented.

In the following discussion, regarding talk 1, identification of unknown parameters, there was a question regarding the choice of optimization algorithms: why genetic algorithms, aren't those inefficient? Answer: genetic algorithms are simple to understand and use and possibly modify. Another advantage is that there is no need to change the model. Another question: how do other methods, e.g., Tabu search, compare? Answer: this has not yet been investigated.

Regarding the optimization talk, there were questions regarding formulating the upper and lower bounds, needs for a special backend. A program called Socks was mentioned that should be somewhat similar to the presented work. Can we switch optimization algorithms without changing the model?

Finally, regarding the robust initialization, there were questions regarding the scalability: will the method work efficiently with 100 or more state variables instead of 6 as in the example? According to the presenter, the approach should scale up. The optimization algorithm is fairly efficient, and even complex applications have seldom more than a hundred or a few hundred state variables. Another question concerned if-equations: which region should be optimized? Answer: keep one branch constant while varying the other, then keep the second branch constant while varying the first.

To summarize: tools and methods for analyses related to modeling and simulation are becoming increasingly important to help prepare models for solution, e.g., parameter identification and initialization, or post processing and additional analysis such as optimization, which uses simulation for a particular purpose.

5 Discussion of Future Directions of Equation-Based Languages

The workshop ended with a general discussion about possible future directions of EOO languages and tools. The discussion was roughly divided into the following topics.

5.1 New Directions

What new directions can be discerned in the area? Optimization was mentioned as one such area. Metamodeling, model unification (see below) is another. Static analysis of models for verification is already established in the embedded systems community, and should increasingly be relevant here.

A current trend is increased emphasis on model-based development for embedded systems, not just simulation. This includes generation of embedded code, e.g., in controllers, perhaps with fixed-point support, and more emphasis on real-time issues in general.

5.2 Tool Integration and Tool Interfaces

There is increasing recognition that tools need to be more modular with clearly defined interfaces/APIs and interface formats between the phases/modules. This will have advantages such as:

- Enables extensible plugin development e.g., as in Eclipse.
- Enables tool certification.

There was also some discussion on the availability of the flat structure of equations. Is this enough? The main reason is that it is easier for many tools to operate on the flat structure.

5.3 Variable Structure Systems

Support for variable structure systems is a hot future topic that needs to find good solutions. The challenge is to combine the advantages of efficient code and static checking of fixed-structure models with the flexibility of variable structured systems. For example, what is the cost of restructuring, and can that be brought down? These, and similar, issues need to be studied more closely.

5.4 Metamodeling, Reflection, Model Unification

Metamodeling, operations on models, and model transformations are topics of increasing importance and tools become more capable and extensible. The models themselves could be made extensible by including new analyses and transformations in the models instead of in monolithic tools.

There is a trend to use separate untyped scripting languages together with modeling languages. Instead, it might be desirable to generalize the modeling languages themselves to handle models, have functions that return models, and operate on models with a type system that includes all this.

5.5 Integrated Modeling Approaches

Integrated modeling approaches could mean approaches for metamodeling by combining black box models, co-simulation, or tool integration in general. This is an increasing trend and strongly dependent on the tool integration mentioned previously.

6 Conclusions

The participants felt that this was a successful workshop, the first in its series. The area of equation-based object-oriented (EOO) languages and tools is of rapidly increasing importance. It is important to engage more computer scientists in this area, which is one of the motivations of co-locating the workshop with ECOOP.

It is important to bring in a wider spectrum of languages and tools, with less dominance of Modelica-related work. For example, why not include also PDE or FEM modeling languages and tools? It was felt that the workshop should be continued and possibly expanded. The discussions in the workshop were good. In case there will be more papers presented at future workshops, the time per presentation has to be reduced in order to keep enough time for discussions.

Some references are given below as a background to this area.

References

[1] Accellera, Cadence: Verilog-AMS Language Reference Manual Version 2.2, Published by: Accellera, 1370 Trancas Street, #163, Napa, CA 94558 (November 2004)

[2] Augustin, D.C., Fineberg, M.S., Johnson, B.B., Linebarger, R.N., Sansom, F.J., Strauss, J.C.: The SCi Continuous System Simulation Language (CSSL). Simulation (9), 281–303 (1967)

[3] Birtwistle, G.M., Dahl, O.J., Myhrhaug, B., Nygaard, K.: SIMULA BEGIN. Auerbach Publishers, Inc. (1973)

[4] Breunese, A.P.J., Broenink, J.F.: Modeling Mechatronic Systems Using the SIDOPS+ Language. In: Proceedings of ICBGM 1997, 3rd International Conference on Bond Graph Modeling and Simulation, Phoenix, Arizona. Simulation Series, vol. 29(1), pp. 301–306. SCS Publishing, San Diego, California (1997), http://www.rt.el.utwente.nl/proj/modsim/modsim.htm

[5] Cellier, F.E.: Continuous System Modelling, p. 755. Springer, New York (1991)

[6] Cellier, F.E., Kofman, E.: Continuous System Simulation, p. 643. Springer, New York (2006)

[7] Christen, E., Bakalar, K.: VHDL-AMS – A Hardware Description Language for Analog and Mixed-Signal Applications. IEEE Transactions on Circuits and Systems II: Analog and Digital Signal Processing 46(10), 1263–1272 (1999)

[8] Clabaugh, J., Tolsma, J.E., Barton, P.I.: Abacuss II: Advanced Modeling Environment and Embedded Simulator, and Abacuss II Syntax Manual. Massachusetts Institute of Technology, Chemical Engineering System Research Group (1999), Available at http://yoric.mit.edu/abacuss2/abacuss2.html

[9] Elmqvist, H.: A Structured Model Language for Large Continuous Systems. Ph.D. thesis, TFRT-1015, Department of Automatic Control, Lund Institute of Technology, Lund, Sweden (1978)

[10] Ernst, T., Jähnichen, S., Klose, M.: The Architecture of the Smile/M Simulation Environment. In: Proceedings 15th IMACS World Congress on Scientific Computation, Modelling and Applied Mathematics, Berlin, Germany, vol. 6, pp. 653–658 (1997)

[11] Fritzson, P.: Principles of Object-Oriented Modeling and Simulation with Modelica 2.1, p. 940. Wiley-IEEE Press (2004) ISBN 0-471-471631

[12] Fritzson, P., Viklund, L., Fritzson, D., Herber, J.: High Level Mathematical Modeling and Programming in Scientific Computing, IEEE Software, pp. 77–87 (July 1995)

[13] Mattsson, S.-E., Andersson, M.: The Ideas Behind Omola. In: CADCS 1992. Proceedings of the 1992 IEEE Symposium on Computer-Aided Control System Design, Napa, California, March 17-19, 1992, pp. 23–29 (1992)

[14] Oh, M., Pantelides, C.C.: A modelling and Simulation Language for Combined Lumped and Distributed Parameter Systems. Computers and Chemical Engineering 20(6–7), 611–633 (1996)

[15] Piela, P.C., Epperly, T.G., Westerberg, K.M., Westerberg, A.W.: ASCEND: An Object-Oriented Computer Environment for Modeling and Analysis: The Modeling Language. Computers and Chemical Engineering 15(1), 53–72 (1991)

[16] Sahlin, P., Sowell, E.F.: A Neutral Format for Building Simulation Models. In: Proceedings of the Conference on Building Simulation, IBPSA, Vancouver, Canada, pp. 147–154 (1989)

[17] Sargent, R.W.H., Westerberg, A.W.: Speed-Up in Chemical Engineering Design. Chemical Engineering Research and Design 42a, 190–197 (1964)

[18] The Mathworks. Simulink – Simulation and Model-Based Design (Last accessed: March 6, 2007), http://www.mathworks.com/products/simulink/

[19] The Modelica Association. The Modelica Language Specification Version 3.0 (September 2007), http://www.modelica.org

[20] Tiller, M.: Introduction to Physical Modeling with Modelica, p. 368. Springer, New York (2001)

[21] UML Homepage: http://www.uml.org

[22] van Beek, D.A., Man, K.L., Reniers, M.A., Rooda, J.E., Schiffelers, R.R.H.: Syntax, and consistent equation semantics of hybrid Chi. The Journal of Logic and Algebraic Programming 68, 129–210 (2006)

Aliasing, Confinement, and Ownership in Object-Oriented Programming
Report on the Workshop IWACO'07 at ECOOP 2007

Dave Clarke[1], Sophia Drossopoulou[2], James Noble[3], and Tobias Wrigstad[4]

[1] CWI, Amsterdam, The Netherlands
dave@cwi.nl
[2] Imperial College, London, UK
sd@doc.ic.ac.uk
[3] Victoria University of Wellington, New Zealand
kjx@mcs.vuw.ac.nz
[4] Stockholm University, Stockholm, Sweden
tobias@dsv.su.se

Abstract. The power of objects lies in the flexibility of their interconnection structure. But this flexibility comes at a cost. Because an object can be modified via any alias, object-oriented programs are hard to understand, maintain, and analyse. Aliasing makes objects depend on their environment in unpredictable ways, breaking the encapsulation necessary for reliable software components, making it difficult to reason about and optimise programs, obscuring the flow of information between objects, and introducing security problems.

Aliasing is a fundamental difficulty, but we accept its presence. Instead we seek techniques for describing, reasoning about, restricting, analysing, and preventing the connections between objects and/or the flow of information between them. Promising approaches to these problems are based on ownership, confinement, information flow, sharing control, escape analysis, argument independence, read-only references, effects systems, and access control mechanisms.

1 Introduction

The aim of the IWACO workshop was to address the question how to manage interconnected object structures in the presence of aliasing. In, particular the following issues were covered:

- models, type and other formal systems, programming language, separation logic, mechanisms, analysis and design techniques, patterns, tools and notations for expressing object ownership, aliasing, confinement, uniqueness, and/or information flow;
- optimisation techniques, analysis algorithms, libraries, applications, tools, and novel approaches exploiting object ownership, aliasing, confinement, uniqueness, and/or information flow;

M. Cebulla (Ed.): ECOOP 2007 Workshop Reader, LNCS 4906, pp. 40–49, 2008.

- empirical studies of programs or experience reports from programming systems designed with these issues in mind;
- novel applications of aliasing management techniques such as ownership types, ownership domains, confined types, region types, and uniqueness.

1.1 History

IWACO 2007 was the third ECOOP workshop focussing on aliasing. The previous workshops were IWACO 2003 [2] and the Intercontinental Workshop on Aliasing in Object-oriented Systems (IWAOOS) in 1999. The issues addressed in this workshop were first brought into focus with the Geneva Convention on the Treatment of Object Aliasing [5].

2 Invited Talk

The invited speaker, Vijay Saraswat, affiliated with IBM T. J. Watson Research Lab and Penn State University, talked about X10, an experimental new language currently under development at IBM [8]. X10 sports a few concepts of interest to the IWACO crowd, most notably the notion of place types which are dependent types expressing that data lives (or computation happens) at a specific place and what places are available to a computation. In addition, X10's use of constraint-based type systems, rather than more direct-style type systems, generated quite a bit of discussion, as the constraint-based approach gels well with the idea of automatically generating ownership and aliasing conditions. The type system Saraswat presented was undecidable, as it relied heavily on dependent types, but he argued that this was not a big problem, as the programs that cause problems are pathological.

3 The Presentations

In addition to the invited talk, there were 15 presentations at IWACO. These were of 5, 10, or 25 minutes in length, depending upon how well-developed the submission was, and thus ample time for discussion was available.

4 Comparative Summary of Contributions and Debates

Although many ideas from each talk related to ideas in other talks, and the discussions that were triggered cross-cut the entire spectrum of topics, for coherency, we have grouped the presentations into the following categories:

- (ownership) inference—techniques to overcome the syntactic overhead of extant aliasing annotation and ownership types systems;
- ownership in the real world—case studies applying ownership types to real world applications or corpora of real world programs;

- project overviews—the state of the art and plans of various groups working on aliasing;
- theoretical developments—contributions to the (type) theory underlying ownership types and other approaches to dealing with (the effects of) aliasing in object-oriented programming; and
- (re)emerging techniques—new approaches to addressing aliasing, or existing techniques seen in a new light.

4.1   (Ownership) Inference

Aliasing analyses and ownership types [4] systems rely on annotations to work. Important issues that need to be addressed include the annotating of existing code bases, techniques to reduce the volume of annotations that a programmer needs to add, and tools to provide programmer assistance to determine what the best annotations are. Three presentations addressed these issues.

Rather than applying a pure static analysis technique, Werner Dietl and Peter Müller attempted *Runtime Universe Type Inference*. Their approach relies on runtime information to determine the annotations. The paper describes the architecture and implementation of a system that infers Universe ownership types from the run-time access patterns of Java programs. Although the Universe type system has a low annotation overhead, annotating existing software is a considerable effort. The paper described how to analyze the execution of programs and infer ownership modifiers from the resulting execution traces. An Eclipse plug-in was demonstrated. It was based on a C program that traces JVM execution and a Java application that infers the Universe annotations.

The idea of using both static and dynamic techniques was also presented in *Compile-Time Views of Execution Structure Based on Ownership*, by Marwan Abi-Antoun and Jonathan Aldrich. They argued that developers need to understand both the static and dynamic structure of object-oriented programs, and that class diagrams are not sufficient to understand the static code structure. Furthermore, they argued that raw object graphs produced either via static or dynamic analysis also tend not to convey design intent and do not scale to large programs. The approach taken was to use the stronger (hierarchical) encapsulation guarantees of ownership types systems to produce more intuitive and appealing visualizations of a system's dynamic structure. By taking ownership information into account, a hierarchical representation can be built and uses of the same class in different domains are kept separate. Two case studies of 15,000 line large programs were presented and the results look promising, as in both cases, the automatically generated visualization fitted on one page, and provided insights into the dynamic structure that would be otherwise hard to obtain by looking at the code or at existing class diagrams.

Not everyone was convinced that dynamic techniques were required. Instead, annotations on the boundaries of 'modules' significantly improve the scalability of analysis. This was essentially the point argued by by Mike Barnett, Manuel Fähndrich, Diego Garbervetsky and Francesco Logozzo in their talk *Annotations for (more) Precise Points-to Analysis*. They extended Salcianu's existing points-to analysis to support .NET's structs and parameter passing by reference, and increased precision by handling *non-analyzable* methods—those whose code is unavailable because it is abstract, virtual (and unresolved) or native. For such methods, an extension that models potentially affected heap locations was introduced. A combined points-to/effects annotation language was designed to provide modular analysis without the loss of too much precision. A preliminary evaluation was described, showing the benefits of the aliasing declarations for verifying purity annotations.

The discussion revolved around the degree to which various subtleties of the approaches produced the best results. Pure static analysis seemed to be insufficient in general to produce good annotations of programs. This is where the dynamic approach helped, by seeding the analysis process with a first approximation. Visualization tools enabled the annotations to be refined to closer match programmer expectations. After the boundaries of certain modules were annotated, static analysis techniques could leverage that information to more effectively analyze smaller code fragments. It was noted that the additional benefit of ownership and alias inference was that they can identify bad design 'smells' in existing systems. Some evidence for this idea was presented from the case studies.

4.2   Ownership in the Real World

Ownership types have been around for nearly 10 years, though insufficient work has been done in applying them in the context of large systems. A number of researchers are addressing this issue, either on an application-by-application basis, or by (semi-)automatically analyzing large corpora of programs.

The paper *Using ownership types to support library aliasing boundaries*, by Luke Wagner, Jaakko Järvi and Bjarne Stroustrup, applied ownership to concurrent library design in C++. Their key concept is the notion of a *tether*, which is a (smart) object pointer that is only valid inside the right thread (its owner). The paper presented a case study on the use of object ownership to prevent concurrency problems. The case study was a 3D computer game, in a 6 month, 10 developer project. Interactive games need concurrency, but concurrency is hard to get right. A system of ownership-based rules and an explicit representation of ownership were proposed to prevent bugs from the incorrect concurrency. Although the developers were inexperienced, there were no problems with data races in the multi-threaded application. This paper thus demonstrated the benefit of having ownership in the language and argued that this can apply not just to concurrency libraries, but also to memory, security, and resource management.

Marwan Abi-Antoun presented *Ownership Domains in the Real World*, joint work with his supervisor Jonathan Aldrich. His talk described the publicly available tool that supports the Ownership Domains type system. As their original implementation was not backwards compatible with Java and ran on research infrastructure, it was difficult to conduct substantial case studies on interesting systems. Consequently, they re-implemented their system using Java 1.5 and Eclipse. The resulting tool was used to annotate two real 15,000-line Java programs, with the aid of refactoring tools.

The first paper differed from most of the remainder of the presentations at the workshop as it considered both ownership and concurrency. Discussion revolved around the relationship between the authors' approach and some existing attacks on concurrency using ownership. The paper seemed to present a new approach, by tying the dynamics of a program to the ownership relationship, and thereby points to a useful direction for future research. These two papers illustrate that various kinds of ownership type systems can express and enforce design intent related to object encapsulation and communication. Some expressiveness gaps in the various approaches were described, and audience members posed possible solutions, or noted the problems as topics for future work. In addition, there was some postulation about other situations that could benefit from the various approaches discussed.

4.3   Project Overviews

A number of groups around the world are working on ownership types and aliasing. Two groups took the opportunity to present an overview of what they have been doing in the last few years, and what their plans for the future are. The talks *Ownership Meets Java* by Christo Fogelberg, Alex Potanin and James Noble and *2007 State of the Universe Address* by Werner Dietl and Peter Müller described the research in their groups. Noble's talk focussed on piggy-backing ownership types on top of Java's generics. An alternative approach, also used by other researchers, is to use Java's annotation system. In both talks, the idea is to exploit existing programming language features as much as possible to be able to re-use existing programming tools, such as Eclipse. The observation is that proposals not using existing language constructs will not be able to be, for example, parsed by IDE's or checking tools.

The idea of integrating ownership types into Java has a number of problems, as many audience members pointed out. As there are numerous distinct ownership type systems, each having its own uses and limitations, it is not clear, should push come to shove, which one is the best candidate, nor is it clear whether it is possible to unify them.

4.4   Theoretical Developments

Techniques for dealing with aliasing are often founded in type theory and programming language semantics. Such theoretical techniques not only guarantee the soundness of various proposals addressing aliasing problems, but also are a rich source of new ideas for the more practical approaches to these problems.

Typed intermediate languages and typed assembly languages for optimizing compilers require types to describe stack-allocated data. Frances Perry, Chris Hawblitzel and Juan Chen's *Simple and Flexible Stack Types* improved on existing type systems by resolving the undecidability problem, and enabling a stronger treatment of arguments passed by reference. The result was a simple, sound and decidable type system, suitable for low-level intermediate languages, such as Micro-CLI. Unlike most of the other papers presented at the workshop, this paper used alias types, singleton pointers and a small subset of linear logic.

One of the trends in aliasing and ownership types system research is to investigate hybrid type systems that combine elements of ownership with read-only references and/or immutability. Johan Östlund's talk *Ownership, Uniqueness and Immutability* reported on joint work with Tobias Wrigstad, Dave Clarke and Beatrice Åkerblom. This talk described the benefits of such a hybrid type system. Specifically, the combination of access modes with unique-reference based ownership transfer could express patterns such as fractional permissions [1] and much of flexible alias protection [7]. This research illustrated that one can relatively easily exploit the infrastructure provided by a basic layer of ownership types to achieve a lot more without much more effort, illustrating the robustness of ownership types as a concept. A lot of discussion revolved around precisely what was the right formulation of various concepts in order to obtain the most flexibility whilst retaining strong guarantees.

Adrian Fiech and Ulf Schünemann presented the *potential access path* methodology for reasoning about composite objects. The presentation, *Formalizing Composite State Encapsulation*, in spite of being short and technical, seemed to offer a different attack on the *owner-as-modifier* discipline imposed by Müller's Universe Types [6]. The novel contribution of the system was its treatment of uniqueness, enabling the transfer of subobjects (similar to Clarke and Wrigstad's External Uniqueness [3]). The audience agreed that this research represented another point on the design space worth exploring.

An audience member pointed out a problem with the various approaches based on or related to external uniqueness. They seem to be incompatible with (internal) threads. Even if all external references to an object do not allow modification, an active internal thread with a mutable view of the object can break invariants that depend on the perceived immutability. This open problem will surely attract some research in the near future.

4.5   (Re)emerging Techniques

The workshop provided the perfect forum for researchers to present ideas that were relatively immature. Such presentation generally provide fresh input to stimulate new directions of research. Some of these presentations took a controversial stance, expressing dissatisfaction with a particular approach or suggesting a totally different perspective on the problems the workshop was interested in. Sometimes casting an older technique in terms of object-oriented programming offered a source of new ideas.

Four talks proposed research that shifted invariants and other reasoning techniques from focussing on single objects to groups of objects. As most abstractions are implemented using more than one object, this direction of research is natural. The difficulty is that object-oriented programs are expressed in terms of classes, which do not have the same granularity as the abstractions they are used to implement.

Iterators can be Independent "from" Their Collections by John Boyland, William Retert and Yang Zhao focussed on the particular example of iterators, which have caused problems for alias control mechanisms since their inception.

Iterators have access to the elements of a collection, but can be used in contexts that are unaware of the existence of the collection. Consequently, iterators may fail unexpectedly when their collections are modified. Boyland *et al.* proposed to use fractional permissions [1] to control the interaction between the iterator and the collection, and sketched a static analysis to detect concurrent modification exceptions.

Matthew Parkinson presented a controversial and deliberately provocative talk, *Class Invariants: The End of the Road?*, which revealed a number of complications in scaling class invariants to real programs, namely, that class invariants depend upon multiple objects and invariants need to be broken temporarily owing to call-backs. Parkinson proposed the question: "Is the class invariant the correct foundation for verifying object-oriented programs?" The example focussed on the subject-observer pattern, and the talk presented a heavy use of invariants to show what can be done without class invariants. The challenge is that class invariants have the advantage of being easy to understand for the programmer, and this seems to be lost by using predicates. One audience member suggested that family polymorphism/virtual classes could solve the problem, by shifting the class invariants to talk about a family of classes instead of just a single class.

In some respects, the talk *Maintaining Invariants Through Object Coupling Mechanisms*, by Eric Kerfoot and Steve McKeever, presented a possible counter-argument to Parkinson's contention. They focussed on the problems that arise when an object's invariant relies on objects that are externally aliased and modified, as the changes to the external object are uncontrolled and may invalidate an object's invariant. The talk informally described a technique for coupling objects (called the *colleague technique*), which defined additional conditions upon objects involved in a strong relationship. Examples from the Java programming language and the JML specification language were used to illustrate the approach. Possible programming language support for this technique could be provided by Erik Ernst's *primitive associations*. These atomically maintained the coupling relationship between objects. His idea is strongly related to those posed by the other authors in this group, and it grows out of the mechanisms for ownership, controlled aliasing, sharing, escape analysis, and so on.

Overall, it was clear that one of the main challenges for future research is extending alias control mechanisms and formal reasoning systems to deal better with groups of objects. The discussion mentioned a number of recent papers that are taking steps in that direction.

The talk by Franz Puntigam, entitled *See the Pet in the Beast: How to Limit Effects of Aliasing*, described a means for ensuring exclusive access to objects by passing around tokens, without limiting the aliasing in the system. The approach also enabled objects to enforce a state-based protocol to ensure that they were used properly. Discussion revealed that there was a close relationship between this idea and the older ideas of *software protocol* or *type states* [9], as these have recently garnered some interest in the PLDI community. Transferring these ideas to an object-oriented setting is non-trivial, and Puntigam's approach offers some insight on how this transfer could take place.

5   Discussion

In addition to the talks and debates already described, there was discussion about the future direction of ownership. In particular, the question was raised as to whether a JSR should be written so that a standard approach to ownership could be devised and incorporated into Java. The conclusion seemed to be that this is premature.

Another important issue was the lack of more longitudinal experience with ownership (types), in particular, within the context of refactoring existing code bases to support ownership. How do ownership annotations interplay with refactoring, program design and maintenance? Simple patterns such as "move field" might require changes to class headers which will have (potentially severe) propagating effects throughout the entire program. It was concluded that more research in this area was needed in order to incorporate ownership (types) into a programmers' toolset and workflow.

6   Future

It appears that the community working on aliasing and ownership has reached critical mass, if the number of submissions, participants and presentations are any indication. Consequently, we plan to repeat the workshop in conjunction with ECOOP 2008.

References

1. Boyland, J.: Checking interference with fractional permissions. In: Cousot, R. (ed.) SAS 2003. LNCS, vol. 2694, pp. 55–72. Springer, Heidelberg (2003)
2. Clarke, D., Drossopoulou, S., Noble, J.: Aliasing, confinement, and ownership in object-oriented programming. In: Buschmann, F., Buchmann, A., Cilia, M.A. (eds.) ECCV-WS 2003. LNCS, vol. 3013, pp. 197–207. Springer, Heidelberg (2004)
3. Clarke, D., Wrigstad, T.: External uniqueness is unique enough. In: Cardelli, L. (ed.) ECOOP 2003. LNCS, vol. 2743, pp. 176–200. Springer, Heidelberg (2003)
4. Clarke, D.G., Potter, J., Noble, J.: Ownership types for flexible alias protection. In: OOPSLA, pp. 48–64 (1998)
5. Hogg, J., Lea, D., Wills, A., de Champeaux, D., Holt, R.: The Geneva Convention on the treatment of object aliasing. OOPS Messenger 3(2), 11–16 (1992)
6. Müller, P., Poetzsch-Heffter, A. (eds.): Universes: A Type System for Controlling Representation Exposure, pp. 131–140 (1999)
7. Noble, J., Vitek, J., Potter, J.: Flexible alias protection. In: Jul, E. (ed.) ECOOP 1998. LNCS, vol. 1445, pp. 158–185. Springer, Heidelberg (1998)
8. Saraswat, V.A., Sarkar, V., von Praun, C.: X10: concurrent programming for modern architectures. In: Yelick, K.A., Mellor-Crummey, J.M. (eds.) PPOPP 2007. Proceedings of the 12th ACM SIGPLAN Symposium on Principles and Practice of Parallel Programming (2007)

9. Strom, R., Yemini, S.: Typestate: A programming language concept for enhancing software reliabiity. IEEE Transactions on Software Engineering 12(1), 157–171 (1986)

A Participants

IWACO gathered 38 participants from 16 different countries.

Marwan Abi-Antoun	Carnegie Mellon University (USA)
Jonathan Aldrich	Carnegie Mellon University (USA)
Frank de Boer	CWI (The Netherlands)
John Boyland	University of Wisconsin-Milwaukee (USA)
Einar Broch Johnsen	University of Oslo (Norway)
Nicholas Cameron	Imperial College (UK)
Dave Clarke	CWI (The Netherlands)
Curt Clifton	Rose-Hulman Institute of Technology (USA)
Markus Degen	Universität Freiburg (Germany)
Mariangiola Dezani-Ciancaglini	University of Turin (Italy)
Werner Dietl	ETH Zürich (Switzerland)
Sophia Drossopoulou	Imperial College (UK)
Erik Ernst	University of Århus (Denmark)
Manuel Fähndrich	Microsoft Research (USA)
Yishai Feldman	IBM Research (Israel)
Adrian Fiech	Memorial University (Canada)
Diego Garbervetsky	Universidad De Buenos Aires (Argentina)
Philippe Haller	EPFL (Switzerland)
Clément Hurlin	Inria (France)
Jaako Järvi	Texas A&M University (USA)
Eric Kerfoot	Oxford University (UK)
Ondřej Lhoták	University of Waterloo (Canada)
Fracesco Logozzo	Microsoft Research (USA)
Yi Lu	University of New South Wales (Australia)
Peter Müller	Microsoft Research (US)
James Noble	Victoria University of Wellington (New Zeeland)
Johan Östlund	Stockholm University (Sweden)
Matthew Parkinson	University of Cambridge (UK)
Frances Perry	Princeton University (USA)
Arnd Poetzsch-Heffter	University of Kaiserslauten (Germany)
John Potter	University of New South Wales (Australia)
Franz Puntigam	TU Wien (Austria)
Vijay Saraswat	IBM TJ Watson Research Lab (USA)
Peter Thiemann	Universität Freiburg (Germany)
Jan Vitek	Purdue University (USA)
Luke Wagner	Texas A&M University (USA)
Stefan Wehr	Uni Freiburg (Germany)
Tobias Wrigstad	Stockholm University (Sweden)

B   Organisers

Dave Clarke	CWI (The Netherlands)
Sophia Drossopoulou	Imperial College (UK)
James Noble	Victoria University of Wellington (New Zealand)
Tobias Wrigstad	Stockholm University (Sweden)

C   Program Committee

Jonathan Aldrich	Carnegie Mellon University (USA)
Chandrasekhar Boyapati	University of Michigan (USA)
Dave Clarke	CWI (The Netherlands)
Sophia Drossopoulou	Imperial College (UK)
Rustan Leino	Microsoft Research (USA)
Peter Müller	ETH Zurich (Switzerland)
James Noble	Victoria University of Wellington (New Zealand)
Peter O'Hearn	Queen Mary, University of London (UK)
Alex Potanin	Victoria University of Wellington (New Zealand)
Jan Vitek	Purdue University (USA)
Tobias Wrigstad	Stockholm University (Sweden)

Implementation, Compilation, Optimization of Object-Oriented Languages, Programs and Systems

Report on the Workshop ICOOOLPS 2007 at ECOOP 2007

Olivier Zendra[1], Eric Jul[2], Roland Ducournau[3], Etienne Gagnon[4], Richard Jones[5], Chandra Krintz[6], Philippe Mulet[7], and Jan Vitek[8]

[1] INRIA-LORIA, France
[2] DIKU, Denmark
[3] LIRMM, France
[4] UQAM, Canada
[5] Univ. of Kent, UK
[6] UCSB, USA
[7] IBM, France
[8] Purdue University, USA

Abstract. ICOOOLPS'2007 was the second edition of the ECOOP-ICOOOLPS workshop. ICOOOLPS intends to bring researchers and practitioners both from academia and industry together, with a spirit of openness, to try and identify and begin to address the numerous and very varied issues of optimization. After a first successful edition, this second one put a stronger emphasis on exchanges and discussions amongst the participants, progressing on the bases set last year in Nantes.

The workshop attendance was a success, since the 30-people limit we had set was reached about 2 weeks before the workshop itself. Some of the discussions (e.g .annotations) were so successful that they would required even more time than we were able to dedicate to them. That's one area we plan to further improve for the next edition.

1 Objectives and Call for Papers

Programming languages, especially object-oriented ones, are pervasive and play a significant role in computer science and engineering life. They sometime appear as ubiquitous and completely mature. However, despite a large number of works, there is still a clear need for solutions for efficient implementation and compilation of OO languages in various application domains ranging from embedded and real-time systems to desktop systems.

The ICOOOLPS workshop series thus aims to address this crucial issue of optimization in OO languages, programs and systems. It intends to do so by bringing together researchers and practitioners working in the field of object-oriented

M. Cebulla (Ed.): ECOOP 2007 Workshop Reader, LNCS 4906, pp. 50–64, 2008.

languages implementation and optimization. Its main goals are identifying fundamental bases and key current issues pertaining to the efficient implementation, compilation and optimization of OO languages, and outlining future challenges and research directions.

Topics of interest for ICOOOLPS include but are not limited to:

- implementation of fundamental OOL features:
  - inheritance (object layout, late binding, subtype test...)
  - genericity (parametric types)
  - memory management
- runtime systems:
  - compilers
  - linkers
  - virtual machines
- optimizations:
  - static and dynamic analyses
  - adaptive virtual machines
- resource constraints:
  - real-time systems
  - embedded systems (space, low power)...
- relevant choices and tradeoffs:
  - constant time vs. non-constant time mechanisms
  - separate compilation vs. global compilation
  - dynamic loading vs. global linking
  - dynamic checking vs. proof-carrying code
  - annotations vs. no annotations

This workshop thus tries to identify fundamental bases and key current issues pertaining to the efficient implementation and compilation of languages, especially OO ones, in order to spread them further amongst the various computing systems. It is also intended to extend this synthesis to encompass future challenges and research directions in the field of OO languages implementation and optimization.

Finally, as stated from the very beginning and the very first edition in Nantes in 2006, ICOOOLPS is intended to be a recurrent workshop in ECOOP. Since the feedback from first year attendants was very positive, this second edition was set up. We organizers integrated most of the suggestions for improvements made in 2006, so as to further improve the workshop. The main adaptation was that less time was given to presentations, in order to free extra time for discussions.

In order to increase bases on which the discussions could be based and to keep them focused, each prospective participant was encouraged to submit either a short paper describing ongoing work or a position paper describing an open issue, likely solutions, drawbacks of current solutions or alternative solutions to well known problems. Papers had to be written in English and their final version could not exceed 8 pages in LNCS style (4 pages recommended).

2   Organizers

Olivier ZENDRA (chair),   INRIA-LORIA, Nancy, France.
Email: olivier.zendra@inria.fr
Web: http://www.loria.fr/~zendra
Address: INRIA / LORIA
            615 Rue du Jardin Botanique
            BP 101
            54602 Villers-Lès-Nancy Cedex, FRANCE

Olivier Zendra is a full-time permanent computer science researcher at IN-RIA / LORIA, in Nancy, France. His research topics cover compilation, optimization and automatic memory management. He worked on the compilation and optimization of object-oriented languages and was one of the two people who created and implemented SmartEiffel, The GNU Eiffel Compiler (at the time SmallEiffel). His current research topics and application domains are program analysis, compilation, memory management and embedded systems, with a specific focus on low energy.

Eric JUL (co-chair),   DIKU, Copenhagen, Denmark.
Email: eric@diku.dk
Web: http://www.diku.dk/~eric
Address: DIKU
            Universitetsparken 1
            DK-2100 København Ø, DANMARK

Eric Jul is Professor of Computer Science at the University of Copenhagen and head of the Distributed Systems Group. He is one of the principal designers of the distributed, object-oriented language Emerald. He implemented fine-grained object mobility in Emerald. His current research is in Grid Computing. He is currently Vice-President of AITO.

Roland DUCOURNAU,   LIRMM, Montpellier, France.
Email: ducour@lirmm.fr
Web: http://www.lirmm.fr/~ducour
Address: LIRMM,
            161, rue Ada
            34392 Montpellier Cedex 5, FRANCE

Roland Ducournau is Professor of Computer Science at the University of Montpellier. In the late 80s, while with Sema Group, he designed and developed the YAFOOL language, based on frames and prototypes and dedicated to knowledge based systems. His research topics focuses on class specialization and inheritance, especially multiple inheritance. His recent works are dedicated to implementation of OO languages.

Etienne GAGNON,   UQAM, Montréal, Québec, Canada.
Email: egagnon@sablevm.org
Web: http://www.info2.uqam.ca/~egagnon
Address: Département d'informatique
              UQAM
              Case postale 8888, succursale Centre-ville
              Montréal (Québec) Canada / H3C 3P8

Etienne Gagnon is a Professor of Computer Science at Université du Québec à Montréal (UQAM) since 2001. Etienne has developed the SableVM portable research virtual machine for Java, and the SableCC compiler framework generator. His research topics include language design, memory management, synchronization, verification, portability, and efficient interpretation techniques in virtual machines.

Richard JONES,   University of Kent, Canterbury, UK.
Email: R.E.Jones@kent.ac.uk
Web: http://www.cs.kent.ac.uk/~rej
Address: Richard Jones, Reader in Computer Systems,
              Computing Laboratory,
              University of Kent at Canterbury,
              Canterbury CT2 7NF, UK

Richard Jones is Reader in Computer Systems and Deputy Director of the Computing Laboratory at the University of Kent, Canterbury. He leads the Systems Research Group. He is best known for his work on garbage collection: his monograph Garbage Collection remains the definitive book on the subject. His memory management research interests include techniques for avoiding space leaks, scalable yet complete garbage collection for distributed systems, flexible techniques for capturing traces of program behaviour, and heap visualisation. He was made a Distinguished Scientist of the Association for Computer Machinery (ACM) in 2006 and awarded an Honorary Fellowship at the University of Glasgow in 2005.

Chandra KRINTZ,   UC Santa Barbara, CA, USA.
Email: ckrintz@cs.ucsb.edu
Web: http://www.cs.ucsb.edu/~ckrintz
Address: University of California
              Engineering I, Rm. 1121
              Department of Computer Science
              Santa Barbara, CA 93106-5110, USA

Chandra Krintz is an Assistant Professor at the University of California, Santa Barbara (UCSB); she joined the UCSB faculty in 2001. Chandra's research interests include automatic and adaptive compiler and virtual runtime techniques for object-oriented languages that improve performance and increase battery life. In particular, her work focuses on exploiting repeating patterns in the time-varying behavior of underlying resources, applications, and workloads to guide dynamic optimization and specialization of program and system components.

Philippe MULET,   IBM, Saint-Nazaire, France.
　　Email:　　　philippe_mulet@fr.ibm.com
　　Address:　　IBM France - Paris Laboratory
　　　　　　　　69, rue de la Vecquerie
　　　　　　　　44600 Saint-Nazaire, France

Philippe Mulet is the lead for the Java Development Tooling (JDT) Eclipse subproject, working at IBM since 1996; he is currently located in Saint-Nazaire (France). In late 1990s, Philippe was responsible for the compiler and codeassist tools in IBM Java Integrated Development Environments (IDEs): VisualAge for Java standard and micro editions. Philippe then became in charge of the Java infrastructure for the Eclipse platform, and more recently of the entire Java tooling for Eclipse. Philippe is a member of the Eclipse Project PMC. Philippe is also a member of the expert group on compiler API (JSR199), representing IBM. His main interests are in compilation, performance, scalability and meta-level architectures.

Jan VITEK,   Purdue Univ., West Lafayette, IN, USA.
　　Email:　　　jv@cs.purdue.edu
　　Web:　　　　http://www.cs.purdue.edu/homes/jv
　　Address:　　Dept. of Computer Sciences
　　　　　　　　Purdue University
　　　　　　　　West Lafayette, IN 47907, USA

Jan Vitek is an Associate Professor in Computer Science at Purdue University. He leads the Secure Software Systems lab. He obtained his PhD from the University of Geneva in 1999, and a MSc from the University of Victoria in 1995. Prof. Vitek research interests include programming language, virtual machines, mobile code, software engineering and information security.

3   Participants

ICOOOLPS attendance was limited to 30 people for technical reasons. Unlike in the 2006 edition, it was not mandatory for ICOOOLPS 2007 to submit a paper to participate. We indeed intended to further open the discussion by making the attendance easier, and had learned from the numerous walk-ins during ICOOOLPS 2006. The 30-people limit was reached about 2 weeks before the workshop itself, which lead us to put a note on the website to stop new registrations.

Finally, 27 people from 12 countries — up from 22 people from 8 countries in 2006 — attended this second edition, which is an encouraging sign of an increasing audience for ICOOOLPS. These attendants are listed in table 1.

Table 1. ICOOOLPS 2007 list of attendees

First name	NAME	Affiliation	Country	Email
Philippe	ALTHERR	Google	Switzerland	paltherr@google.com
Maurizio	CIMADAMORE	DEIS, Università di Bologna	Italy	Maurizio.Cimadamore@unibo.it
Marcus	DENKER	Ubiversity of Bern	Switzerland	denker@iam.unibe.ch
Iulian	DRAGOS	EPFL	Switzerland	iulian.dragos@epfl.ch
Gilles	DUBOCHET	EPFL - LAMP	Switzerland	Gilles.Dubochet@epfl.ch
Burak	EMIR	EPFL	Switzerland	Burak.Emir@gmail.com
Michael	FRANZ	UC Irvine	USA	franz@uci.edu
Etienne	GAGNON	UQAM	Canada	egagnon@sablevm.org
Michael	HAUPT	Hasso-Plattner-Institut, Univ. Potsdam	Germany	michael.haupt@hpi.uni-potsdam.de
Raymond	HU	Imperial College, London	United Kingdom	rh105@doc.ic.ac.uk
Christine	HUNDT	TU-Berlin	Germany	resix@cs.tu-berlin.de
Maha	IDRISSI AOUAD	INRIA / LORIA	France	Maha.IdrissiAouad@loria.fr
Eric	JUL	DIKU	Denmark	eric@diku.dk
Stéphane	MICHELOUD	EPFL	Switzerland	Stephane.MICHELOUD@epfl.ch
Anders Bach	NIELSEN	University of Århus	Denmark	abachn@daimi.au.dk
Meir	OVADIA	Cadence	Israel	meiro@cadence.com
Laurent	PLAGNE	EDF R&D	France	Laurent.Plagne@edf.fr
Andreas	PRIESNITZ	Chalmers University of Technology	Sweden	priesnit@cs.chalmers.se
Yannis	SMARAGDAGKIS	University of Oregon	USA	yannis@cs.uoregon.edu
Alexander	SPOON	EPFL	Switzerland	lex@lexspoon.org
Witawas	SRISA-AN	University of Nebraska - Lincoln	USA	witty@cse.unl.edu
Darko	STEFANOVIC	University of New Mexico	USA	darko@cs.unm.edu
Jan	SZUMIEC	Cracow University of Technology	Poland	jps@wieik.pk.edu.pl
Howard	THOMSON	UKUUG Council	United Kingdom	howard.thomson@dial.pipex.com
Stijn	TIMBERMONT	Vrije Universiteit Brussel	Belgium	stimberm@vub.ac.be
Jan	VITEK	Purdue Univ.	USA	v@cs.purdue.edu
Olivier	ZENDRA	INRIA-LORIA	France	Olivier.Zendra@loria.fr

4   Contributions

The presentations and discussions at ICOOOLPS 2007 were organized in 4 sessions: annotations vs. no annotation, lookup and dispatch mechanisms, miscellaneous implementation issues and continuations and synchronizations.

Here are the main contributions for the sessions. More details (papers, presentations slides, etc.) are available from `http://icooolps.loria.fr`. They are reported here in a lively an rather informal way, so as to keep some of the spontaneity of the workshop, with of course extra organization.

4.1   Annotations vs. No Annotation

This first technical session was a discussion-only one, chaired by Olivier Zendra, who introduced it by a talk synthesizing the contributions of ICOOOLPS 2006 discussion "written down in code vs. inferred". It was a very lively and interesting discussion, with a lot of attendees participating. Unfortunately, to respect the schedule, we had to stop the discussion before it was over. This first indicates this discussion topic is still open and should probably be continued in 2008, then that discussion times should be even longer and/or more flexible.

A quote from last year stated that "Annotations are too serious to be left to developers". But this triggers the question "And what about code ?!"

Some answers pointed that there is room for the compiler to do consistency checking. Others argued it was better to let people do their own mistakes, since that's part of the learning process. It was objected that this reasoning, pushed to the extreme, could lead to directly writing assembly code. Everyone agreed that of course we still need higher level because we want people be more productive.

The issue was raised whether we actually needed different levels of annotations. One level would we the "How-level", where we express how things are done. This is very useful for optimization. Not so many people in the room considered this level appealing to them, though. Another level would be the "What-level", where we express properties (eg security) of the program, algorithms, ie. what has to be done to some extent. Many people in the room considered this level appealing to them.

But a flag was waived: annotations that change the meaning of a program are just ... code ! So annotations should not change the semantic of a program, otherwise we obtain a new language. Annotations, to remain genuine ones, should be intrinsically optional: they should be *hints*. Annotations can be constraints. They thus express domain-specific things and pertain to checking. However, annotations should not grow so much as to have their own type system, otherwise this makes the program much more complex.

A very interesting point was that we may need different hints, for different uses, for different people (annotations for security, for speed optimization, for .... ?) So one remarked that maybe they should stay *outside* the code of the program itself. We could have source (code) files and annotations files, each pertaining to a specific domain.

But wouldn't it be better to be able to modify the language easily (extension, reflexivity...) ? That could be an opening question for next year !

Reflexive annotations (with run-time changes) were mentioned, but the discussion did not go very far on this.

4.2 Lookup, Dispatch Mechanisms

The second session, chaired by Eric Jul, consisted of 2 paper presentations, one insightful introductory talk by Eric on AbCons, and a discussion. This session topic was a brand new one from this year.

The first paper, "One method at a time is quite a waste of time", by Andreas Gal, Michael Bebenita and Michael Franz (University of California, Irvine, USA), made a very convincing case that optimizing on a per method basis is not a good granularity level. Instead their compiler optimizes on at the granularity of hot traces, especially for loops.

The second paper, "Type feedback for bytecode interpreters", by Michael Haupt, Robert Hirschfeld (Univ. of Potsdam, Germany) and Marcus Denker (Univ. of Bern, Switzerland), explained the advantages pertaining to the use of polymorphic inline caches (PICs) in interpreters, and some implementation details in Squeak Smalltalk.

After these nice research works and the introduction on AbCons by Eric, the discussion itself unfortunately did not really catch up, it seems. Things were probably not mature enough. It is also possible that the attendees were not concerned by this kind of implementation "details"... Maybe we could check this for next year (survey ?). The timing — just before lunch — may also have had an impact.

A few points of interest nonetheless emerged:

- Lookup can be implemented in many different ways.
- Lookup tends to increase memory size. This is not too good for caches, hence performance.
- Similarly, lookup tends to increase register pressure, with again a negative impact on performance.
- There was some discussion about the use of fat pointers, to reduce the cost of lookup. Some participants argued that fat pointers are too expensive.
- Most calls can be solved statically, hence alleviating the need for (run-time) lookup. Of course, this may imply whole system analysis, possibly at link time.

4.3 Miscellaneous Implementation Issues

This third session, chaired by Eric Jul, begun the afternoon with three papers.

Titled "A Survey of Scratch-Pad Memory Management Techniques for low-power and -energy", the first paper by Maha Idrissi Aouad (Univ. Henri-Poincaré, Nancy, France) and Olivier Zendra (INRIA-LORIA, Nancy, France) presented various existing SPM (scratch-pad memory) management techniques aimed at low-power. It mostly focused on optimal placement of data according to existing techniques and outlined unexplored directions.

The second paper, "Language and Runtime Implementation of Sessions for Java" by Raymond Hu, Nobuko Yoshida (Imperial College, London, United Kingdom) and Kohei Honda (Univ. of London, United Kingdom), explained how session types could provide type-safe communications in Java. An implementation validating this was shown, with important protocol and communications points detailed.

Finally, "Ensuring that User Defined Code does not See Uninitialized Fields" by Anders Bach Nielsen (Univ. of Aarhus, Denmark) was the third and last paper of this sessions. It discussed some of the problems and solutions found in implementing gbeta, a generalization of the BETA language. This ongoing work focused on a smart handling of object initialization so as to guarantee that user code only uses fully initialized object, thus strengthening the type system promises.

4.4   Continuations and Synchronizations

This fourth session of ICOOOLPS 2007 was chaired by Etienne Gagnon and comprised one paper, one detailed presentation by Etienne on fat locks and Java synchronization and a discussion. It continued ICOOOLPS 2006 unfinished discussion about threads in Java.

The paper in this session was presented by Iulian Dragos (EPFL, Switzerland), Antonio Cunei and Jan Vitek (Purdue Univ., USA). Titled "Continuations in the Java Virtual Machine", it was an introduction to the nontrivial addition of first-class continuation in a Java VM. It outlined the issues such an addition raises, studying interactions with existing features of the Java language such as exceptions, threads, security model and garbage collector.

After a very detailed and complete talk on "Keeping fat locks on a diet, eager deadlock detection, and looking beyond the current Java synchronization model" by Etienne, the discussion on "Java threads and synchronization model." took place.

This was a follow-up and extension to last year's discussion "Do (Java) threads make sense ?". This topic sparked a lot of interest, unlike last year, which indicates that the topic had somehow matured in participants minds.

The current statu quo is "rely on the developer" to express and manage concurrency/synchronization. However, Java was about protecting programmers from themselves. Is it really still the case with threads and synchronization as done in Java ? Threads are not part of the language in Java, but the "synchronized" keyword is. Shouldn't they both be part of the language ? The current situation is somewhat unbalanced.

We then considered what was in the future. Cooperative synchronization ? Synchronization is harder than GC (Garbage collection): indeed automating synchronization is not possible, it is part of the semantics (which is not the case for a GC's work). Synchronization is akin to parallel programming. It's an unsolved problem. On a high level, writing a language that prevents deadlocks (or tells you there are none) would be great. But isn't it like solving the halting problem ? That's not a promising path...

Once again, participants asked whether Java threads were really useful. Indeed, threads and their synchronization seem very low level. But to go lower level than Java, we have C... Shared memory and parallelism is ugly but convenient for scientific programming.

The actual problem for developers is to express that they want to use parallelism, not how. On a higher level, we have parallel programming, join, merge...

Would "actors" and asynchronous message sending be appropriate ?

Overall, the consensus seems to be that threads and synchronization in Java is flawed, not at the appropriate level. Higher-level means should be provided to express these concerns. Those who need lower-level or very fine control of things should rely on going through C code.

5   Conclusion

This second edition of ICOOOLPS was a successful successor to ICOOOLPS 2006, where it had been decided ICOOOLPS should go on recurrently, on a yearly basis. This year, we managed to increase the audience of ICOOOLPS, gathering 27 people from 12 countries — up from 22 people from 8 countries in 2006 — from academia and industry, researcher as well as practitioners. This clearly bides well for the future and the building of a small, informal, community.

A number of positive aspects can be mentioned about ICOOOLPS 2007.

First, this year, the workshop was officially open to anyone, not only authors/speakers. This was coherent with the fact that an ECOOP workshop aims at fostering discussions and exchanges, and the fact we had had many unregistered (but welcome) walk-ins in 2006.

Thanks to our correct forecast for a larger attendance, this year the room allocated by the ECOOP organizers was able to comfortably host all the attendants.

The name tags for attendants were also a small but welcome improvement.

On a more scientific level, once again thanks to the skills of the speakers and active participation of the attendants, the discussions were lively, open-minded and allowed good exchanges. We had allocated more time for discussions than last year, but it was barely enough.

Another encouraging aspect is that some discussions (annotations, Java threads) recurred from 2006, which shows there is interesting work to be done in these areas. Furthermore, the fact that the discussion on Java threads, which did not caught up in 2006, was successful this year, indicates that some topics are maturing.

As we had mentioned last year identifying the main challenges for optimization is not that easy, if only because optimizations for object-oriented languages come in variety of contexts with very different constraints (embedded, real-time, dynamic, legacy...) hence different optimizations criteria (speed, size, memory footprint, energy...). One thing that emerged more clearly in this second edition is the fact that some of our concerns extend beyond object-oriented languages (to functional languages, for example). Another important point is that to optimize, it is difficult to consider separately implementation and language design, or at least specifications. In this respect, the consensus we reached in the workshop that threads and synchronization in Java are flawed and not at the appropriate level is an interesting outcome.

6   Perspectives: ICOOOLPS Future

The perspectives for the ECOOP-ICOOOLPS workshop are very good. When surveyed at the very end of the workshop, 16 attendees amongst the 18 still present intended to come next year. We are thus very confident for ICOOOLSP 2008 to happen, in Cyprus.

Like every year, we try to draw lessons from each edition to further improve the following ICOOOLPS editions. This year, we noted several aspects to improve, amongst which the main ones are:

- This year, we had shorter presentations and longer discussions than in 2006. That was good. But in 2008 we should *devote even more time to discussions*, with even shorter presentations: the purpose of a workshop is not papers, but brainstorming. Presentations should be 10 minutes *max* + 10 minutes for questions.
- We must be *very strict with presentations times*, and not hesitate to stop a speaker who's exceeding her/his time.
- The *papers* do have to be available on the website *before* the workshop.
- Session report drafts should be written during a session (papers and talks) and maybe briefly discussed at the end of each session (not after the workshop).
- Prior registration with the workshop organizers, like in ICOOOLPS 2006, is better. It helps keeping track of attendants, gathering their topics of interest, etc.
- We have to provide *a list of suggested discussion topics* at registration time, so that attendees can vote for them (or suggest new ones). Having discussion time open for topics suggested during the workshop did not work very well in 2007.

Of course, some of these points put an increased burden on the organizers, but are key to an even more successful and enjoyable workshop.

We also intend to selectively enlarge the audience to other — possibly non-OO — communities who face the same kind of issues as the one we focus on in ICOOOLPS.

7   Background

In order to provide a fixed access point for ICOOOLPS related matters, the web site for the workshop is maintained at http://icooolps.loria.fr. All the papers and presentations done for ICOOOLPS'2007 are freely available there.

References

1. Absar, M.J., Catthoor, F.: Compiler-based approach for exploiting scratch-pad in presence of irregular array access. In: DATE, pp. 1162–1167 (2005)
2. Amme, W., Dalton, N., Franz, M., von Ronne, J.: Safetsa: A type safe and referentially secure mobile-code representation based on static single assignment form. In: PLDI, pp. 137–147 (2001)
3. Angiolini, E., Benini, L., Caprara, A.: Polynomial-time algorithm for on-chip scratchpad memory partitioning. In: CASES (2003)
4. Arnold, M., Fink, S., Grove, D., Hind, M., Sweeney, P.F.: Adaptive optimization in the jalapeno jvm. In: OOPSLA, pp. 47–65 (2000)
5. Arnold, M., Fink, S.J., Grove, D., Hind, M., Sweeney, P.F.: A survey of adaptive optimization in virtual machines. Proceedings of the IEEE 93(2), 449–466 (2005)
6. Athavale, R., Vijaykrishnan, N., Kandemir, M.T., Irwin, M.J.: Influence of array allocation mechanisms on memory system energy. In: IPDPS, p. 3 (2001)
7. Avissar, O., Barua, R., Stewart, D.: An optimal memory allocation scheme for scratch-pad-based embedded systems. Transaction on Embedded Computing Systems 1(1), 6–26 (2002)
8. Bacon, D.F., Cheng, P., Rajan, V.T.: A real-time garbage collector with low overhead and consistent utilization. In: POPL, pp. 285–298 (2003)
9. Bacon, D.F., Konuru, R.B., Murthy, C., Serrano, M.J.: Thin locks: Featherweight synchronization for java. In: PLDI, pp. 258–268 (1998)
10. Banakar, R., Steinke, S., Lee, B.-S., Balakrishnan, M., Marwedel, P.: Scratchpad memory: design alternative for cache on-chip memory in embedded systems. In: CODES, pp. 73–78. ACM Press, New York (2002)
11. Baynes, K., Collins, C., Fiterman, E., Ganesh, B., Kohout, P., Smit, C., Zhang, T., Jacob, B.: The performance and energy consumption of three embedded real-time operating systems. In: CASES 2001. 4th Workshop on Compiler and Architecture Support for Embedded Systems, pp. 203–210 (2001)
12. Beers, M.Q., Stork, C., Franz, M.: Efficiently verifiable escape analysis. In: Odersky, M. (ed.) ECOOP 2004. LNCS, vol. 3086, Springer, Heidelberg (2004)
13. Benini, L., Macii, A., Macii, E., Poncino, M.: Increasing Energy Efficiency of Embedded Systems by Application Specific Memory Hierarchy Generation. IEEE Design and Test 17(2), 74–85 (2000)
14. Benini, L., De Micheli, G.: System-level power optimization: techniques and tools. IEEE Design and Test 17(2), 74–85 (2000)
15. Blackburn, S., Jones, R., McKinley, K.S., Moss, J.E.B.: Beltway: Getting around garbage collection gridlock. In: PLDI, pp. 153–164 (2002)
16. Blackburn, S.M., Cheng, P., McKinley, K.S.: Oil and water? high performance garbage collection in java with mmtk. In: ICSE, pp. 137–146 (2004)
17. Blanchet, B.: Escape analysis for java^{tm}: Theory and practice. ACM Trans. Program. Lang. Syst. 25(6), 713–775 (2003)
18. Bollella, G., Gosling, J.: The real-time specification for java. IEEE Computer 33(6), 47–54 (2000)
19. Bruggeman, C., Waddell, O., Dybvig, R.K.: Representing control in the presence of one-shot continuations. In: PLDI, pp. 99–107 (1996)
20. Chambers, C., Ungar, D., Lee, E.: An efficient implementation of self a dynamically-typed object-oriented language based on prototypes. In: OOPSLA, pp. 49–70 (1989)

21. Cherem, S., Rugina, R.: Region analysis and transformation for java programs. In: ISMM, pp. 85–96 (2004)
22. Cofer, D.D., Rangarajan, M.: Formal modeling and analysis of advanced scheduling features in an avionics rtos. In: Sangiovanni-Vincentelli, A.L., Sifakis, J. (eds.) EMSOFT 2002. LNCS, vol. 2491, pp. 138–152. Springer, Heidelberg (2002)
23. Colnet, D., Coucaud, P., Zendra, O.: Compiler support to customize the mark and sweep algorithm. In: ISMM, pp. 154–165 (1998)
24. Delaluz, V., Kandemir, M., Vijaykrishnan, N., Irwin, M.J., Sivasubramaniam, A., Kolcu, I.: Compiler-directed array interleaving for reducing energy in multi-bank memories. In: ASP-DAC 2002. 2002 conference on Asia South Pacific design automation/VLSI Design, p. 288. IEEE Computer Society Press, Los Alamitos (2002)
25. Deters, M., Cytron, R.: Automated discovery of scoped memory regions for real-time java. In: MSP/ISMM, pp. 132–142 (2002)
26. Detlefs, D.: A hard look at hard real-time garbage collection. In: ISORC, pp. 23–32 (2004)
27. Dezani-Ciancaglini, M., Mostrous, D., Yoshida, N., Drossopoulou, S.: Session types for object-oriented languages. In: Thomas, D. (ed.) ECOOP 2006. LNCS, vol. 4067, pp. 328–352. Springer, Heidelberg (2006)
28. Dominguez, A., Udayakumaran, S., Barua, R.: Heap data allocation to scratch-pad memory in embedded systems. Journal of Embedded Computing (JEC) 1(4) (2005)
29. Dwyer, M.B., Hatcliff, J.R., Ranganath, V.P.: Exploiting object escape and locking information in partial-order reductions for concurrent object-oriented programs. Formal Methods in System Design 25(2–3), 199–240 (2004)
30. Egger, B., Lee, J., Shin, H.: Scratchpad Memory Management for Portable Systems with a Memory Management Unit. In: EMSOFT (2006)
31. Ernst, E.: Family polymorphism. In: Knudsen, J.L. (ed.) ECOOP 2001. LNCS, vol. 2072, pp. 303–326. Springer, Heidelberg (2001)
32. Fitzgerald, R.P., Tarditi, D.: The case for profile-directed selection of garbage collectors. In: ISMM, pp. 111–120 (2000)
33. Ben Fradj, H., El Ouardighi, A., Belleudy, C., Auguin, M.: Energy aware memory architecture configuration. 33(3), 3–9 (2005)
34. Gagnon, E.M., Hendren, L.J.: Sablevm: A research framework for the efficient execution of java bytecode. In: Java Virtual Machine Research and Technology Symposium, pp. 27–40 (2001)
35. Graybill, R., Melhem, R.: Power aware computing. Kluwer Academic Publishers, Norwell (2002)
36. Grove, D., Chambers, C.: A framework for call graph construction algorithms. ACM Trans. Program. Lang. Syst. 23(6), 685–746 (2001)
37. Hall, R.S.: A policy-driven class loader to support deployment in extensible frameworks. In: Component Deployment, pp. 81–96 (2004)
38. Hallnor, G., Reinhardt, S.K.: A fully associative software-managed cache design. In: ISCA (2000)
39. Harris, T.L.: Dynamic adaptive pre-tenuring. In: ISMM, pp. 127–136 (2000)
40. Higuera-Toledano, M.T., Issarny, V., Banâtre, M., Cabillic, G., Lesot, J.-P., Parain, F.: Region-based memory management for real-time java. In: ISORC, pp. 387–394 (2001)
41. Hirzel, M., Diwan, A., Hertz, M.: Connectivity-based garbage collection. In: OOPSLA, pp. 359–373 (2003)

42. Hiser, J.D., Davidson, J.W.: EMBARC: An Efficient Memory Bank Assignment Algorithm for Retargetable Compilers. In: LCTES, pp. 182–191. ACM Press, New York (2004)
43. Hölzle, U., Ungar, D.: Optimizing dynamically-dispatched calls with run-time type feedback. In: PLDI, pp. 326–336 (1994)
44. Hom, J., Kremer, U.: Inter-program optimizations for conserving disk energy. In: ISLPED, pp. 335–338. ACM Press, New York (2005)
45. Jones, R., Lins, R.: Garbage Collection: Algorithms for Automatic Dynamic Memory Management. Wiley, Chichester (1996)
46. Kandemir, M., Vijaykrishnan, N., Irwin, M.J., Ye, W., Demirkiran, I.: Register relabeling: A post compilation technique for energy reduction. In: COLP (October 2000)
47. Krintz, C., Calder, B.: Using annotation to reduce dynamic optimization time. In: PLDI, pp. 156–167 (2001)
48. LCTES. Compilation Challenges for Network Processors. In: Compilers and Tools for Embedded Systems. Industrial Panel, ACM Conference on Languages (June 2003)
49. Lee, M., Tiwari, V., Malik, S., Fujita, M.: Power analysis and minimization techniques for embedded dsp software. IEEE Transactions on Very Large Scale Integration, 5 (March 1997)
50. Moreau, P.-E., Zendra, O.: GC²: a generational conservative garbage collector for the ATterm library. J. Log. Algebr. Program. 59(1–2), 5–34 (2004)
51. Muchnick., S.S. (ed.): Advanced compiler design and implementation. Morgan Kaufmann Publishers Inc., San Francisco (1997)
52. Nagpurkar, P., Krintz, C., Hind, M., Sweeney, P.F., Rajan, V.T.: Online phase detection algorithms. In: CGO, pp. 111–123 (2006)
53. Necula., G.C.: Proof-carrying code. In: POPL, pp. 106–119 (1997)
54. Nguyen, N., Dominguez, A., Barua, R.: Memory allocation for embedded systems with a compile-time-unknown scratch-pad size. In: CASES (2005)
55. Nystrom, N., Clarkson, M.R., Myers, A.C.: Polyglot: An extensible compiler framework for java. In: CC (2003)
56. Palacz, K., Vitek, J.: Java subtype tests in real-time. In: Cardelli, L. (ed.) ECOOP 2003. LNCS, vol. 2743, pp. 378–404. Springer, Heidelberg (2003)
57. Panda, P.R., Dutt, N., Nicolau, A.: Efficient utilization of scratch-pad memory in embedded processor applications. In: DATE (1997)
58. Pizlo, F., Fox, J.M., Holmes, D., Vitek, J.: Real-time java scoped memory: Design patterns and semantics. In: ISORC, pp. 101–110 (2004)
59. Poletti, F., Marchal, P., Atienza, D., Benini, L., Catthoor, F., Mendias, J.M.: An integrated hardware/software approach for run-time scratchpad management. In: DAC, pp. 238–243 (2004)
60. Privat, J., Ducournau, R.: Link-time static analysis for efficient separate compilation of object-oriented languages. In: PASTE, pp. 20–27 (2005)
61. Ravindran, R.A., Senger, R.M., Marsman, E.D., Dasika, G.S., Guthaus, M.R., Mahlke, S.A., Brown, R.B.: Partitioning variables across register windows to reduce spill code in a low-power processor. IEEE Transaction on Computers 54(8), 998–1012 (2005)
62. Reynolds, J.C.: The discoveries of continuations. Lisp Symb. Comput. 6(3–4), 233–248 (1993)
63. Siebert., F.: Hard real-time garbage-collection in the jamaica virtual machine. In: RTCSA, pp. 96–102 (1999)

64. Soman, S., Krintz, C., Bacon, D.F.: Dynamic selection of application-specific garbage collectors. In: ISMM, pp. 49–60 (2004)
65. Steinke, S., Grunwald, N., Wehmeyer, L., Banakar, R., Balakrishnan, M., Marwedel, P.: Reducing Energy Consumption by Dynamic Copying of Instructions onto Onchip Memory. In: ISSS (2002)
66. Steinke, S., Knauer, M., Wehmeyer, L., Marwedel, P.: An accurate and fine grain instruction-level energy model supporting software optimizations. In: Proc. of PATMOS (2001)
67. Suganuma, T., Yasue, T., Nakatani, T.: A region-based compilation technique for a java just-in-time compiler. In: PLDI, pp. 312–323. ACM Press, New York (2003)
68. Tallam, S., Gupta, R.: Bitwidth aware global register allocation. In: POPL, pp. 85–96 (2003)
69. Tofte, M., Talpin, J.-P.: Region-based memory management. Inf. Comput. 132(2), 109–176 (1997)
70. Udayakumaran, S., Dominguez, A., Barua, R.: Dynamic allocation for scratch-pad memory using compile-time decisions. Embedded Comput. Syst. 5(2), 472–511 (2006)
71. Verma, M., Wehmeyer, L., Pyka, R., Marwedel, P., Benini, L.: Compilation and Simulation Tool Chain for Memory Aware Energy Optimizations. In: Vassiliadis, S., Wong, S., Hämäläinen, T.D. (eds.) SAMOS 2006. LNCS, vol. 4017, pp. 279–288. Springer, Heidelberg (2006)
72. Whaley, J., Rinard, M.C.: Compositional pointer and escape analysis for java programs. In: OOPSLA, pp. 187–206 (1999)
73. Woo, S., Yoon, J., Kim, J.: Low-power instruction encoding techniques. In: SOC Design Conference (2001)
74. Xie, F., Martonosi, M., Malik, S.: Intraprogram dynamic voltage scaling: Bounding opportunities with analytic modeling. ACM Transactions on Architure and Code Optimization (TACO) 1(3), 323–367 (2004)
75. Zendra, O., Driesen, K.: Stress-testing control structures for dynamic dispatch in java. In: Java Virtual Machine Research and Technology Symposium, pp. 105–118 (2002)
76. Zhang, Y., Gupta, R.: Data compression transformations for dynamically allocated data structures. In: Horspool, R.N. (ed.) CC 2002 at ETAPS 2002. LNCS, vol. 2304, pp. 14–28. Springer, Heidelberg (2002)
77. Zhuang, X., Lau, C., Pande, S.: Storage assignment optimizations through variable coalescence for embedded processors. In: LCTES, pp. 220–231. ACM Press, New York (2003)

Models and Aspects -
Handling Crosscutting Concerns in MDSD
Report on the Workshop MA'07 at ECOOP 2007

Andrew Jackson[1], Iris Groher[2], Christa Schwanninger[2], and Markus Völter[3]

[1] Distributed Systems Group, Department of Computer Science,
Trinity College, Dublin 2, Ireland
anjackson@cs.tcd.ie
[2] Siemens AG, Corporate Technology, Munich, Germany
{iris.groher.ext,christa.schwanninger}@siemens.com
[3] Independent Consultant, Heidenheim, Germany
voelter@acm.org

Abstract. This report summarizes the presentations and discussions of the Third Workshop on Models and Aspects Handling Crosscutting Concerns in MDSD, held in conjunction with the 21st European Conference on Object-Oriented Programming (ECOOP) in Berlin, Germany on July, 31, 2007. This workshop was motivated by the fact that both Model-Driven Software Development (MDSD) and Aspect-Oriented Software Development (AOSD) are important new paradigms that both promise to change the way software is developed. Both approaches provide opportunities for concern separation. AOSD separates concerns horizontally and MDSD enables concern separation vertically. This workshop identified two key integration strategies to achieve the complementary benefits of both aspect-oriented and model-driven development. The first is the use of aspects within transformation languages to separate transformational concerns making model transformations easier to write. The second is the separation of concerns within models defined as aspects. This workshop established the key benefits of these. The major benefit of the first is easing the complexity of development and maintainability of transformations. The major benefit of the second is means to reduce the problems associated with aspects, such as, aspect interactions, fragile pointcuts and understandability.

1 Introduction

Model-Driven Software Development (MDSD) and Aspect-Oriented Software Development (AOSD) are important new paradigms that both promise to change the way software is developed. Both approaches provide opportunities for concern separation. AOSD separates concerns horizontally and MDSD enables concern separation vertically. Although the benefits of AOSD and MDSD are clear, the benefits of their integration into one paradigm remain ambiguous and prone to mis-interpretation. These benefits are unclear because the key integration strategies for combining these paradigms are unclear.

M. Cebulla (Ed.): ECOOP 2007 Workshop Reader, LNCS 4906, pp. 65–74, 2008.
© Springer-Verlag Berlin Heidelberg 2008

This ambiguity is the product of two distinct communities overlapping with their goals, outlooks and experiences. The goals of the AOSD community are to reduce the problems associated with aspects. These problems include the aspect interaction issue, fragile pointcut problem and problems related to the understandability of systems decomposed into aspect modules. The goals of the MDSD community are to improve the ease with which model transformations are written.

This workshop identified two key integration strategies to achieve the complementary benefits of both aspect-oriented and model-driven development. The first is the use of aspects within transformation languages to separate transformational concerns, making model transformations easier to write. The second is the separation of crosscutting concerns within models defined as aspects. This workshop established the key benefits of these. The major benefit of the first is easing the complexity of development and maintainability of transformations. The major benefit of the second is the reduction of evolutionary problems related to composition, more commonly referred to as pointcut fragility.

The remainder of this report is structured as follows. In Section 2 a synopsis of each paper is provided. In Section 3 we list the questions that were tackled in the workshop. In Section 4 we list the participants of the workshop. In Section 5, we characterise and report on the discussion that took place during the workshop. Our conclusions from the workshop are presented in Section 6.

2   Synopsis of Accepted Papers

In this section we present a synopsis of each submitted paper. Typically, we have based this synopsis on abstracts from each paper and where papers did not have abstracts we have provided suitable text. These papers are available on the workshop website http://www.kircher-schwanninger.de/workshops/MDD&AOSD/.

2.1   Using Aspect Oriented Modeling to Localize Implementation of Executable Models [1]

Executable models are essential to define the behavior of models, such as constraints put on model elements. However their implementation crosscut multiple model elements. Model semantics will facilitate Model Driven Development, without it, Design and Implementation won't necessarily represent different abstractions of the same system. This paper introduces a mechanism to query executable models and weave constraints in order to localize their implementation, which improves code redundancy and modularity.

2.2   Interests and Drawbacks of AOSD Compared to MDE a Position Paper [3]

Separation of concern is an essential design process. Two challenges are how to describe a concern and how apply it? The aspect approach makes the choice to offer an universal, generic, mechanism of weaving and requires that the concern designer adopt it and expresses concerns knowing this universal mechanism. All the flexibility is in the concern description. On the contrary, the model driven approach offers more flexibility. In fact, the concern designers decides first the way he describes the concern, selecting a concern meta-model, and after, elaborates a transformation that injects concerns into the base model. No universal merging (weaving) transformation is required. Every transformation is tailored. We argue the MDE approach can be used to separate concerns in a more flexible way that the usual AOP does. Transformations implement automatized steps of the design process. Parts of this process are related to the woven concern and, hence, can be implemented thanks to model transformations. We also argue that concerns must be selected, analyzed, specified, modeled prior to their weaving process. The concern model influence the weaving transformation, but the implementability of the transformation may also influence the concern model. This is why the flexibility offered by MDE is so important.

2.3   Identification of Crosscutting Concerns in Constraint-Driven Validated Model Transformations [4]

Domain-specific model processors facilitate the efficient synthesis of application programs from software models. Often, model compilers are realized by graph rewriting-based model transformation. In Visual Modeling and Transformation System (VMTS), metamodel-based rewriting rules facilitate to assign Object Constraint Language (OCL) constraints to model transformation rules. This approach supports validated model transformation. Unfortunately, the validation introduces a new concern that often crosscuts the functional concern of the transformation rules. To separate these concerns, an aspect-oriented solution is applied for constraint management. This paper introduces the identification method of the crosscutting constraints in metamodel-based model transformation rules. The presented algorithms make both the constraints and the rewriting rules reusable, furthermore, supports the better understanding of model transformations.

2.4   Towards a Generic Aspect-Oriented Modeling Framework [5]

Aspect Oriented Modelling approaches propose to model reusable aspects, or crosscutting concerns, that can be later on composed into various base systems. These approaches are often limited to a particular domain: UML Class diagrams, UML Sequence diagrams .... and therefore they cannot be easily adapted to other domains. In this paper the authors propose to extend the notion of aspects to encompass an open ended number of domains. They present a Generic Aspect Oriented Modeling Framework and show how it can easily be specialised for any specific domain.

2.5   Towards a Run-Time Model Based on Colored Petri-nets for the Execution of Model Transformations [6]

Existing model transformation languages, which range from purely imperative to fully declarative approaches, have the advantage of either explicitly providing statefulness and the ability to define control flow, or offering a raised level of abstraction through automatic rule ordering and application. Existing approaches trying to combine the strengths of both paradigms do so on the language level, only, without considering the benefits of integrating imperative and declarative paradigms in the underlying execution model. Hence, this paper proposes a transformation execution model based on colored Petri-nets, which allows to combine the statefulness of imperative approaches as well the raised level of abstraction from declarative approaches. Furthermore, we show how a Petri-net based execution model lends itself naturally to the integration of an aspect-oriented style of transformation definition, as transformation rules can be triggered not only upon the input model, but on the state of the transformation execution itself.

2.6 Improving Traceability through AOSD [7]

Tracing artefacts throughout the whole development process is a key issue in industry, driven by internal and external forces. Handling variability and documenting decisions on variations is the core issue of traceability. AOSD approaches introduce interesting concepts to modularise cross-cutting concerns at various development stages but it also complicates traceability. Explicit aspect interfaces are one requirement for easier tracking of dependencies between AO and non-AO artefacts. In the paper the authors share their industry perspective on how AOSD and MDSD could further fertilise each other for improving traceability issues, among other challenges.

2.7 Reducing Aspect-Base Coupling through Model Refinement [8]

Aspect-Oriented Programming languages allow pointcut descriptors to quantify over the implementation points of a system. Such pointcuts are problematic with respect to independent development because they introduce strong mutual coupling between base modules and aspects. This position paper addresses the aspect-base coupling problem by defining pointcut descriptors in terms of abstract views of the base module. These abstract views should be towards the architectural viewpoints of the system under development.

3 Workshop Questions Tackled

The aim of this workshop was to explore issues for new approaches to using Model-Driven and Aspect-Oriented Software Development together. We invited researchers and practitioners to present their approaches and discuss the relevance for practical software development. Seven papers, summarised in Section 2, were accepted in total. These papers raised the following questions:

1. Does AOSD improve traceability? [7,3,5,1]
2. What is the relationship between traceability and the fragile pointcut problem in AOSD? [8,3,5]

3. Can the use of models and aspects reduce coupling issues between aspects? [8,3,5]
4. Is MDSD more flexible than AOSD and does this flexibility make AOSD redundant? [3,5,6]
5. Should model transformations and aspects be combined? [4,6,3]
6. What kinds of crosscutting concerns exist in model transformations? [4,6,3]

4 Participants

The following people participated in the workshop:

- Iris Groher, PhD student at Siemens AG, Corporate Technology, Munich, Germany, iris.groher.ext@siemens.com
- Andrew Jackson, PhD student at the Distributed Systems Group, Trinity College Dublin, Ireland, anjackso@cs.tcd.ie
- Thomas Reiter, PhD student, University of Linz, Austria, reiter@bioinf.jku.at
- Benoit Baudry, IRISA/INRIA, Rennes, France, Benoit.Baudry@irisa.fr
- Katharina Mehner, Siemens AG, Munich, Germany, katharina.mehner@siemens.com
- Birgit Grammel, SAP AG, Dresden, Germany, birgit.grammel@sap.com
- Meir Ovadin, Cadence, meiro@cadence.com
- Wilfried Rupflin, University of Dortmund, wilfried.rupflin@cs.uni-dortmund.de
- Laszlo Lengyel, BUTE DAAI, lengyel@aut.bme.hu
- Antoine Beugnard, ENST-Bretagne, Antoine.beugnard@enst-bretagne.fr
- Florian Heidenreich, Technical University Dresden, florian.heidenreich@tu-dresden.de
- Piotr Jacak, Technical University Berlin, jacak@cs.tu-berlin.de
- Gerti Kappel, Technical University Vienna, gerti@big.tuwien.ac.at
- Linda Badri, UQTR, linda.badri@uqtr.ca
- Mourad Babei, UQTR, mourad.babei@uqtr.ca
- Zaid Altahat, IIT, zaid.altahat@ge.com
- Awais Rashid, University of Lancaster, marash@comp.lancs.ac.uk
- Nelly Bencomo, University of Lancaster, nelly@acm.org
- Marco Mosconi, Technical University Berlin, mosconi@cs.tu-berlin.de
- Aswin v. d. Berg, Motorola Labs, aswin.vandenberg@mot.com

5 Discussion

Following in the footsteps of the previous Models and Aspects workshops held at ECOOP the enduring debate over what the core benefits are of using Aspect-Oriented Software Development in conjunction with Model-Driven Software Development. The value of model driven software development was firstly discussed. In this discussion we agreed that the expected benefit of MDSD is that it raises the level of abstraction in software development. Unlike previous instances of this workshop, participants' opinions varied on the most significant benefits of the integration of these complementary approaches to software development. The list of benefits previously considered in this workshop series included maintainability, extensibility, reusability, testability, comprehensibility, scalability, traceability, parallel development and reduced complexity [2]. In contrast, in this installment of the workshop showed a dramatic narrowing of the benefits expected from combining models and aspects. This narrowing has separated the benefits along community lines (the Aspect Oriented Modeling (AOM)[1] community and Model Transformation (MODELS) community [2]). Through this workshop it quickly became apparent that the AOM community was looking towards models to reduce some of the know problems associated with aspects. The MODELS community in contrast was looking toward aspects to ease with which model transformations can be developed, reused and maintained. To facilitate focused discussion for both communities the discussion was separated along these lines.

5.1   Discussion 1: Models to Reduce Problems with Aspects

Andrew Jackson led this discussion and Aswin van den Berg, Birgit Grammel and Zaid Altahat were among the main discussion participants. In this discussion we firstly investigated the idea that traceability was a major benefit when combining aspects and models. The idea here was a more direct alignment between requirements, architecture, design and implementation that aspects in a model-driven environment when AOSD is employed across the development life cycle.

Through our discussion it became clear from experiences and insights within the group that although following an AOSD decomposition would improve the alignment of artifacts in a model-driven approach, it would not improve traceability. The consensus was that traceability would just be between different artifacts and this would not be a marked improvement over other approaches to decomposition. It was agreed that strong traceability should be a side effect of model transformation regardless of decomposition. This discussion dealt with question one defined in Section 2.

With this misconception fully laid to rest we then turned to questions two and three. These questions focused on the ability to use models to reduce coupling between aspects at the code level. The idea forwarded was that by having higher-level representations of aspects the coupling between these models is reduced. The reduction in coupling is due to the fact that composition at higher levels of abstractions is based on the model semantics rather than syntax based composition at lower levels of abstraction.

This move from syntactic to semantic composition mechanisms is an attempt to reduce the negative implications of the fragile pointcut problem. The fragile pointcut problem arises where syntax based composition is employed in development. Pointcut fragility is a byproduct of evolution. Syntax based pointcuts are dependent on the structures and control flow of the elements being composed.

---

[1] http://www.aspect-modeling.org/
[2] http://www.model-transformation.org/

When these structures change this can cause the composition specified by point-cuts to become incorrect. This incorrect composition in turn can then cause the composed software product to be faulty.

To facilitate this move from syntactic to semantic composition the group discussed the possibility of employing a model-driven approach whereby composition is semantically defined between software models and these models are used to automatically generate corresponding syntactic realizations of this at the code level. It was acknowledged by the group that the automated generation of code would produce a skeletal realization of the model which could be embellished by developers where deemed necessary. Allowing embellishment of the generated code can be problematic. The group identified that embellishment causes issues with regeneration from the a changed model. If the model has been embellished and the model that from which the embellished code changes then there is a problem as embellishments may become lost, incorrect or inappropriate when the changed model is regenerated. There is the an associated cost with refactoring the embellishments to ensure the efforts invested in embellishments are not wasted. If the embellished code changes outside the scope of the model then there is a problem of reverse engineering these changes into the model.

Towards the end of this discussion the group reflected on these problems and agreed that round-trip engineering was needed in an Aspect-Oriented Model-Driven approach to software development. Based on our original discussion we conceded that one way to provide round trip engineering in such an approach was by ensuring strong traceability between higher and lower levels of abstraction. From this changes at either level can be more easily propagated between the various levels of abstraction. Through the combination of a model-driven approach, aspect-orientation and round trip engineering the maintainability of the resulting software is expected to be increased.

Our discussion ended by noting that round trip engineering is a complex task that requires an excellent level of tooling to be employed practically at all. We also noted that the benefits of integration of models and aspects requires many more empirical studies at the model level to quantify the true benefits of aspects and models.

5.2   Discussion 2: Aspects in Transformations

Iris Groher led this discussion. In the discussion we first talked about if we should combine model transformations and aspects at all. Some participants were of the opinion that model transformations are very complex in general and aspects could further complicate them. Also, the question was raised if we already know enough about model transformations that we are able to judge what kinds of crosscutting concerns exist in transformations. We agreed that might first have to get a better understanding of transformations and then identify typical crosscutting concerns (CCCs). Experts in the domain of transformations might already know some typical CCCs. Testing is one of the unsolved issues in transformations in general and in AO transformations in particular. We then discussed the issue of development aspects vs. production aspects. Development aspects such as tracing or logging could be added as features of the transformation language to ease the life of transformation developers. Developers can make use of those aspects if they like, similar to the separation of several (mostly non-functional) concerns in component containers.

Another discussion point was how much is actually influenced by the transformation language itself. The question raised was: Depending on the type of transformation language, might there be a need for aspects or not? This question led us to the idea of domain specific transformation languages. As some participants raised the issue of constraints being potential CCCs on transformation level, some domain constraints could already be built in a domain specific transformation language.

We also talked about how aspects on transformation level could look like at all. Are they more then just macro expansion or process interception? It was agreed that only the fact that transformation steps are repeated does not make them crosscutting. Also, participants agreed that the transformation should make sense without the aspect and should be able to be executed without the aspect being applied to it.

The last point we discussed about are software product lines. The transformation language Xtend provides support for aspects (as part of openArchitectureWare 4.2) which has successfully been applied in product line development. Here, features were expressed on model level. The feature dependent parts of the transformation were separated as aspects. We all agreed that this might be a very useful application of aspects on transformation level.

The following example shows what Xtend aspects look like. The function *Interface2Service* transforms an interface into a service. The advice shown below advises the function. The advice is a before advice, ctx.proceed() calls the original function.

create Service Interface2Service (Interface intf) :

setName (intf.name) -> setOperations ((List)intf.operations.clone());

around Interface2Service (Interface intf) :

ctx.proceed() -> ... do additional stuff ;

AO on model transformation level also brings in the opportunity of defining variants of model transformers. By doing so, families of transformers can be created. Aspects applied to transformation functions can change the actual behavior of transformations. In general it was agreed that good tool support is vital for model transformation in general and AO model transformations in particular. It is clear that aspects can make the transformation work-flow harder to understand. openArchitectureWare 4.2 for example provides a debugger for transformations that is also able to debug transformation aspects.

6   Conclusions

This workshop was highly successful. Participants were highly involved and interesting debates raged all day, chaperoned and guided by the organisers. The questions that were tackled arose from the papers that were accepted.

One conclusion of the first discussion (Section 5.1) was that one way that models and aspects can be used together is to use models to raise the level of abstraction to a semantic level where the fragile pointcut problem is overcome. Another outcome from that discussion was the identification of particular fallacies about traceability. We concluded that traceability is not improved through the combination of models and aspects.

In the second discussion (Section 5.2) it was agreed that good tool support is vital for model transformation in general and AO model transformations in particular. It also was concluded that aspects can make the transformation workflow harder to understand.

A final conclusion of the workshop is that more work need to be done to reveal and fully quantify what the main benefits of integrated AOSD-MDSD are; this integration may be at too early stage of research to really identify what needs to be done in the future and current tooling needs to be extended to support integrated AOSD-MDSD approaches.

Acknowledgements

This workshop is supported by European Commission grant IST-2-004349: European Network of Excellence on Aspect-Oriented Software Development (AOSD-Europe), 2004-2008.

References

1. Altahat, Z., Elrad, T., Vojtisek, D.: Using aspect oriented modeling to localize implementation of executable models. In: Proceedings of the Third Workshop on Models and Aspects, Handling Crosscutting Concerns in MDSD at the 21st European Conference on Object-Oriented Programming, Berlin, Germany, pp. 3–7 (2007) (Forschungsberichte der Fakultät IV, Elektrotechnik und Informatik, Bericht Nr. 6, 2007)
2. Groher, I., Jackson, A., Volter, M., Schwanniger, C.: Models and aspects, handling crosscutting concerns in mdsd. In: Südholt, M., Consel, C. (eds.) ECOOP 2006 Ws. LNCS, vol. 4379, pp. 21–25. Springer, Heidelberg (2007)
3. Kabore, C.E., Beugnard, A.: Interests and drawbacks of aosd compared to mde a position paper. In: Proceedings of the Third Workshop on Models and Aspects, Handling Crosscutting Concerns in MDSD at the 21st European Conference on Object-Oriented Programming, Berlin, Germany, pp. 1–2 (2007) (Forschungsberichte der Fakultät IV, Elektrotechnik und Informatik, Bericht Nr. 6, 2007)
4. Lengyel, L., Levendovszky, T., Charaf, H.: Identification of crosscutting concerns in constraint-driven validated model transformations. In: Proceedings of the Third Workshop on Models and Aspects, Handling Crosscutting Concerns in MDSD at the 21st European Conference on Object-Oriented Programming, Berlin, Germany, pp. 13–18 (2007) (Forschungsberichte der Fakultät IV, Elektrotechnik und Informatik, Bericht Nr. 6, 2007)
5. Morin, B., Barais, O., Jezequel, J.-M., Ramos, R.: Towards a generic aspect-oriented modeling framework. In: Proceedings of the Third Workshop on Models and Aspects, Handling Crosscutting Concerns in MDSD at the 21st European Conference on Object-Oriented Programming, Berlin, Germany, pp. 25–29 (2007) (Forschungsberichte der Fakultät IV, Elektrotechnik und Informatik, Bericht Nr. 2007, 6)

6. Reiter, T., Wimmer, M., Kargl, H.: Towards a runtime model based on colored petri-nets for the execution of model transformations. In: Proceedings of the Third Workshop on Models and Aspects, Handling Crosscutting Concerns in MDSD at the 21st European Conference on Object-Oriented Programming, Berlin, Germany, pp. 19–23 (2007) (Forschungsberichte der Fakultät IV, Elektrotechnik und Informatik, Bericht Nr. 6, 2007)
7. Rummler, A., Pohl, C., Grammel, B.: Improving traceability through aosd. In: Proceedings of the Third Workshop on Models and Aspects, Handling Crosscutting Concerns in MDSD at the 21st European Conference on Object-Oriented Programming, Berlin, Germany, pp. 9–10 (2007) (Forschungsberichte der Fakultät IV, Elektrotechnik und Informatik, Bericht Nr. 6, 2007)
8. van den Berg, A., Cottenier, T., Elrad, T.: Reducing aspect-base coupling through model refinement. In: Proceedings of the Third Workshop on Models and Aspects, Handling Crosscutting Concerns in MDSD at the 21st European Conference on Object-Oriented Programming, Berlin, Germany, pp. 11–12 (2007) (Forschungsberichte der Fakultät IV, Elektrotechnik und Informatik, Bericht Nr. 6, 2007)

Aspects, Dependencies and Interactions
Report on the Workshop ADI at ECOOP 2007

Frans Sanen[1], Ruzanna Chitchyan[2], Lodewijk Bergmans[3],
Johan Fabry[4], Mario Sudholt[5], and Katharina Mehner[6]

[1] K.U.Leuven, Leuven, Belgium
frans.sanen@cs.kuleuven.be
[2] Lancaster University, Lancaster, UK
rouza@comp.lancs.ac.uk
[3] University of Twente, Enschede, The Netherlands
L.M.J.Bergmans@ewi.utwente.nl
[4] Computer Science Department (DCC),
University of Chile
jfabry@dcc.uchile.cl
[5] Ecole des Mines de Nantes, Nantes, France
Mario.Sudholt@emn.fr
[6] Siemens, Germany
Katharina.Mehner@siemens.com

Abstract. The topics on aspects, dependencies and interactions are among the key remaining challenges to be tackled by the Aspect-Oriented Software Development (AOSD) community to enable a wide adoption of AOSD technology. This second workshop, organized and supported by the AOSD-Europe project, aimed to continue the wide discussion on aspects, dependencies and interactions started at ADI 2006.

Keywords: Aspects, dependencies, interactions.

1 Introduction

Aspects are crosscutting concerns that exist throughout the software development life cycle - from requirements through to implementation. While crosscutting other concerns, aspects often exert broad influences on these concerns, e.g., by modifying their semantics, structure or behaviour. These dependencies between aspectual and non-aspectual elements may lead to either desirable or (more often) unwanted and unexpected interactions. The goal of this second workshop was to continue the wide discussion on aspects, dependencies and interactions started at ADI 2006, thus investigating the problems of aspects, dependencies and interactions and handling them at all levels:

- starting from the early development stages (i.e., requirements, architecture, and design), looking into dependencies between requirements (e.g., positive/negative contributions between aspectual goals) and interactions caused by aspects (e.g., quality attributes) in requirements, architecture, and design;

M. Cebulla (Ed.): ECOOP 2007 Workshop Reader, LNCS 4906, pp. 75–90, 2008.

- analyzing these dependencies and interactions both through modeling and formal analysis;
- considering language design issues which help to handle such dependencies and interactions (e.g., 'declare precedence' mechanism of AspectJ);
- studying such interactions in applications.

In the rest of this workshop report, we present the main topics that were discussed at the workshop, including a comparative overview of the main topics of the accepted papers, a summary of the keynote speech by Gary T. Leavens on "Concerning efficient reasoning in AspectJ-like languages, a summing-up of the debates hold in the different discussion breakout groups and a synthesis of the panel chaired by Awais Rashid on "Does AO equal quantification and obliviousness?"

2   Accepted Papers

Papers accepted to the workshop covered a broad spectrum of problems related to aspects, dependencies and interactions. We have clustered these papers into three sets, with each set briefly summarized below.

2.1   Requirements, Analysis and Design

This set of papers focuses mainly on the early stages of AOSD: requirements engineering, analysis and design modeling.

In [3], a method is proposed that supports the identification of functional requirements that crosscut other functional requirements. In addition, guidelines about how to generate derived or modified requirements are provided. The authors of the paper use actions as the primary means for identifying match-points between functional requirements. The authors propose to manually define a list of all actions that are directly used by each action, i.e., the implied actions. These implied actions are then used to check whether requirements crosscut each other. Modes or states of the different entities in the system are also important for determining whether requirements crosscut: requirements related to the same mode crosscut while requirements with mutually exclusive modes do not crosscut each other. Next to implied actions and modes, action modifiers are described to help to decide whether two requirements crosscut each other. The authors distinguish between three action modifiers: restrict, unconditional and none. If a requirement restricts the use of an action X, then all actions that imply action X are also restricted. A similar observation is made for requirements that can be used unconditionally.

In [19], the authors argue that currently it is difficult to verify whether a base model is correctly structured and if the weaving reflects the intention of a modeler. They propose a verification method for weaving in AspectM: an extensible aspect-oriented modeling language [20,21]. The paper focuses on the verification of the base model. AspectM provides not only major join point mechanisms but also a mechanism called meta-model access protocol that allows a modeler to modify the meta-model, which is an extension of the UML meta-model. Prototype tool support for the reflective model editor and model weaver has been developed. The tool consists of a meta-model checker for verifying whether a base model conforms to the meta-model, a module structure checker for detecting the aspect interference and an assertion checker.

2.2 Language-Level Problems

This set of papers looks at novel AO language concepts regarding aspect interaction management and issues of interaction between aspects written in different AO domain-specific languages.

In [4], novel concepts regarding aspect interaction management are defined. The paper proposes some extensions to the AspectJ [2] language for detecting unintended aspect interactions. These extensions are aspect and advice cardinality, and meta-aspects. The authors start off by providing a classification of seven different types of aspect interactions. Some fundamental causes of undesired interactions also are discussed. Next, aspect and advice cardinality is defined to represent the absolute and relative proportions of aspect use and advice weaving. Aspect cardinality is the measure of the expected number of aspect bindings to an application while advice cardinality represents the expected number of advice weavings per aspect binding. It's the developer's responsibility to ensure that multiple weavings at the same join point behave coherently depending on a certain applicable execution order. Finally, meta-aspects are generic, abstract specifications of concrete aspects with a number of advantages. These concrete aspects usually can be derived automatically with all generic pointcut definitions being instantiated into specific, narrow-scoped expressions.

In [14], the authors focus on understanding interactions between foreign aspects, i.e., aspects written in different aspect domain-specific languages. They distinguish between two categories: co-advising and foreign advising. Co-advising is the application of multiple pieces of advice to the same join point while foreign advising captures the situation where an aspect also advises aspects written in languages other than the base. A classification and comparison of a set of composition approaches according to whether these resolve the interactions at the language level or at the program level is covered in the paper. In order to understand why resolving these interactions at the language level is fundamentally different than resolving them at the program level, the authors elaborate on both the Reflex [18] and Awesome [13] frameworks. The latter handles both foreign advising and co-advising interactions.

2.3 Contract-Based Approaches

This set of papers addresses contract-based approaches for managing aspect interactions in an AO middleware or for controlling use of aspects without constraining the power of AOSD.

In [9], the authors aim to manage interaction issues in an aspect-oriented middleware platform by allowing interaction contracts to be specified which then are enforced at runtime. Explicitly specifying these contracts improves the management and control of such interactions. The work focuses on two broad categories of aspect interactions: conflicts (two aspects being incompatible) and dependencies (one aspect requiring another). The solution in the paper includes a component model with a well-defined interaction model that supports a variety of relationships. These relationships are specified using interaction contracts that are evaluated at runtime to ensure conflicts do not occur and dependencies are fulfilled. The interaction model is based on shared elements (such as a common join point, a component instance or the base application). It's possible to specify both basic (requires and provides) and advanced (conflict, precedence and resolution) interaction contracts. The approach has been validated by applying it to a series of interaction issues that occurred when implementing services for a flexible and customizable AO middleware platform, CustAOMWare.

In [16], an overview is given of approaches that address two important challenges for AOSD's mainstream adaption: the evolution paradox problem and the invasive nature of aspects. The evolution paradox encompasses the difficulties that arise when an application created using AOSD tries to evolve and is hampered by the fragile pointcut problem. Invasive aspects enable us to specify harmful advice that breaks encapsulation. As a consequence, aspects can invalidate some of the already existing desirable properties of a system resulting in, among others, security problems. Current approaches that solve or reduce one or both of these problems are categorized according to the means they use: guidelines, code-based, analysis, model-based and contract-based. Next, a solution to deal with these problems is sketched. The aim is not to constrain the power of AOSD, but rather control aspect invasiveness and fit aspects to better support evolution.

3   Keynote Speech by Gary T. Leavens on "Concerning Efficient Reasoning in AspectJ-Like Languages"

The work presented in this keynote was concerned with efficient forms of reasoning. The approach taken was based on static analysis of source code that is annotated with meta-information, to determine (non-)interference of the aspect with the base code. What was specified in this approach is object state and method preconditions, heap effects and control effects. Heap effects include postconditions such as changes to static variables. Control effects treat how the control flow of the method is changed. Specification is done by the developer through annotations of the source code. Some of these annotations are deducible, however no support for automatic deduction is provided. Implementation verification is performed by a conservative static analysis. The reasoner accumulates facts as the program is processed, and verifies these with regard to the given specifications.

The innovative part of this approach over existing reasoning with contracts approaches was that it has been effectively tailored towards aspects. This is because the classical subtyping relationships used in these approaches are not applicable to aspects. Around advice can be considered like an overriding method, but is often used to change the behavior in different ways than what an overriding method would do. For example, advice introduces a number of control effects, such as running the original method multiple times. The existing specification approaches cannot reflect this, and their verification steps are not designed for it.

Multiple possible and existing approaches for specification of advice were then discussed. The first approach was using the semantics directly, which is maximally expressive, but implies re-verification for all changes, and provides no abstraction. A second approach is considering functional advice, which has no heap or control effects, which does not affect reasoning over the base code. This advice cannot do anything however, and is therefore useless. Third, the concept of *harmless advice* [6] was discussed. Here no information flows from the advice to the base code, which has as benefits that no heap effects on the base occur. The downsides are that this does not address control effects, there is a loss of expressiveness and inference amongst advice is not addressed. A fourth approach is a refinement of behavioral subtyping, using an object-oriented analogy of around advices as overriding methods, and proceed as a super call. This allows the base code to be verified independent of the advice. This has a number of downsides such as that quantification is limited, and that much advice falls outside of this paradigm, as said above. In general the downsides are too important to make this feasible. A fifth approach is specifying at the language level which join points can be advised, as proposed by multiple authors. This poses no limits on expressive power, but has as downside, amongst others, that interference amongst advices is not considered.

The last approach discussed was reasoning about the level of specifications, written in the aspect, that are woven. The presenter expects that this is the direction that the community is taking. If successful, this has the benefits that it is at a more abstract level than code, and will allow changes in methods and advice without the need for re-verification. The downsides are that there is less expressiveness and that the weaving of specifications is difficult and expensive. However, there are some optimizations that are possible, e.g., ignoring inapplicable advice and spectator advice, which do not affect the heap nor has control effects. A second form of optimization is via effect analysis: an advice heap interferes with base code if it writes a field that is read in the base code. This is efficient because it only needs to look at signatures, and furthermore the analysis can also apply to two pieces of advice.

The last part of the talk then gave an overview of concern domains. It follows the specification weaving approach above, by declaring concern domains, i.e., partitions of the heap, in which write effects are declared. A form of type and effect analysis is then used to detect potential interference. This has been proven to be sound for checking possible heap interference. A further benefit is that spectators can be ignored in the verification phase. Downsides are the cost incurred by manually declaring the effects of methods and advice, and a number of restrictions placed on assertions.

4   Discussion Topics

A large part of the afternoon sessions of the workshop was devoted to group discussions. Four main discussion topics were discussed. These group discussions are summarized below.

4.1   Discussion Group 1: Aspects, Dependencies and Interactions Due to and/or Prohibited by Languages

The goal of this discussion group was to investigate the role of programming language design as a cause or a means to avoid unwanted interactions. The idea behind this topic was that (a) the features of programming languages, such as aspects, can be the enabler for certain interactions, both desired and undesired, and (b) hence there are trade-offs to be made such as expressiveness versus interactions. Some examples are listed next:

- If there were no join points within advice code, there would be no undesired infinite loops caused by advice that is called while executing itself.
- Allowing for pointcuts or advice to ignore the regular OO encapsulation rules, creates potential for unwanted dependencies between aspects and base code.
- The ability to affect the control flow of the base code (e.g., by omitting a *proceed()* statement within *around* advice) is powerful, but can also easily destroy the correctness of the application.

One of the first issues that was discussed was whether or not a language should allow to specify interactions, and/or avoid conflicts. Avoiding conflicts in general is very hard, though, without severely reducing the expressiveness of the language. Hence, the group considered that additional specifications would be necessary to allow for the static detection (and hence avoidance) of interference: for example in the form of contracts or relation specifications.

It was questioned by Shigeru Chiba that many new features for AOP are proposed, often without convincing cases to motivate them, and raising the question whether these features are not merely useful for certain applications or application domains only. In particular, he suggested that many examples of aspects were the codification of program idioms, where there might be other, more conventional ways, such as mix-ins, generics or C++ templates, to express the same behavior.

Further, the group discussed the kind of interferences that are caused by AOP. First, it was proposed that these must be strongly related to the identifying properties AOP, such as obliviousness and quantification. However, it was concluded that in fact, AOP does not introduce new types of interference, but only makes it easier to create them. The reason is that AOP offers new and more powerful composition mechanisms, but in the end, these result in the same types of behavioral combination that can be created manually in procedural or object-oriented languages.

4.2   Discussion Group 2: Aspects, Dependencies and Interactions in Applications

People that joined this discussion group came from two different backgrounds: software product lines and middleware services. Discussion started by agreeing on the fact that a feature in the product line world matches a service in a middleware context. In addition, all discussion participants believed that the true power of AOSD lies in quantification (i.e., composition) rather than in obliviousness. One of the main problems with complete obliviousness is that the aspect developer needs to be aware of the entire system. We refer the reader for the remainder of this discussion topic to Section 5.

Second topic within this discussion group was crosscutting programming interfaces, XPI's, work from Griswold et al. [10] It was concluded that these XPI's would be a very nice idea especially in the context of feature development because a more safe evolution and composition becomes possible. The discussants highlighted the issue of defining such a crosscutting programming interface. At first sight, the base code developer seems more appropriate to define this interface because he/she knows the code the best. But it's hard to imagine that the base code developer knows of all other pieces of code that will cooperate with the base code. Obviously, one of the real problems in specifying pointcuts is that they are mainly syntax-based, which gives rise to the fragile pointcut problem. The group concluded that domain-specific aspect languages might be used as a source of inspiration when trying to raise the level of abstraction.

The next discussion topic in this group consisted of the notion of two-sided contracts as in [16]. The group considered this to be a very interesting idea. The idea of aspect categories and explicitly stating which categories are allowed at a certain point seems a useful thing to do. In addition, the approach enables manageability and safety at the same time. However, the question was posed if the contracts as proposed in [16] are expressive enough.

The group ended this discussion session by reflecting on what should be expressed? On the one hand, expressing what is allowed depends on the specific requirements within a particular application context while expressing what is not allowed seems to pose difficulties taking evolution into account.

4.3   Discussion Group 3: State and Future of Formal Methods for Aspects

A lively discussion on the state and future for formal methods focused on two main questions:

1. What kind of properties are of particular interest for AOSD?
2. What methods can be used to analyze and ensure such properties?

Aspect interactions were discussed as a prime example of properties relevant to AOSD. The current notion of interactions between aspects that are applied to the same joinpoint was identified as a major stumbling block for the handling of interactions among aspects. This coarse notion of interactions forbids the analysis of the frequent case where interactions are caused by two aspects manipulating a common state at different joinpoints. As a second group of aspect-relevant properties, security properties at different levels of abstraction (e.g., on the heap level, on the level of calls to higher-level services) have been discussed.

The discussion on formal methods for the analysis and verification of aspect-relevant properties centered on the need for easy to use, robust and scalable tools. Currently, almost no existing tool supports more than one of those criteria. A major underlying cause for this state of affairs is a lack of modular analysis and verification methods for aspects: specifications of formal properties therefore are rather unwieldy and require time-consuming whole-program analyses. Approaches that restrict aspects on the basis of traditional module boundaries as well as pre-computation of analysis information for program parts that can be reused in the context of analyses on larger programs were discussed as potential solutions to these problems.

4.4 Discussion Group 4: A Classification of Aspect Dependencies and Interactions

The topic of this discussion group was classifications for aspect dependencies and interactions. As it was clear that the group would not be able to provide such a classification or a classification framework, it looked into the characteristics of classifications for aspect dependencies and interactions.

The discussion started from the following question: "Why are there so many classifications for aspect dependencies and interactions?" By this question, the group referred to the situation that in ADI there are relatively many different classifications given that it is still a small community and compared to the overall number of papers on ADI. Some of the noteworthy classifications are [17,5,7] but this list is by no means complete.

Firstly, the group agreed on the fact that classifications are useful because they are a means for understanding the problem space, i.e., the possible dependencies and interactions among aspects or among aspects and other kind of modules. Classifications are also a means to classify the solution space, i.e., the approaches to detect or handle such dependencies. Classifications help with building tools and allow comparing different approaches and tools. A useful classification should cover commonalities and variabilities. Lastly, a useful classification should have been successfully used more than once.

Classifications for aspect dependencies and interactions differ in the following dimensions. These dimensions apply to the problem space that is introduced above. The group considered these dimensions as orthogonal to each other.

- Development phases of the software development life cycle, i.e., requirements engineering, architecture, design modeling, implementation, and testing.
- Expressive power of aspect languages.
- Level of abstraction.

It equally makes sense to think of classifications for the solution space, i.e., for the approaches that detect or even solve aspect dependencies and interactions.

These approaches will use theoretical foundations. Therefore, the solution space can be classified according to the complexity and limitations of the theoretical foundations used.

Getting back to the question that the group asked itsef at the beginning of the discussion, our conclusion is that there is potential for harmonization and unification of classifications.

5 Panel on "Does AO Equal Quantification and Obliviousness?"

The workshop hosted a panel that discussed the question "Does AO equal quantification and obliviousness?" [8]. In particular, the panelists had to formulate an answer to the following three questions.

1. Are quantification and obliviousness fundamental to AO?
2. If yes, why should we embrace them?
3. If no, then what is AO about?

We first elaborate on the different panel positions in which each of the four panelists presented his personal view on the matter. Next, an overview is given from the panel discussion based on questions from the workshop attendants.

5.1 Panel Positions

Michael Haupt started by declaring that we shouldn't be dogmatic: AOSD is about getting some constructs to modularize crosscutting concerns. There are some concerns we can modularize with OO, others we can't. For these, we introduced the term aspects and that's also what AO should be about: modularizing those crosscutting concerns. W.r.t. obliviousness, concerns are already there even before any code is being written. They are an inherent part of a system instead of imposed on (part of) a system. In addition, crosscutting concerns are crosscutting by nature: we can't do anything about it. Obliviousness, however, means in its original definition that aspects can just be imposed on (parts of) a system. The analogy with patches was thrown, where modules don't know they are being patched similar to modules that are oblivious to the fact if there is an aspects imposed on them. This clearly results in a contradiction with crosscutting concerns being there from the start. Michael concluded his statement on obliviousness with requiring that any part of the system should not be more obliviousness to any other part than in traditional OO. For the quantification part of the questions, a very important question in his opinion regards what we should quantify over? Nowadays, we are able to quantify over both static and dynamic parts of a system. We definitely must not quantify over internals of modules, but over interfaces. This way, modules are allowed to express themselves in terms of situations that may be of interest to other modules without giving away too many details.

Klaus Ostermann doesn't like the word obliviousness much because it refers to code locations and as a result, an aspect refers to a module. But an aspect affects a point in the dynamic flow of a program and not a module. Aspects should offer a modular implementation of global invariants of the form: "whenever X happens, do Y". Otherwise, it is implied that we only can understand programs in a step-by-step manner rather than having some higher level of understanding, while the latter is exactly what we should aim for. Many examples have proven this to be true: thread yielding, garbage collection, lazy evaluation, email filtering, etc. A major problem in AOSD so far is that one aspect may destroy the higher-level invariant that is assumed by another aspect. Therefore, in future work, more attention should go to the more controlled interaction between the invariants, in such a way that the problem is composed of modules where each module is responsible for maintaining one or more invariants.

Hidehiko Masuhara rephrased the title of the panel slightly to "AO = quantification (+ obliviousness not necessary) + join point abstraction" because the latter is often overlooked. AO mechanisms can be seen as means of identifying join points and affecting the behavior at those join points, in parallel with the 3-part model that Masuhara et al. have proposed at ECOOP 2003 [15]. When comparing both pieces of work, quantification nicely matches with the means of identifying join points. On the other hand, obliviousness more or less equals how the means of identifying and affecting are modeled, which is not an essential part of the 3-part model. However, join point abstraction, which is not explicitly mentioned in both models, should enable us to capture multiple join points at once. This is often supported by giving a name to a set of join points, so the details are hidden from the user. One of the other panelists asked the speaker about the difference between quantification and join point abstraction. This was countered by explaining that both are not the same thing. The speaker ended with the open question "Is naming sufficient to provide abstraction?"

Wouter Joosen sketched the following historical perspective. When we moved from procedural to OO programming, we went for localization. In this regard, encapsulation can be considered as a first wave of modularization. When we moved to aspects, this only happened because the modularization in OO was not enough: crosscutting concerns still existed. But when going to a next, extended, paradigm, we should not throw away OO ideas. Transactions, persistence and security are the three reusable services that one wants to configure without re-implementing everything over and over again. And, (un)fortunately, obliviousness here exactly is the crime for AO, such as for instance motivated by [22,12]. Due to the current context, we should choose another term (suggestion: dependencies) and take it from there. Finally, some observations were given to the audience. Firstly, the time to ship a software product is essential and makes shifting to components necessary. Aspect should be combined with components if they want to be useful in production environments. Secondly, quantification needs to be over interfaces. Last, but not least, the idea to document the effect of advice next to the effect of aspects [5] is a very valuable one.

5.2 Panel Discussion

Discussions were centered around three more specific topics: obliviousness, interfaces and abstraction. Summaries for each of these discussions are provided below.

Obliviousness. At the beginning of the discussion, the workshop participants agreed that the developer of a module best knows what the module can expose and what not. This should not be influenced by aspects. This is exactly what was pointed out before by some of the panelists. Hidehiko Masuhara complemented this line of thinking, which is similar to Aldrich's open modules [1], by pointing out that the abstraction itself is important, no matter who defines the abstraction where. Hidehiko Masuhara reminded us of the meta-level programming world of computational reflection and asked the question "How do we distinguish AO from meta-level programming?". Klaus Ostermann pointed out that meta-level programming goes about a program with its syntax while AO, at least, tries to talk about the semantics of a program.

According to the panelists, *obliviousness* seems to be a negative thing. Is there any idea about how to design AO technologies without obliviousness? Given the fact that AspectJ has built in some property of obliviousness, is it possible to take it away? In other words, are quantification and obliviousness truly essential? For obliviousness, the answer would be that it is not essential, but useful. Obviously, not all AO technologies must have obliviousness mechanisms. One example would be using AspectJ only with pointcuts on annotations. As a consequence, obliviousness is not essential, since AO technologies can do without it. Languages of course also carry more or less obliviousness than others with different degrees of coupling and cohesion. Klaus Ostermann complemented this with stating that, in his opinion, a pointcut can involve private methods as long as the implementation details are kept hidden. To illustrate, if an aspect depends on the name of a method in AspectJ, one would interpret this as anti-modular because changing implementation details can invalidate aspects. However, pointcuts can either be formulated by referring to method names or by using higher level pointcuts. The latter clearly does not break encapsulation.

Interfaces. A member of the audience also pointed out that the revised definitions of quantification and obliviousness have been overlooked in the discussion so far. Wouter Joosen responded that obliviousness stays a crime and in essence is all about dependencies. Looking at the base code, do we have to know there are dependencies? XPI's [10] and Open Modules [1] are about specifying points that you cannot see in code. We certainly do not want annotations everywhere and a limited form of obliviousness sounds appealing. In any case, we need a mechanism to express what we expect. If you say in an AO composition that you imposed behaviour, then there should be contracts that say which compositions are allowed or not. We can be more precise about what we may want in terms of aspect composition. But if we don't want to be that precise, then we should not violate existing contracts and break encapsulation of, e.g., private elements. Michael Haupt illustrated this further by indicating that there exist different ways in AspectJ to interact with a module ending up with something not being a module any longer if encapsulation gets broken.

An audience member acknowledged Michael Haupt's suggestion that we should plan ahead. However, he claimed that some crosscutting concerns arise because of requirements changes, often after the code is in place. Aspects were compared to patches in this regard. Immediately, the panel intervened by declaring we have a choice. For instance, if there is something in an OO system that doesn't fit my needs, I ask the developer of the module to create a new abstraction. The audience questioned how that developer then could create that new abstraction? One would think using obliviousness, probably. Michael Haupt responded that another option is to have the ability in future AO languages for a module to expose its own interface, and not have an external entity responsible for this. Since, the base module developer has full control over the code, he is the best person in place to provide such an abstraction. Another member of the audience raised the concern that you have component programming on the one side and component assembly on the other. At the assembly-level, you absolutely need contracts in a non-oblivious manner. Wouter Joosen complemented this with noting that oblivousness is of little value when the programmer has full control over the code. The latter is very important from the perspective of software industry where things need to be shipped that won't break. Everybody agreed on the following conclusion of this discussion topic. We should differentiate between obliviousness w.r.t. interfaces and obliviousness w.r.t. implementation. We should avoid the former while the latter is acceptable.

Abstraction. On a question what makes AO different, Hidehiko Masuhara answered with join point abstraction. Klaus Ostermann's view on this matter regards the ability to declaratively describe interesting events and to use this mechanism to implement invariants. Among others, the parallel with macros was drawn. The position of the panel was that an aspect is exposed as a first-class construct dynamically while a macro is done completely statically. The power of using *proceed()* to manipulate the control flow of the program dynamically is not available when working with macros. At the moment, aspects seem to be a sort of swiss army knife doing everything from replacing a byte code rewriter to implementing different crosscutting concerns. This highlights the importance to recognise different needs for obliviousness instead of discouraging obliviousness all together.

The audience started another discussion from the viewpoint of long term maintenance of a product. What happens if changes are required in the next release of a product? If in the previous release the base programmers weren't aware, then in this next release they should be. The relevance is clear if changes to the base code are needed of which the base programmers know that it would affect the aspects that rely on it. Wouter also pointed out the relevance of verifying any interaction that is modeled in a contract, such as for instance in [9], by the compiler or a dedicated verifier. This relates to the ideas in [19].

Finally, Awais Rashid challenged the panel asking what abstraction is essentially? Is naming a sufficient property for abstraction? Hidehiko Masuhara acknowledged the fact that, nowadays, the only property we have at our disposal is naming. Klaus Ostermann completed the position of the panel by stating that naming alone probably will not be enough. Everyone agreed that join point abstraction will be one of the key differentiating factors. A join point definition is abstract if and only if it is in terms of the domain at hand rather than a projection to the code. An audience member asked if it was realistic to try to abstract the pointcut specifications from the code and turn that into an interface and then find an aspect that matches that interface? Would this be sufficient? Hidehiko Masuhara emphasized the resemblance with XPI's [10]. Whether the AspectJ pointcut language suffices to achieve this is another question. Klaus Ostermann also referred to a paper of Kiczales et al. about aspect-aware interfaces [11] at ICSE 2005.

6 Conclusion

This second workshop on Aspects, Dependencies and Interactions provided an opportunity for presentations and lively discussion between researchers working on AOSD, dependencies and interactions from all over the world. The workshop continued the wide discussion on aspects, dependencies and interactions that was started at last years' ADI 2006. It is our intention to continue encouraging the challenging work on this topic by further organizing a number of follow-up workshops.

7 Workshop Organizers and Participants

7.1 List of Organizers

The workshop organizing committee consisted of the following five members.

- Frans Sanen, K.U.Leuven, Belgium (co-chair)
  Email: frans.sanen (at) cs.kuleuven.be
- Ruzanna Chitchyan, Lancaster University, UK (co-chair)
  Email: rouza (at) comp.lancs.ac.uk
- Lodewijk Bergmans, University of Twente, The Netherlands
  Email: L.M.J.Bergmans (at) ewi.utwente.nl
- Johan Fabry, Computer Science Department (DCC), University of Chile, Chile
  Email: jfabry (at) dcc.uchile.cl
- Mario Sudholt, Ecole des Mines de Nantes, France
  Email: mario.sudholt (at) emn.fr

7.2 List of Attendees

The list of attendees officially registered for the workshop is presented alphabetically below. It should be noted that a number of unregistered attendees also participated, but these are not listed here.

1. Zaid Altahat (Illinois Institute of Technology, USA)
2. Mourad Badri (Universit du Qubec Trois-Rivires, Canada)
3. David Bar-On (Open University of Israel, Israel)
4. Jorge Barreiros (Instituto Politecnico de Coimbra, Portugal)
5. Benoit Baudry (IRISA, France)
6. Alexandre Bergel (University of Potsdam, Germany)
7. Lodewijk Bergmans (University of Twente, The Netherlands)
8. Julien Charles (INRIA, France)
9. Shigeru Chiba (Tokyo Institute of Technology, Japan)
10. Johan Fabry (University of Chile, Chile)
11. Gael Fraeteur (PostSharp, Czech Republic)
12. Birgit Grammel (SAP AG, Germany)
13. Phil Greenwood (Lancaster University, UK)
14. Florian Heidenreich (Dresden University of Technology, Germany)
15. Kevin Hoffman (Purdue University, USA)
16. Atsushi Igarashi (Kyoto University, Japan)
17. Jendrik Johannes (Dresden University of Technology, Germany)
18. Wouter Joosen (K.U.Leuven, Belgium)
19. Bert Lagaisse (K.U.Leuven, Belgium)
20. Gary T. Leavens (IOWA State University, USA)
21. Hidehiko Masuhara (University of Tokyo, Japan)
22. Katharina Mehner (Siemens, Germany)
23. Klaus Ostermann (Technical University of Darmstadt, Germany)
24. Meir Ovadia (Cadence Design Systems, USA)
25. Marco Piccioni (ETH Zurich, Switserland)
26. Awais Rashid (Lancaster University, UK)
27. Frans Sanen (K.U.Leuven, Belgium)
28. Hans Schippers (University of Antwerp, Belgium)
29. Sergio Soares (Universidade de Pernambuco, Brazil)
30. Guido Soldner (FAU Erlangen, Germany)
31. Fredrik Sorensen (University of Oslo, Norway)
32. Mario Sudholt (Ecole des Mines de Nantes, France)
33. Shmuel Tyszberowicz (Open University of Israel, Israel)
34. Naoyasu Ubayashi (Kyushu Institute of Technology, Japan)

References

1. Aldrich, J.: Open modules: Modular reasoning about advice. In: Black, A.P. (ed.) ECOOP 2005. LNCS, vol. 3586, pp. 144–168. Springer, Heidelberg (2005)
2. Aspectj, http://www.eclipse.org/aspectj
3. Bar-On, D., Tyszberowicz, S.: Derived requirements generation. In: Proceedings of the Second International Workshop on Aspects, Dependencies and Interactions (held at ECOOP), pp. 5–10 (2007)

4. Barreiros, J., Moreira, A.: Aspect interaction management with meta-aspects and advice cardinality. In: Proceedings of the Second International Workshop on Aspects, Dependencies and Interactions (held at ECOOP), pp. 11–16 (2007)
5. Clifton, C., Leavens, G.T.: Spectators and assistants: Enabling modular aspect-oriented reasoning. Technical Report TR02-10, Iowa State University (2002)
6. Dantas, D.S., Walker, D.: Harmless advice. In: 33rd ACM SIGPLAN - SICACT Symposium on Principles of Programming Languages (POPL06), vol. 41(1), pp. 383–396 (2006)
7. Douence, R., Fradet, P., Südholt, M.: Composition, reuse, and interaction analysis of stateful aspects. In: Proceedings of the 3rd international Conference of Aspect-oriented Software Development, ACM Press, New York (2004)
8. Filman, R., Friedman, D.: Aspect-oriented programming is quantification and obliviousness. In: OOPSLA 2000. Proceendings of Workshop on Advanced Separation of Concerns, October 2000, Minneapolis (2000), http://ic-www.arc.nasa.gov/ic/darwin/oif/leo/filman/text/oif/aop-is.pdf
9. Greenwood, P., Coulson, G., Rashid, A., Lagaisse, B., Sanen, F., Truyen, E., Joosen, W.: Interactions in aspect-oriented middleware. In: Proceedings of the Second International Workshop on Aspects, Dependencies and Interactions (held at ECOOP), pp. 17–22 (2007)
10. Griswold, W.G., Sullivan, K., Song, Y., Shonle, M., Tewari, N., Cai, Y., Rajan, H.: Modular software design with crosscutting interfaces. IEEE Software 23(1), 51–60 (2006)
11. Kiczales, G., Mezini, M.: Aspect-oriented programming and modular reasoning. In: ICSE 2005. Proceedings of the 27th international conference on Software engineering, pp. 49–58. ACM Press, New York (2005)
12. Kienzle, J., Gélineau, S.: Ao challenge - implementing the acid properties for transactional objects. In: Proceedings of the 5th International Conference on Aspect-Oriented Software Development, pp. 202–213. ACM Press, New York (2006)
13. Kojarski, S., Lorenz, D.H.: Awesome: A co-weaving system for multiple aspect-oriented extensions. In: Proceedings of the 22nd Annual Conference on Object-Oriented Programming Systems, Languages and Applications, ACM Press, New York (2007)
14. Lorenz, D.H., Kojarski, S.: Understanding aspect interactions, co-advising and foreign advising. In: Proceedings of the Second International Workshop on Aspects, Dependencies and Interactions (held at ECOOP), pp. 23–28 (2007)
15. Masuhara, H., Kiczales, G.: Modeling crosscutting in aspect-oriented mechanisms. In: Cardelli, L. (ed.) ECOOP 2003. LNCS, vol. 2743, Springer, Heidelberg (2003)
16. Munoz, F., Barais, O., Baudry, B.: Vigilant usage of aspects. In: Proceedings of the Second International Workshop on Aspects, Dependencies and Interactions (held at ECOOP), pp. 29–35 (2007)
17. Rinard, M., Sălcianu, A., Bugrara, S.: A classification system and analysis for aspect-oriented programs. In: Proceedings of SIGSOFT 2004/FSE-12, pp. 147–158. ACM, New York (2004)
18. Tanter, É., Noyé, J.: A versatile kernel for multi-language AOP. In: Glück, R., Lowry, M. (eds.) GPCE 2005. LNCS, vol. 3676, pp. 173–188. Springer, Heidelberg (2005)
19. Ubayashi, N., Maeno, Y., Noda, K., Otsubo, G.: A verification mechanism for weaving in extensible aom languages. In: Proceedings of the Second International Workshop on Aspects, Dependencies and Interactions (held at ECOOP), pp. 36–41 (2007)

20. Ubayashi, N., Tamai, T., Sano, S., Maeno, Y., Murakami, S.: Model compiler construction based on aspect-oriented mechanisms. In: Glück, R., Lowry, M. (eds.) GPCE 2005. LNCS, vol. 3676, pp. 109–124. Springer, Heidelberg (2005)
21. Ubayashi, N., Tamai, T., Sano, S., Maeno, Y., Murakami, S.: Aspect-oriented and collaborative systems metamodel access protocols for extensible aspect-oriented modeling. In: Zhang, K., Spanoudakis, G., Visaggio, G. (eds.) SEKE, pp. 4–10 (2006)
22. Win, B.D.: Engineering application-level security through aspect-oriented software development. PhD dissertation (2004)

Enabling Software Evolution Via AOP and Reflection
Report on the Workshop RAM-SE at ECOOP 2007

Manuel Oriol[1], Walter Cazzola[2], Shigeru Chiba[3], Gunter Saake[4],
Yvonne Coady[5], Stéphane Ducasse[6], and Günter Kniesel[7]

[1] ETH Zurich, Zurich, Switzerland
moriol@inf.ethz.ch
[2] Università degli Studi di Milano, Milano, Italy
cazzola@dico.unimi.it
[3] Tokyo Institute of Technology, Tokyo, Japan
chiba@is.titech.ac.jp
[4] Otto-von-Guericke-Universität Magdeburg, Magdeburg, Germany
saake@iti.cs.uni-magdeburg.de
[5] University of Victoria, Victoria, Canada
ycoady@cs.uvic.ca
[6] INRIA, Lille, France
stephane.ducasse@inria.fr
[7] University of Bonn, Bonn, Germany
gk@cs.uni-bonn.de

Abstract. Following last three years' RAM-SE (Reflection, AOP and
Meta-Data for Software Evolution) workshop at the ECOOP conference,
the RAM-SE'07 workshop was a successful and popular event. As its
name implies, the workshop's focus was on the application of reflective,
aspect-oriented and data-mining techniques to the broad field of software
evolution. Topics and discussions at the workshop included mechanisms
for supporting software evolution, technological limits for software evolution and tools and middleware for software evolution. The workshop's
main goal was to bring together researchers working in the field of software evolution with a particular interest in reflection, aspect-oriented
programming and meta-data. The workshop was organized as a full day
meeting, partly devoted to presentation of submitted position papers
and partly devoted to panel discussions about the presented topics and
other interesting issues in the field. In this way, the workshop allowed
participants to get acquainted with each other's work, and stimulated
collaboration.

1 Workshop Description and Objectives

Software evolution and adaptation is a research area that offers stimulating challenges for both academic and industrial researchers. The evolution of software
systems, to face unexpected situations or just for improving their features, relies

M. Cebulla (Ed.): ECOOP 2007 Workshop Reader, LNCS 4906, pp. 91–98, 2008.
© Springer-Verlag Berlin Heidelberg 2008

on software engineering techniques and methodologies. Nowadays a similar approach is not applicable in all situations e.g., for evolving nonstopping systems or systems whose code is not available.

Features of reflection such as transparency, separation of concerns, and extensibility seem to be perfect tools to aid the dynamic evolution of running systems. Aspect-oriented programming (AOP) can simplify code instrumentation whereas techniques that rely on meta-data can be used to inspect the system and to extract the necessary data for designing the heuristic that the reflective and aspect-oriented mechanism use for managing the evolution.

We feel the necessity to investigate the benefits brought by the use of these techniques on the evolution of object-oriented software systems. In particular we would determine how these techniques can be integrated with more traditional approaches to evolve a system and the benefits we get from their use.

The overall goal of this workshop was that of supporting circulation of ideas between these disciplines. Several interactions were expected to take place between reflection, aspect-oriented programming and meta-data for the software evolution, some of which we cannot even foresee. Both the application of reflective or aspect-oriented techniques and concepts to software evolution are likely to support improvement and deeper understanding of these areas. This workshop has represented a good meeting-point for people working in the software evolution area, and an occasion to present reflective, aspect-oriented, and meta-data based solutions to evolutionary problems, and new ideas straddling these areas, to provide a discussion forum, and to allow new collaboration projects to be established. The workshop was a full day meeting. One part of the workshop was devoted to presentation of papers, and another to panels and to the exchange of ideas among participants.

2   Workshop Topics and Structure

Every contribution that exploits reflective techniques, aspect-oriented programming and/or meta-data to evolve software systems were welcome. Specific topics of interest for the workshop have included, but were not limited to:

- aspect-oriented middleware and environments for software evolution;
- adaptive software components and evolution as component composition;
- evolution planning and deployment through aspect-oriented techniques and reflective approaches;
- aspect interference and composition for software evolution;
- feature- and subject-oriented adaptation;
- unanticipated software evolution supported by AOSD or reflective techniques;
- MOF, code annotations and other meta-data facilities for software evolution;
- software evolution tangling concerns;
- techniques for refactoring into AOSD and to get the separation of concerns;
- early aspect evolution, i.e., to design evolution by evolving the design information or the application in its early stages of development.

To ensure lively discussion at the workshop, the organizing committee has chosen the contributions on the basis of topic similarity that will permit the beginning of new collaborations. To grant an easy dissemination of the proposed ideas and to favorite an ideas interchange among the participants, accepted contributions are freely downloadable from the workshop web page:

http://homes.dico.unimi.it/RAM-SE07.html.

The workshop was a full day meeting organized in four sessions. The first session was devoted to the Shigeru Chiba's keynote speech on *"How We Should Use Aspects"*. Each of the remaining sessions has been characterized by a dominant topic that perfectly describes the presented papers and the related discussions. The two dominant topics were: *Classic Software Evolution,* and *Aspect-Oriented and Reflection for Software Evolution.* During each session, paper presentations took 15 minutes with a 5 minutes discussion. At the end of the day a special session was devoted to discussions. The discussion related to each session has been brilliantly lead respectively by Mario Südholt, Walter Cazzola, Manuel Oriol and Gunter Saake.

The workshop has been very lively, the debates very stimulating, and the high number of participants (see appendix A) testifies the interest in the application of reflective, aspect- and meta-data oriented techniques to software evolution as well as software evolution in general.

3   Important References

The following publications are important references for people interested in learning more about the topics of this workshop:

- Pattie Maes. Computational Reflection. PhD thesis, Vrije Universiteit Brussel, Brussels, Belgium, 1987.
- Gregor Kiczales, John Lamping, Anurag Mendhekar, Chris Maeda, Cristina Videira Lopes, Jean-Marc Loingtier, and John Irwin. Aspect-Oriented Programming. In *11th European Conference on Object Oriented Programming (ECOOP'97),* LNCS 1241, pages 220–242, Helsinki, Finland, June 1997. Springer-Verlag.
- The proceedings of the International Conference on Aspect-Oriented Software Development (AOSD) from 2002 onward. See also http://aosd.net/archive/index.php.
- Several tracks related to aspect-oriented software development and evolution at the International Conference on Software Maintenance (ICSM) and the Working Conference on Reverse Engineering (WCRE), from 2002 onward.
- The software evolution website at the Program Transformation wiki:

http://www.program-transformation.org/twiki/bin/view/
Transform/SoftwareEvolution.

- The workshops proceedings of the USE workshop series:

http://www.informatik.uni-bonn.de/~gk/use/.

4　Workshop Overview: Session by Session

Session on How We Should Use Aspects

In the first morning session, Shigeru Chiba gave a keynote talk that was moderated by Mario Südholt:

How We Should Use Aspects

Abstract. *Besides classic logging and the observer pattern, several applications of aspect-oriented programming (AOP) have been proposed so far. This talk reviews those applications and discusses what properties of AOP are significant and promising for software evolution. It will also discuss what are unique features of AOP against related technology such as reflection and mixin layers.*

Chiba's provocative talk presented several applications where AOP should be used. The first application presented is logging as it consists of a multitude of similar calls that can be located anywhere in the code. This is one of the possibilities used by IBM field engineers. The Aspect-Oriented interactive debuggers [1], high performance computing [2] could also be interesting. Application-level scheduling [3] is also a possible use of AOP and as an example, the application level scheduling achieved better performances than the Linux scheduler. Non-functional requirements do not appear to be the best fields to which aspects can be best applied as they are generally very class centric. One of the lessons drawn is that most aspects are heterogeneous and thus AOP does not avoid iterative code of programming idioms. Another lesson is that pointcut advices are seldom used, thus the question is if pointcut is a primary mechanism.

The keynote talk fostered further discussions which triggered the following points:

- It was suggested that AOP is better than the meta-object protocol (MOP) for persistence.
- The lessons outlined by Chiba are mostly valid because he is drawing them from AspectJ, using another aspect language (e.g., a higher level one) could lead to very different results.
- There are a handful of applications that use AOP (MySQL, WebSphere,...) while many applications use MOP. The reason for such a fact may be that the AOP community did not focus on a simple set of "evident" applications to help people getting in the methodology.

Session on Classic Software Evolution

Classical software evolution was the main focus of the second session. The session was moderated by Walter Cazzola.

[4] Toward Computer-Aided Usability Evaluation Evolving Interactive Software. *Yonglei Tao* (Grand Valley State University, USA).

Yonglei Tao gave the presentation.

[5] Towards Runtime Adaptation in a SOA Environment. *Florian Irmert, Marcus Meyerhofer* and *Markus Weiten* (Friedrich-Alexander Universität Erlagen-Nürnberg, Germany).

Florian Irmert gave the presentation.

[6] IDE-integrated Support for Schema Evolution in Object-Oriented Applications. *Marco Piccioni, Manuel Oriol,* and *Betrand Meyer* (ETH Zürich, Switzerland).

Marco Piccioni gave the presentation.

[7] Property-preserving Evolution of Components Using VPA-Based Aspects. *Dong Ha Nguyen* and *Mario Südholt,* Ecole des Mines de Nantes, France.

Mario Südholt gave the presentation.

Session on Aspect-Oriented and Reflection for Software Evolution

Aspect-oriented and reflection for software evolution was the main focus of the third session. The session was moderated by Manuel Oriol.

[8] Characteristics of Runtime Program Evolution. *Mario Pukall,* and *Martin Kuhlemann* (Otto von Guericke University Magdeburg, Germany).

Mario Pukall gave the presentation.

[9] Aspect-Based Introspection and Change Analysis for Evolving Programs. *Kevin Hoffman, Murali Krishna Ramanathan, Patrick Eugster,* and *Suresh Jagannathan* (Purdue University, USA).

Kevin Hoffman gave the presentation.

[10] Morphing Software for Easier Evolution. *Shan Shan Huang* and *Yannis Smaragdakis* (University of Oregon, USA).

Yannis Smaragdakis gave the presentation.

[11] AOP vs Software Evolution: a Score in Favor of the Blueprint. *Walter Cazzola* (DICo Università degli Studi di Milano, Italy), and *Sonia Pini* (DISI Università degli Studi di Genova, Italy).

Sonia Pini gave the presentation.

Session on Future Evolutions of RAM-SE

The workshop ended with a session led by Gunter Saake on the future of the RAM-SE workshop and fostered lively discussions. Most of the discussion focused on the fact that aspects are polarizing people either positively or very negatively. In order to develop aspects further, it is needed to show very simple examples in which aspects have an evident applicability and ease the task. Even if it is probably not possible to find use cases where only aspects could solve the problem there are numerous areas in which the most elegant solution would use aspects. The cost of having people understand and use aspects is probably to propose and advocate emblematic simplifications. This is inspired by reflection being what probably stands out of the meta-object protocol.

5   Tendencies in Reflection, AOP and Meta-data for Software Evolution

The workshop outlined at least three major areas which are currently active:

- Evolution enabling technologies.
- Applications of aspects to understanding or controlling the evolution of programs.
- New trends in AOP for smooth evolution.

The first area consists of technologies that improve the direct evolution capabilities of programs. As such, the work of Piccioni *et al.* on schema evolution [6] enables the easy programming of persistent applications by using reflexive techniques. The work of Irmert *et al.* on dynamic adaptation of applications through the use of dynamic aspects [5] opens new directions in the runtime evolution of applications. The work from Nguyen *et al.* on the dynamic evolution of pushdown automata [7] opens new leads in the correctness of dynamic updates. The work of Pukall *et al.* [8] analyzes languages and technologies according to the time of evolution and the type of evolution that they enable while effecting runtime evolution.

The second area consists of applications of the aspects technologies that ease the understanding of the state or of the evolution of programs. For example the work by Tao on the evaluation of usability of interactive software [4] uses aspects to trace users actions. The work by Hoffman *et al.* [9] instruments programs using aspects to gather information on the state of a program while it executes in order to understand the changes that were performed at runtime when updated.

The third area consists of new trends in AOP that ease the evolution of applications coded with aspects. As an example the work by Huang *et al.* [10] allows for a better evolvability of programs by defining the morphing technique. The work of Cazzola *et al.* [11] proposes a new aspect language that solves the fragile pointcut issue and evaluate the solution with evolving programs.

6   Final Remarks

The main goal of the workshop was to bring together researchers interested in the field and have them communicate on their respective work. The workshop lived up to its expectations, with high-quality submissions and presentations, and lively and stimulating discussions. The vitality of the work as well as the lively discussions that took place during the workshop show that the issues addressed by the workshop are plainly relevant and need such a forum to be discussed. We hope participants found the workshop interesting and useful, and encourage them to finalize their position papers and submit them as full papers to international conferences interested in the topics of this workshop.

Acknowledgements. We wish to thank Mario Südholt both for his interest in the workshop and for his help during the workshop as chairman and speaker. We wish also to thank all the researchers that have participated to the workshop.

We have also to thank the Department of Informatics and Communication of the University of Milan, the Department of Mathematical and Computing Sciences of the Tokyo institute of Technology, ETH Zurich and the Institute für Technische und Betriebliche Informationssysteme, Otto-von-Guericke-Universität Magdeburg for their various supports.

References

1. Usui, Y., Chiba, S.: Bugdel: An aspect-oriented debugging system. In: APSEC 2005. 12th Asia-Pacific Software Engineering Conference, December 15-17, 2005, Taipei, Taiwan, pp. 790–795 (2005)
2. Nishizawa, M., Chiba, S., Tatsubori, M.: Remote pointcut: a language construct for distributed aop. In: AOSD 2004. Proceedings of the 3rd International Conference on Aspect-Oriented Software Development, pp. 7–15 (2004)
3. Kourai, K., Hibino, H., Chiba, S.: Aspect-oriented application-level scheduling for j2ee servers. In: AOSD 2007. Proceedings of the 6th International Conference on Aspect-Oriented Software Development, pp. 1–13 (2007)
4. Tao, Y.: Toward Computer-Aided Usability Evaluation Evolving Interactive Software. In: In Cazzola, W., Chiba, S., Coady, Y., Ducasse, S., Kniesel, G., Oriol, M., Saake, G. (eds.) Proceedings of ECOOP 2007. Workshop on Reflection, AOP and Meta-Data for Software Evolution (RAM-SE 2007), Berlin, Germany (2007)
5. Irmert, F., Meyerhöfer, W.M.: Towards Runtime Adaptation in a SOA Environment. In: Cazzola, W., Chiba, S., Coady, Y., Ducasse, S., Kniesel, G., Oriol, M., Saake, G. (eds.) Proceedings of ECOOP 2007 Workshop on Reflection, AOP and Meta-Data for Software Evolution (RAM-SE 2007), Berlin, Germany (2007)
6. Piccioni, M., Oriol, M., Meyer, B.: IDE-integrated Support for Schema Evolution in Object-Oriented Applications. In: Cazzola, W., Chiba, S., Coady, Y., Ducasse, S., Kniesel, G., Oriol, M., Saake, G. (eds.) Proceedings of ECOOP 2007 Workshop on Reflection, AOP and Meta-Data for Software Evolution (RAM-SE 2007), Berlin, Germany (2007)

7. Nguyen, D.H., Südholt, M.: Property-preserving Evolution of Components Using VPA-Based Aspects. In: Cazzola, W., Chiba, S., Coady, Y., Ducasse, S., Kniesel, G., Oriol, M., Saake, G. (eds.) Proceedings of ECOOP 2007 Workshop on Reflection, AOP and Meta-Data for Software Evolution (RAM-SE 2007), Berlin, Germany (2007)
8. Pukall, M., Kuhlemann, M.: Characteristics of Runtime Program Evolution. In: Cazzola, W., Chiba, S., Coady, Y., Ducasse, S., Kniesel, G., Oriol, M., Saake, G. (eds.) Proceedings of ECOOP 2007 Workshop on Reflection, AOP and Meta-Data for Software Evolution (RAM-SE 2007), Berlin, Germany (2007)
9. Hoffman, K., Ramanathan, M.K., Eugster, P., Jagannathan, S.: Aspect-Based Introspection and Change Analysis for Evolving Programs. In: Cazzola, W., Chiba, S., Coady, Y., Ducasse, S., Kniesel, G., Oriol, M., Saake, G. (eds.) Proceedings of ECOOP 2007 Workshop on Reflection, AOP and Meta-Data for Software Evolution (RAM-SE 2007), Berlin, Germany (2007)
10. Huang, S.S., Smaragdakis, Y.: Morphing Software for Easier Evolution. In: Cazzola, W., Chiba, S., Coady, Y., Ducasse, S., Kniesel, G., Oriol, M., Saake, G. (eds.) Proceedings of ECOOP 2007 Workshop on Reflection, AOP and Meta-Data for Software Evolution (RAM-SE 2007), Berlin, Germany (2007)
11. Cazzola, W., Pini, S.: AOP vs Software Evolution: a Score in Favor of the Blueprint. In: Cazzola, W., Chiba, S., Coady, Y., Ducasse, S., Kniesel, G., Oriol, M., Saake, G. (eds.) Proceedings of ECOOP 2007 Workshop on Reflection, AOP and Meta-Data for Software Evolution (RAM-SE 2007), Berlin, Germany (2007)

A   Workshop Attendee

The success of the workshop is mainly due to the people that have attended it and to their effort to participate to the discussions. The following is the list of the attendees in alphabetical order.

Name	Affiliation	Country	e-mail
Blair, Gordon	Lancaster University	United Kingdom	gordon@comp.lancs.ac.uk
Cazzola, Walter	Università degli Studi di Milano	Italy	cazzola@dico.unimi.it
Chiba, Shigeru	Tokyo Institute of Technology	Japan	chiba@is.titech.ac.jp
Greenwood, Phil	Lancaster University	United Kingdom	greenwood@comp.lancs.ac.uk
Hoffman, Kevin	Purdue University	USA	KevinJohnHoffman@gmail.com
Huang, Shan Shan	Georgia Tech	USA	ssh@cc.gatech.edu
Irmert, Florian	Universität Erlagen-Nürnberg	Germany	florian.irmert@informatik.uni-erlagen.de
Kienle, Holger	University of Victoria	Canada	kienle@cs.uvic.ca
Masuhara, Hidehiko	University of Tokyo	Japan	masuhara@graco.c.u-tokyo.ac.jp
Mens, Kim	Université Catholique de Louvain	Belgium	km@info.ucl.ac.be
Mosser, Sebastian	University of Nice/CNRS	France	mosser@polytech.unice.fr
Oriol, Manuel	ETH Zürich	Switzerland	moriol@inf.ethz.ch
Piccioni, Marco	ETH Zürich	Switzerland	marco.piccioni@inf.ethz.ch
Pini, Sonia	Università degli Studi di Genova	Italy	pini@disi.unige.it
Pukall, Mario	University of Magdeburg	Germany	pukall@iti.cs.uni-magdeburg.de
Rashid, Awais	Lancaster University	United Kingdom	marash@comp.lancs.ac.uk
Südholt, Mario	École des Mines de Nantes	France	sudholt@emn.fr
Sørensen, Fredrik	University of Oslo	Norway	fredrso@ifi.uio.no
Saake, Gunter	University of Magdeburg	Germany	saake@iti.cs.uni-magdeburg.de
Smaragdakis, Yannis	University of Oregon	USA	yannis@cs.uoregon.edu
Tanter, Éric	University of Chile	Chile	etanter@dcc.uchile.cl
Tao, Yonglei	Grand Valley State University	USA	taoy@gvsu.edu
Ueyama, Jó	University of Campinas	Brazil	joueyama@ic.unicamp.br
Yonezawa Akinori	University of Tokyo	Japan	yonezawa@is.s.u-tokyo.ac.jp

Formal Techniques for Java-Like Programs
Report on the Workshop FTfJP at ECOOP 2007

John Boyland[1,2], Dave Clarke[3], Gary Leavens[4], Francesco Logozzo[5],
and Arnd Poetzsch-Heffter[6]

[1] University of Wisconsin–Milwaukee, USA
`boyland@uwm.edu`
[2] Nanjing University, China
[3] CWI, Amsterdam, Netherlands
`dave@cwi.nl`
[4] University of Central Florida, USA
`leavens@eecs.ucf.edu`
[5] Microsoft Research, USA
`logozzo@microsoft.com`
[6] Universität Kaiserslautern, Germany
`poetzsch@informatik.uni-kl.de`

Abstract. Formal techniques can help analyze programs, precisely describe program behavior, and verify program properties. Newer languages such as Java and C# provide good platforms to bridge the gap between formal techniques and practical program development, because of their reasonably clear semantics and standardized libraries. Moreover, these languages are interesting targets for formal techniques, because the novel paradigm for program deployment introduced with Java, with its improved portability and mobility, opens up new possibilities for abuse and causes concern about security.

Work on formal techniques and tools for programs and work on the formal underpinnings of programming languages themselves naturally complement each other. This workshop aims to bring together people working in both these fields, on topics such as: specification techniques and interface specification languages, specification of software components and library packages, automated checking and verification of program properties, verification logics, language semantics, program analysis, type systems, security.

1 Call for Papers

The Call for Papers included the text from the abstract above and the following text:

Contributions are sought on open questions, new developments, or interesting new applications of formal techniques in the context of Java or similar languages, such as C#. Contributions should not merely present completely finished work, but also raise challenging open problems or

M. Cebulla (Ed.): ECOOP 2007 Workshop Reader, LNCS 4906, pp. 99–107, 2008.
© Springer-Verlag Berlin Heidelberg 2008

propose speculative new approaches. We particularly welcome contributions that simply suggest good topics for discussion at the workshop, or raise issues that you feel deserve the attention of the research community. Submissions must be in English and are limited to 10 pages using LNCS style (excluding bibliography). Papers must be submitted electronically via the workshop website: http://cs.nju.edu.cn/boyland/ftjp.

An informal proceedings will be made available to workshop participants. Papers will also be available from the workshop web page. There will be no formal publication of papers. We intend to invite selected papers for a special journal issue as a follow-up to the workshop, as has been done for some previous FTfJP workshops.

Indeed, after the workshop, we invited eight papers to submit updated papers for a special issue of JOT (Journal of Object Technology). Six teams of authors have responded positively thus far.

2   People

2.1   Programme Committee

- Cyrille Valentin Artho (RCIS/AIST, Japan),
- Frank S. de Boer (CWI, Netherlands),
- Fabrice Bouquet (University of Franche Comté, France),
- John Boyland (Nanjing University, China and University of Wisconsin-Milwaukee, USA) chair,
- Alex Buckley (Sun Microsystems, UK),
- Patrice Chalin (Concordia University, Canada),
- Dave Clarke (CWI, Netherlands),
- Paola Giannini (University of Piemonte Orientale, Italy),
- Marieke Huisman (INRIA Sophia Antipolis, France),
- Giovanni Lagorio (Università di Genova, Italy),
- Gary T. Leavens (Iowa State University, USA, now Central Florida University, USA),
- Francesco Logozzo (Microsoft Research, USA),
- Wojciech Mostowski (Radboud University Nijmegen, Netherlands),
- Wolfram Schulte (Microsoft Research, USA).

2.2   Organizers

- John Boyland (University of Wisconsin-Milwaukee, USA) co-chair,
- Sophia Drossopoulou (Imperial College, UK),
- Susan Eisenbach (Imperial College, UK),
- Gary T. Leavens (Central Florida University, USA),
- Peter Müller (ETH Zürich, Switzerland),
- Arnd Poetzsch-Heffter (Universität Kaiserlautern, Germany),
- Erik Poll (Radboud University Nijmegen, Netherlands), co-chair.

2.3 Participants

Suad Alagic, University of South Maine, alagic@cs.usm.maine.edu
Jonathan Aldrich, Carnegie Mellon University, aldrich@cs.cmu.edu
Philippe Altherr, Google, paltherr@google.com
Davide Ancona, DISI - University of Genova, davide@disi.unige.it
Eric Bodden, McGill University, eric.bodden@mail.mcgill.ca
John Boyland, University of Wisconsin-Milwaukee, boyland@uwm.edu
Alex Buckley, Sun Microsystems, alex.buckley@sun.com
Nicholas Cameron, Imperial College, London, ncameron@doc.ic.ac.uk
Patrice Chalin, Concordia University, chalin@encs.concordia.ca
Julien Charles, INRIA, julien.charles@inria.fr
Dave Clarke, CWI, Amsterdam, dave@cwi.nl
Curt Clifton, Rose-Hulman Institute of Technology,
clifton@rose-hulman.edu
Mario Coppo, Università di Torino, coppo@di.unito.it
Vincent Cremet, (no institution specified), vincent.cremet@gmail.com
Markus Degen, Universität Freiburg, degen@informatik.uni-freiburg.de
Mariangiola Dezani, Università di Torino, dezani@di.unito.it
Werner Dietl, ETH Zürich, dietlw@inf.ethz.ch
Sophia Drossopoulou, Imperial College, London, sd@doc.ic.ac.uk
Gilles Dubochet, Ecole Polytechnique Fédérale de Lausanne,
gilles.dubochet@epfl.ch
Erik Ernst, University of Aarhus, eernst@daimi.au.dk
Manuel Fähndrich, Microsoft Research, maf@microsoft.com
Diego Garbervetsky, Universidad de Buenos Aires, diegog@dc.uba.ar
Elena Giachino, Università di Torino, giachino@di.unito.it
Paola Giannini, Università Piemonte Orientale, giannini@mfn.unipmn.it
Philipp Haller, Ecole Polytechnique Fédérale de Lausanne,
philipp.haller@epfl.ch
Clément Hurlin, INRIA, clement.hurlin@inria.fr
Atsushi Igarashi, Kyoto University, igarashi@kuis.kyoto-u.ac.jp
Einar Broch Johnsen, University of Oslo, einarj@ifi.uio.no
Christine Kehyayan, Lebanese American University,
christine.kehyayan@lau.edu.lb
Eric Kerfoot, University of Oxford, eric.kerfoot@comlab.ox.ac.uk
Neelakantan Krishnaswami, Carnegie Mellon University, neelk@cs.cmu.edu
Gary T. Leavens, University of Central Florida, leavens@eecs.ucf.edu
Francesco Logozzo, Microsoft Research, logozzo@microsoft.com
Rosemary Monahan, National University of Ireland, Maynooth,
rosemary.monahan@nuim.ie
Peter Müller, Microsoft Research, mueller@microsoft.com
Matthew Parkinson, University of Cambridge,
matthew.parkinson@cl.cam.ac.uk
Arnd Poetzsch-Heffter, Universität Kaiserslautern,
poetzsch@informatik.uni-kl.de

John Potter, University of New South Wales, Sydney,
potter@cse.unsw.edu.au
Chieri Saito, Kyoto University, saito@kuis.kyoto-u.ac.jp
Yannis Smaragdakis, University of Oregon, yannis@cs.uoregon.edu
Daniel Wasserrab, Universität Pasau, daniel.wasserrab@uni-passau.de
Stefan Wehr, Universität Freiburg, wehr@informatik.uni-freiburg.de
Tobias Wrigstad, Stockholm University, tobias@dsv.su.se
Elena Zucca, DISI - University of Genova, zucca@disi.unige.it
Johan Östlund, Stockholm University, johano@dsv.su.se

3   Summary of Contributions

There were 20 submissions. Each submission was reviewed by at least 3 programme committee members. The committee decided to accept 9 papers.

The workshop was structured as a small conference with sessions of paper presentations. Each session specialized in a particular topic. The following summaries were originally written by the session chairs.

3.1   Session 1: Types

The first session of FTfJP was devoted to Types and was chaired by Dave Clarke (CWI). The three papers represent three of the various trends in type systems work, namely, understanding concepts from existing programming languages, transferring constructs from one language (or from theory) to another, and understanding new type-theoretic constructs in terms of more traditional constructs.

Nicholas Cameron presented "Towards an Existential Types Model for Java with Wildcards", which was joint work with Erik Ernst and Sophia Drossopoulou. Wildcards were introduced in to Java generics to soften the mismatch between subtyping and parametric polymorphism. A type system including wildcards has never been proven sound. This paper formalises wildcards using an extension of FGJ (featherweight generic Java) with existential types.

The paper proves that the calculus, called $\exists J$, is type sound, and illustrates how it models Java's wildcards. $\exists J$ is not, however, a full model for Java's wildcards as it does not support lower bounds for wildcards. It turns out that it cannot easily be extended to deal with lower bounds. The paper discusses how this issue can be resolved in a type sound way. The model needed to go beyond the standard existential types model due to peculiarities in Java's Wildcards.

Philippe Altherr presented "Adding Type Constructor Parameterization to Java", which was joint work with Vincent Cremet. This paper presented a generalization of Java's generics to enable parametrization by type constructions, that is, functions from types to types. The extension was formalized as a calculus called $\text{FGJ}\omega$, which is proven safe and decidable. The extension is motivated by two examples, namely the definition of generic datatypes with binary methods and generalized algebraic datatypes (GADTs).

Type constructors are found in the programming language Haskell, as well as higher-order logic and other type theories. This paper follows the trend of transferring ideas from type theory and research programming languages such as Haskell into mainstream languages such as Java.

Chieri Saito presented "The Essence of Lightweight Family Polymorphism", which was joint work with Atsushi Igarashi. The paper discusses the formal calculus .FJ that was introduced to model lightweight family polymorphism, a programming style that supports reusable yet type-safe mutually recursive classes. This style of programming originates in Beta and has received a lot of attention in recent years.

The paper clarifies the essence of .FJ by providing a formal translation from .FJ into a variant of FGJ extended with a variant of F-bounded polymorphism which allows self types to appear in mutually recursive constraints on type variables. The correspondence between the two languages is achieved without losing type safety.

3.2   Session 2: Languages and Verification

The second session was chaired by Gary Leavens.

The paper "Separating Type, Behavior, and State to Achieve Very Fine-grained Reuse," by Viviana Bono, Ferruccio Damiani, and Elena Giachino describes a language design that tries to achieve orthogonality in several mechanisms, with the aim of fostering reuse. In particular it tries to separate the mechanisms that allow reuse of: state declarations (records), types (interfaces), and behavior (traits) from each other and from the mechanism that composes these into objects (classes). In this way the language distinguishes itself from other advanced languages, such as Scala, in which traits are also types. The paper describes a calculus, Featherweight Compositional Java. This calculus combines nominal (by-name) and structural type checking, in that method parameters are nominally typed and uses of this are structurally typed. Its type system and a translation that flattens structures into the calculus Featherweight Trait Java with Interfaces is proved to preserve typings and to be sound.

The paper "Modular Verification of the Subject-Observer Pattern via Higher-Order Separation Logic," by Neelakantan Krishnaswami, Lars Birkedal, and Jonathan Aldrich shows how to use higher-order separation logic to modularly verify uses of the Subject-Observer pattern. Modularity means that the subject and observer are hidden from each other, but must not interfere with each other. Furthermore, different observers may have different invariants. The approach uses quantification over predicates to hide representations. It also uses lists of higher-order predicates to maintain a list of the invariants corresponding to each observer. For reasoning about callbacks, the approach uses hypothetical separation properties. The paper formalizes the programming language and the higher-order separation logic. It gives detailed specifications for an instance of the Subject-Observer pattern, including a client program.

The paper "Automatic verification of textbook programs that use comprehensions," by K. Rustan M. Leino and Rosemary Monahan address the problem of automatic verification of generalized quantifiers, such as sum, min, and max. The paper describes an approach taken in Spec#, a formal specification language for C#. Spec# has quantifiers like sum {int k in (1:3); k*k} which denotes $1 \times 1 + 2 \times 2 = 5$. The difficulties in automating this are: (i) how to encode such generalized quantifiers and comprehensions for an automatic, first-order theorem prover (such as Simplify), and (ii) what "inductive axioms" generalized quantifiers and comprehensions in a first-order prover. The approach to solving the first problem is to specify two new function symbols for each kind of quantifier. The axioms used to solve the second problem make these function symbols synonyms, but only in one direction, which avoids the problem of recursive loop triggers. Differences in such axiomatizations affect performance, sometimes dramatically, and such considerations are described in the paper.

3.3   Session 3: Analysis

This session, unlike the previous session, presented papers for the *automatic* analysis of object-oriented programs. It was chaired by Francesco Logozzo.

Manuel Fähndrich gave a talk on a new static analysis that he developed together with Diego Garbervetsky and Wolfram Schulte. The goal of the analysis is to check the presence of re-entrant calls on objects for which the invariant may not hold. The analysis is divided into two stages. First, it uses a modular point-so analysis to detect re-entrant calls. Then, it performs a simple data-flow propagation to check whether the invariant of the receiver of a re-entrant call holds or not. The analysis is supported by an implementation that was able to find that most re-entrant calls are direct calls. The two main differences of this work with respect to others presented in the FTfJP'07, but also in the IWACO'07 workshop, is (i) that the analysis is run on the full program, and (ii) it does require minimal user annotations.

Patrice Chalin presented the work that Frederic Rioux and himself have conducted on the re-definition of the (concrete) semantics of expressions appearing in JML assertions. The new semantics is based on the notion of *strong validity* which means that an expression is true iff (i) it is defined and (ii) it evaluates to true. Such a definition implies that when checking dynamically an assertion, it evaluates to true iff (i) it does not raise an exception (*e.g.* because a division by zero) and (ii) it evaluates to true. The implementation is built on the top of the MultiJ compiler. There are two main advantages of this approach: (i) it provides a more programmer-friendly semantics of assertions, and (ii) it generates more compact runtime checks.

In his talk Manuel Hermenegildo presented some ongoing work that he is doing with his students Jorge Navas and Mario Méndez-Lojo for developing a generic static analysis framework for the Java bytecode based on Abstract Interpretation. The kernel of the work is the fixpoint computation engine which is smart enough to infer non-trivial postconditions for recursive functions. Manuel illustrated the algorithm, inspired by previous work in Logic programming, and he gave a brief demo of the tool. The main difference with other works presented during the workshop is that this tool (i) is completely automatic, (ii) it is oriented to the inference of numerical properties to be used for the absence of runtime errors, and (iii) it is adaptive, in that if information on the caller context is present, then the analysis makes use of it.

3.4   Session 4: Panel Discussion

In the last session of the workshop, a panel discussion investigated future combinations of object-oriented programming, modeling and verification. The panel consisted of four experts with different foci in the field:

- Jonathan Aldrich: Architectural aspects
- Manuel Hermenegildo: Static analysis
- Manuel Fähndrich: Verification, object-oriented programming
- Gary T. Leavens: Modeling languages, dynamic checking

The panel was moderated by Arnd Poetzsch-Heffter. In the following, we shortly summarize the initiating statements of the panelists and the discussion.

Architectural aspects. Jonathon Aldrich summarized central challenges for the verification of object-oriented programs, in particular aliased state, higher-order and event-based code, inheritance, subtyping, and concurrency. He illustrated the problems to find bugs using a graphical text editor as example: a misbehavior in a text area may result from a long event chain touching many parts of the implementation. A still open question is whether current techniques to modularity like separation logic and ownership disciplines are flexible enough to handle such scenarios. It will be important to use software architecture as a backbone to integrate code-oriented modularization like ownership structures with other techniques like permission-based reasoning and event tracking.

Static analysis. As central goals, Manuel Hermenegildo stressed the need to develop improved programming environments. They should increase programmer efficiency and better integrate verification, analysis and optimization into everyday programming. He sketched the CiaoPP approach in which static analysis, partial evaluation, theorem proving and runtime test generation works hand in hand. It will as well be important to be able to ship the derived abstractions together with the program in the sense of an "abstraction carrying code". Languages with a higher abstraction level will not only be needed to simplify the programming task, but as well to integrate programs, abstract interpretation results and other program properties.

Programming and verification. Manuel Fähndrich opened up the discussion towards new language designs. With software systems increasing in size and a hardware trend to multi-core architectures, it will become crucial to be able to develop less buggy and highly concurrent programs in the future. It might be questioned whether the OO paradigm gives a sufficient answer to this challenge:

Current support for alias control and referential transparency is weak in OO languages; and OO concepts and constructs for concurrency are fairly low level. Functional programming provides better techniques to control mutability, and simplifies verification and concurrent programming. An interesting trend that might combine the programming paradigms are small components encapsulating data and control.

Better help for the programmer. Gary T. Leavens added two further issues to the discussion. Firstly, he reflected on how we can better help the programmer. Instead of straitjacketing ordinary programmers with difficult techniques and theories, academia should package their techniques and tools according to the programmer's needs. In particular, support should be better aligned with the design goals of the programmer. For example, if security is an issue, specific support is needed for this requirement; and such a support can crosscut different areas of technology. Gary Leaven's second issue concerned the extension and integration of new trends and developments in programming and formal methods. E.g. how can XML data handling be integrated into interface specifications, how can formal techniques be applied to aspect-oriented programming and highly dynamic programs? In addition, we still have to realize the treatment of temporal, time and space properties in the current verification and tooling landscape.

During and after these statements we had a lively discussion: How should strong, weak and no typing be used and integrated into programming and specification? Is functional programming a key to meet the challenge of correct concurrent programs? Although the emotions underlying such questions in the last century could still be felt, the bottom line of the discussion seemed to be that a well-engineered combination of the developed techniques is the challenge of today and the way to go.

4   Conclusions

Object-oriented programming in the style of Java or C# is now mainstream. Thus the topic of this workshop, applying formal techniques to these languages, is more important than ever. We are seeing large-scale practical efforts, not least JML and Spec#, being used by growing numbers of people. In this way the hard work of researchers in formal techniques is having a broad impact in programming. It is a privilege to be part of this process.

Acknowledgments

As chair, I (John Boyland) thank the providers of EasyChair which made chairing the workshop much easier than if I had to do everything myself, especially while temporarily residing in China. Thanks also to the programme committee members who put in a lot of work in a very tight reviewing schedule, and for the productive round-the-globe email discussion.

I thank Nanjing University and the State Key Laboratory for Novel Software Technology for hosting my stay in China and helping put together the technical report of contributions.

Web Resources

The homepages of the programme committee members and all the individual papers are available from the workshop web site:

http://www.cs.uwm.edu/faculty/boyland/ftjp/index.html

Roles and Relationships in Object-Oriented Programming, Multiagent Systems and Ontologies

Report on the 2nd Workshop on Roles and Relationships at ECOOP 2007

Guido Boella[1] and Friedrich Steimann[2]

[1] Università di Torino, Italy
`guido@di.unito.it`
[2] Fernuniversität in Hagen, Germany
`steimann@FernUni-Hagen.de`

Abstract. This report describes the "Roles'07 — Roles and Relationships" workshop held at ECOOP'07 in Berlin on July 30 and 31, 2007. The aims and organization of the workshop are described, and the main contributions of the presentations and invited talks are summarized, so to have a useful survey of current issues in the field. The description of the discussion and conclusions end the paper.

1 Introduction

The notion of *role* is almost ubiquitous in computer science: it occurs in fields such as conceptual modeling, programming languages, software engineering, coordination languages, database systems, multiagent systems, knowledge representation, formal ontology, computational linguistics, and security. Also, it appears to be indispensable outside computer science: fields like sociology, cognitive science, organizational science, and linguistics make heavy use of it. In fact, it seems that like objects and relationships, roles are so fundamental a notion that they should be granted the status of an *ontological primitive*.

The definition of roles inherently depends on the definition of relationships. With the advent of Object Technology, however, relationships have moved out of the focus of attention, giving way to the more restricted concept of attributes or, more technically, references to other objects. A reference is tied to the object holding it and as such is asymmetric — at most the target of the reference can be associated with a role. This is counter to the intuition that every role should have at least one counter-role, namely the one it interacts with. It seems that the natural role of roles in object-oriented designs can only be restored by installing relationships (collaborations, teams, etc.) as first-class programming concepts.

By contrast, the relational nature of roles is already acknowledged in the area of Multiagent Systems, since roles are related to the interaction among agents and to communication protocols. However, even in this area there is no convergence on a single definition of roles yet, and different points of view, such as agent software engineering, specification languages, agent communication, or agent programming languages, make different use of roles.

M. Cebulla (Ed.): ECOOP 2007 Workshop Reader, LNCS 4906, pp. 108–122, 2008.

In computer science, the discussion about roles started in the 1970s with Bachman and Daya [1], and since then, it has kept recurring to the attention of the research community. Interestingly, Bachman developed his Role Data Model as an alternative to the then emerging Relational and Entity-Relationship Data Models [2], fully acknowledging the dependency of roles on relationships. More recently, roles have been used in various areas to handle behavior and interaction, for example, role based access control in security with the RBAC model [3], collaboration roles in UML to describe the interaction among classes [4], channels connecting components in coordination languages [5], the separation of concerns to describe the interaction properties of objects in new contexts in programming languages [6], etc. With the rise of the internet, new communication possibilities and interactive computing created a new demand of research about roles, for example, in organizations in open multiagent systems, in role based programming languages, in using roles for the composition of web services, and in defining roles in standards for interoperability.

Notwithstanding this revival of the research about the notion of role, little agreement seems possible among the proposals in the different fields. This lack of agreement leads to considerable problems with transferring the results from one area to the other, even inside a single area, a consequence which is unacceptable in times in which the sharing of knowledge and standardization alone represent added value in many fields. The likely reasons of these divergences are that many papers on the notion of role fail to have an interdisciplinary character, that much work proposes new definitions of roles to deal with particular practical problems, and that role seems an intuitive notion which can be grasped in its prototypical characters, yet is really an elusive one when details must be clarified. Few proposals, like Steimann [7] or Masolo et al. [8], have a more general attitude and try to find a problem independent definition of the role concept and its formalization.

The recognition of the need of a wider agreement on roles lead Guido Boella to organize — together with James Odell, Leendert van der Torre, and Harko Verhagen — the first *Roles* event, titled "Roles, an Interdisciplinary Perspective - Roles'05" [9]. To acknowledge its interdisciplinary character, it was organized as an American Association for Artificial Intelligence (AAAI) Fall Symposium and held on November 3-6, 2005 at Hyatt Crystal City in Arlington, Virginia (http://normas.di.unito.it/zope/roles05). The call for papers of Roles'05 produced 30 submissions, of which 22 were presented at the workshop. From the presented papers five were selected for a special issue in *Applied Ontology — An Interdisciplinary Journal of Ontological Analysis and Conceptual Modeling*, representing the different areas involved in the workshop: ontology, programming languages and multiagent systems. Moreover, the article of Friedrich Steimann [2], the invited speaker of the workshop, complemented the other ones by presenting an historical perspective on the subject, analysing the seminal work of Bachman and Daya [1] on the Role Data Model for databases. No other previous event focussed on roles only, even if some other workshops offered the environment for discussing roles, like AOSE'00-'07, CorOrg'05,'06, NorMas'05,'07,'08, VAR'05, COIN'06,'07. However, they either did not have an interdisciplinary character, or they discussed roles from a specific perspective, for example, NorMas is focused on normative systems.

Like its predecessor Roles'05, Roles'07 aimed at gathering researchers from different disciplines to foster interchange of knowledge and ideas concerning roles and relationships, trying to converge on ontologically founded proposals which can be applied to programming as well as agent languages. Roles'07, organized in the context of the ECOOP'07 conference, attracted 10 submissions (of which 8 got accepted), 10 presentations, and about 30 participants. Invited talks were held by one of the fathers of the notion of roles in modelling languages, Trygve Reenskaug, and by one of today's most active researchers in the study of relationships, James Noble. The proceedings of the workshop are available at http://iv.tu-berlin.de/TechnBerichte/2007/2007-09.pdf, the workshop website is http://normas.di.unito.it/zope/roles07.

The scope of Roles'07 was outlined by the following list topics:

- Roles as first-class constructs in programming, modelling, ontologies, and multiagent systems.
- Relationships as first-class programming constructs.
- Applications that would profit from roles and relationships.
- Patterns dealing with the realization of relationships and roles.
- Roles in foundational ontologies and applicative ontologies.
- Roles in models (e.g. UML) and domain-specific languages.
- Roles in multiagent systems design, specification and programming.
- Experience reports with role-oriented approaches.
- Existing and new programming constructs related to roles.
- Literature surveys on roles.
- Reports on roles from other disciplines, like sociology, organizational theory, linguistics, etc.

2 Organizers

Guido Boella (guido@di.unito.it)
Guido Boella received the PhD degree in Computer Science at Università di Torino in 2000. He is currently professor at Dipartimento di Informatica of this university. His research interests include programming languages, multiagent systems, in particular, normative systems, institutions and roles using qualitative decision theory. He organized the workshops on normative multiagent systems (NorMas'05,'07,'08), on coordination and organization (CoOrg'05,'06), the AAAI Fall Symposium on roles Roles'05 and the COIN@ECAI'06 workshop. He developed the programming language powerJava, an extension of Java with roles.

Steffen Göbel (steffen.goebel@sap.com)
Steffen Göbel works as a senior researcher in the Software Engineering & Architecture program at SAP Research CEC Dresden. He received his Diploma and his doctoral degree in computer science from Technische Universität Dresden. His main research interests are model-driven development, software product lines and component-based software engineering.

Friedrich Steimann (steimann@acm.org)
Friedrich Steimann is currently a full professor at the Fernuniversität in Hagen, Germany. He heads the department of Programming Systems and conducts research on

object-oriented programming concepts, software modelling, and development tools. He is a leading researcher on roles in object orientation. He has a past in computational linguistics and medical informatics.

Steffen Zschaler (sz9@inf.tu-dresden.de)
Steffen Zschaler graduated from Technische Universität Dresden in 2002, where he is now working as a research assistant. His main research interests are model-driven development, non-functional properties and component-based software engineering. He is currently involved in the Modelplex research project.

3   Contributions of the Workshop

The three different sessions in which we can ideally organize the presentations are: roles and programming languages, roles and relationships, and roles and ontologies. For each one of them, we illustrate the main issues faced by the presentations.

3.1   Roles and Programming Languages

BabyUML - Roles and Classes in Object Oriented Programming [10]. The value of a system is greater than the sum of its parts; the system organization giving the added value. Trygve Reenskaug's talk shows how a system description can be split into state and behavior parts. Despite being one of the inspirators of UML, Trygve Reenskaug is still unsatisfied by the modelling language. So it is proposing an alternative project named BabyUML. The project goal is to create a programming environment with explicit specification of system state and behavior.

Trygve Reenskaug starts from a quotation of Steven Pinker's "How the Mind Works" [11]: he claims that the meaning of a system comes from the meaning of its parts and from the way they are combined. Objects encapsulate state and behavior. Object state is represented in the object's instance variables. Object behavior is specified in the object's methods. The execution of a method is triggered by the object receiving a message. The binding of message to method is dynamic and depends on the implementation of the receiving object. But the value of a system is greater than the sum of its parts. The properties of a system are similar to the properties of an unattached object. System state is the accumulated state of its objects and their associations. System behavior is triggered by messages that the system receives from its environment and is accomplished through an organized process of message interaction between its objects.

Current mainstream programming languages are class oriented; they specify sets of objects with common properties. Class based languages work well in simple cases; but they are less than ideal in complex cases where the system as a whole tends to be hidden among the details of the classes and methods. In this article, Trygve Reenskaug remedies this deficiency by showing how class centred programming can be augmented by role centred programming where system behavior is specified explicitly in terms of collaborations and roles.

The role is a slippery concept. Roles cannot be defined by their shape or their constitution, only by what they do in the context of a system. The essence of object orientation is that in a system objects collaborate to achieve a common goal. Roles are references to participating objects; each role represents the contribution these objects make towards a system goal. The concept of role conforms to the common usage of the word:

- A role represents a functionality.
- This functionality can be utilized in its collaboration with other roles.
- A role is bound to one or more objects selected from a universe of objects. These selected objects are called the players of the role.
- A role delegates the performance of its functionality to its players.
- A role specifies requirements for its players. An important property is the set of messages that its players must understand.
- The required properties can be implemented by several classes so the players need not be instances of the same class. Different objects can thus perform the same role in different ways.

A collaboration is a structure of interconnected roles that enables the system to perform one or more tasks. First, a collaboration describes a structure of collaborating roles, each performing a specialized function, which collectively accomplish some desired functionality. Second, a collaboration structure constitutes a graph where the nodes are roles and the edges are the message interaction paths.

One of the crucial points in this work is the link between *role* and *objects*. It is annotated by *select from*; this signifies that objects are dynamically selected from a set of relevant objects to play the roles. Many different selection mechanisms can be used. These methods dynamically select the appropriate player objects. In principle, the methods should perform the selection on each call to ensure up-to-date mapping.

Roles for Robots - Roles and Self-Reconfigurable Robots [12]. A self-reconfigurable robot is a robotic device that can change its own shape. Self-reconfigurable robots are commonly built from multiple identical modules that can manipulate each other to change the shape of the robot. Programming a modular, self-reconfigurable robot is however a complicated task: the robot is essentially a real-time, distributed embedded system, where control and communication paths often are tightly coupled to the current physical configuration of the robot, control is distributed across the modules that constitute the robot constraints on the physical size and power consumption of each module limits the available processing power of each module.

The issue of providing a high-level programming platform for developing controllers remains largely unexplored. To facilitate the task of programming modular, self-reconfigurable robots, Nicolai Dvinge, Ulrik P. Schultz, and David Christensen developed a declarative, role-based language RAPL, for the ATRON modular, self-reconfigurable robot, that allows the programmer to associate roles and behavior to structural elements in a modular robot.

Roles provide the abstraction necessary to focus on the behavior of a specific module in a given context. The conceptual view of a role is that it defines the module structure and the active and reactive behavior of each module in a robot. There is a one-to-one mapping between a role and a module, but modules can change their roles (and thus their behavior) as a reaction to messages from other modules or internal events.

An ATRON robot as a whole is implicitly assigned a role using the object oriented concept of a whole-part structure. Behavior for the robot is declared for each individual role. The functionality of the whole and the role that it can play is thus created in coordination between the individual modules, corresponding to how the control of a modular robot necessarily must be implemented in practice.

A Metamodel for Roles: Introducing Sessions [13]. Role is a widespread concept, it is used in many areas like multiagent systems, databases, programming languages, organizations, security and OO modeling. Unfortunately, it seems that the literature is not actually able to give a uniform definition of roles, there exists several approaches that model roles in many different (and opposite) ways. Valerio Genovese's aim is to build a formal framework through which describe different definitions appeared in the literature or implemented in computer systems by means of different configurations of parameters. In particular, he gives a new role's foundation introducing sessions, which are a formal instrument to talk about role's states and he shows how sessions may be useful to model relationships. In the presented work it has been shown how the great majority of proposed role's accounts can be unified within a general infrastructure which is based on 4 basic notions: Role, Player, Context, Session (where is kept the state of a specific interaction), and where the role notion is pivotal in the interaction of two entities: one that offers the role (context) and the other one that plays it (player). Exploiting the session's formalization, it has been stressed how roles can be employed in specifying relationships in a rich and complete way.

Short presentations. Besides the presentations of papers we had two short presentations. The first one is by Stephan Herrmann, about the definition of a metamodel for the ObjectTeams/Java language he developed [14]. He starts from an intuition of Friedrich Steimann, who in [2] proposes as a criterium for evaluating role models the possibility to use the role model as a metamodel of itself (see Section 5.1).

During the development of ObjectTeams/Java the author developed several metamodels as a way to facilitate implementation in Java. While doing so he fell into the trap of a naive metamodel which contains three fundamental classes: Team (the context of a role), Role and Base (the player of a role). While it looks natural at first, this approach fails to support some combinations, where Teams play roles themselves or Teams contain other Teams. These combinations require a model, where Teams, Roles and Bases are not disjoint sets, but actually each intersection is populated with legal elements, too. Since overlapping classes are problematic in object-oriented design, the author chooses to use Object Teams as the language for the metamodel. The central idea behind this model is to leave the metaclass Class untouched, i.e., to refrain from sub-classing Class to produce Team, Role and Base. Instead the model identifies additional properties that can be attached to a Class if it appears in a certain context. Classes appearing in a Collaboration may play either the role of the Collaboration's Team, or they may play a role of a Role within the Collaboration. This models the fact that Teams and Roles only occur in the context of a Collaboration, where each Collaboration has exactly one defining Team and any number of interacting Roles.

The second presentation is by Roberto Grenna, showing his work with Luisa Leonardelli. This work is based on the intuition of Steimann [7] that design patterns are inherently based on roles, and on the implementation of a role based programming language, powerJava [15]. The target was realizing the implementation in powerJava for some design patterns: the State and the Mediator. The primitives offered by powerJava allows the programmer to use roles in the implementation of the patterns. In particular, the advantages are that the number of parameters decreases, since roles use the principle of Java inner classes, the number of written classes is less than in the correspondent Java code, and when a role is defined, it can be played by each class implementing the requirements needed for that role. However, it is difficult to give a precise measure of the advantages of using roles in design patterns besides the improvement of the conceptual clearness.

3.2   Roles and Relationships

Member interposition: Defining Classes [16]. The collaborations between objects are the key to understand large object oriented programs. Software systems do not accomplish their tasks with a single object in isolation, but only by employing a collection of objects. Conceptual modeling languages, such as the Unified Modeling Language (UML) and the Entity-Relationship (ER) model, allow explicit representation of object collaborations through associations and relationships, respectively.

Today's languages allow the description of objects through the programming language abstraction of a class, yet they lack a peer abstraction for object collaborations. Programmers must resort to the use of references to indicate collaborations and thereby often hide the intent and, at the same time, further complicate any analysis of a program since references are a powerful, all encompassing programming construct. To use Rumbaugh [17]'s words, "class-based object oriented implementations of object collaborations hide the semantic information of collaborations but expose their implementation details".

As classes allow the description of a collection of individual objects, relationships in relationship-based language proposed by Stephanie Balzer and Thomas Gross allow the description of a collection of groups of interacting objects. The description involves the declaration of attributes and methods. Relationships indicate the classes of which the interacting objects are instances to delimit the scope of the collaboration. Relationship-based languages also allow the declaration of multiplicities (consistency constraints).

Roles emerge from relationships. The participants of a relationship declaration can be named to indicate the conceptual role the particular class plays in the relationship. Some properties of objects only apply when the object is fulfilling a particular role.

Member interposition is a mechanism proposed by the authors to accommodate relationship-dependent properties of objects, without resorting to inheritance and role classes. For example, consider the relationship `Assist` between a collaborating student and a course. If the attribute `instructionLanguage` of the role `teachingAssistant` is interposed, then each student uses the same language in all the courses he assists. If, instead, the attribute is not interposed, the attribute describes the language used by the student in each course it teaches, and it can differ from course to course.

Whereas an interposed member describes a class that plays a particular role in a relationship, a non-interposed member describes the collaboration that exists between the participants of a relationship. The authors also refer to interposed members as participant-level members and to non interposed members as relationship-level members. Like non-interposed members, interposed members are part of the interface of their defining relationships (and not part of the interface of the classes they are interposed into).

Relationships define roles, objects offer them [18]. Matteo Baldoni, Guido Boella and Leendert van der Torre show how to use the powerJava language (an extension of Java with roles) to model relationships with roles. The powerJava approach is based on the definition of roles as affordances [19]. Inspired by research in cognitive science, this view sees the properties (attributes and operations) of an object as something not independent from whom is interacting with it. In this way, an object affords different ways of interaction to different kinds of objects. The idea behind roles as affordances is that the interaction with an object does not happen directly with it by accessing its public attributes and invoking its public operations. Rather, the interaction with an object happens via a role: to invoke an operation, it is necessary first to be the player of a role offered by the object the operation belongs to. The roles which can be played depend on the properties of the role player (the requirements), as it follows from the definition of affordance. The language extension implements roles as inner classes, so to associate with them attributes and methods, which share the same namespace of the outer class and of other roles: thus, roles are instances having a different identity respect to the players that play them.

Baldoni *et al.* [20] shows how the relationship as attribute pattern to model relationships in OO can be extended with roles, thus endowing the relationship with a state and a behavior, albeit distributed in the two roles composing the relationship. In [18] the authors show how the relationship object pattern can be extended with roles as well. The authors start from an intuition of Steimann [7] who proposes to model roles as classifiers related to relationships, but such that these classifiers are not allowed to have instances. In Java terminology, roles should be modelled as abstract classes, where some behavior is specified, but not all the behavior, since some abstract methods must be implemented in the classes extending them. These abstract classes representing roles should be then extended by other classes in order to be instantiated. However, given that in a language like Java multiple inheritance is not allowed, this solution is not viable, and roles can be identified with interfaces only.

In [18], the authors overcome the problem of the lack of multiple inheritance, by allowing objects participating to the relationship to offer roles which inherit from abstract roles related to the relationship, rather than imposing that objects extend the roles themselves. The advantage of this solution is a tighter coupling between the relationship and its participants, since the roles belong both to the namespace of the relationship and to the namespace of the player, thus having access to the private state of both of them.

3.3   Roles and Ontologies

Role Representation Model Using OWL and SWRL [21]. Roles are very important in ontology engineering. Although the ontology language OWL is a standard, consideration about roles is not enough. This fact can cause to decrease semantic interoperability of ontologies because of conceptual gaps between OWL and developers who need roles. In this paper Kouji Kozaki, Eiichi Sunagawa, Yoshinobu Kitamura, Riichiro Mizoguchi merge an ontological analysis of roles with practical considerations about designing tools for building ontologies, applying it to the OWL language. The most novel element of their model is the notion of role holder, an abstraction of a composition of a role-playing entity with an instance of a role concept. In turn, the role concept instance can exist only in presence of an instance of the context the role is associated with.

Roles (in the sense of role concept instances) can exist without a player, due to their relation with a context. Conversely, some contexts exist only in presence of the roles which compose the context. For example, a marriage exists only as far as both the roles of wife and husband exist. As Loebe [22] does, the authors provide a classification of roles basing on the type of context they are related to. Besides relational roles, processual roles and social roles, Hozo distinguishes action related roles, attribute roles and composite roles. Composite roles allow to model a role like teacher, which includes both the role of staff member of a school and of agent of a teaching activity, and, thus, they depend on multiple contexts at a time. Details can be found in [23].

The authors represent the Hozo role model in OWL. E.g., hozo:BasicConcept class, hozo:RoleConcept class and hozo:RoleHolder class express basic concepts, role concepts and role-holders respectively. hozo:playedBy property represents a relation between classes of role concept and classes of potential player. Besides concept definitions the authors give rules which are applied into classes and properties. They are implemented as SWRL rules. Rules are not only applied to instance models for inference, but also to imply the policies on using the classes and properties underlying Hozo.

The distinction between role concepts and role-holders is realized via the category hozo:RoleHolder. Role-Holders are described with the property hozo:inheritFrom: it is used for representing that a role-holder inherits definitions both from the role concept and its player. But the property does not imply inheritance of identity, and in that respect hozo:inheritFrom differs from rdfs:subClassOf.

Towards a Definition of Roles for Software Engineering and Programming Languages [24]. Frank Loebe describes an analytic, ontology-oriented view on roles, starting from the plurality of views and definitions that role has in literature. A major goal of the work is the provision of a role definition which maximizes the coverage of applications of the term "role". To the extent possible this should be independent from specific application areas, spanning from conceptual modeling to software engineering to linguistics, etc. This leads to a very general, yet weak, analytical definition for the notion of role:

"Definition 1. A role is an entity which is dependent on two other entities, referred to as the player of the role and the context of the role."

The author classifies three kinds of roles according to the different kinds of contexts they belong to. Roles are parts of contexts (in some sense of the term) and the contexts emerge from the existence of the roles, in a mutual existential dependence. Three kinds of contexts are considered in the classification of role, which determine different playing relations:

- Relational role: corresponds to the way in which an argument participates in the context of some relationship; e.g., two as a factor of four refers to a relationship. Relational roles are special properties, and the "plays" relationship between entities and relational roles is thus subsumed by the "has-property" relation.
- Processual role: corresponds to the manner in which a player behaves in the context of some process (i.e., it participates in the process): e.g., John as the mover of some

pen is categorized as a processual role. Processual roles are parts of processes, and, therefore, processes themselves.

– Social role: corresponds to the involvement of a social object within the context of some society; e.g., a student in a university. Social roles are often defined with their own properties, relations and processes in which they (may) participate (confirming the view of roles as "patterns of behavior"). This means that social roles are considered as objects.

Theories of programming and software engineering, in different shapes like object-, agent-, or aspect-orientation, form a major area of using and applying roles in computer science. In this context it does not appear reasonable to argue for the direct adoption of Definition 1 above, which would be too weak while the broadness of coverage is not necessary. Most occurrences of roles in this area seem to require properties for roles and involvement in complex systems, closely resembling social roles from above (a slight generalization to non-social objects may be required). For a common use of "role" in this area, Loebe proposes the following adaptation of Definition 1 as a working hypothesis:

"Definition 2. A role R is an entity which mediates between a context C, comprehended as a system or a society of interrelated entities E_1, E_2,..., and exactly one of these entities, E_i. R depends on both, E_i and C, and it exhibits specific properties and behavior."

Note that this definition exhibits some similarity to the UML 2.0 definition of role [4, p.575]: "Role: A constituent element of a structured classifier that represents the appearance of an instance (or possibly, a set of instances) within the context defined by the structured classifier."

4   Invited Talks

4.1   The OOram Software Engineering Method

For this workshop Trygve Reenskaug, one of the fathers of object orientation and ideator of the model-view-controller pattern for GUI software design in 1979, while visiting Xerox Parc, resurrected the software for modelling with the OOram Software Engineering Method. OOram is a precursor of the UML modelling language, but it is still impressive the simplicity it offers to model a system in terms of roles, only later passing to the design of classes.

On his webpage (http://folk.uio.no/trygver/) Trygve Reenskaug says:

"Roles are about objects and how they interact to achieve some purpose. For thirty years I have tried to get them into the main stream, but haven't succeeded. I believe the reason is that our programming languages are class oriented rather than object oriented. So why model in terms of objects when you cannot code them? And why model at all when you cannot keep model and code synchronized?"

So the discussion after his invited talk could not but lead to the question: what are the reasons of the difficulty of introducing the notion of role in the object oriented community? Under the light of his long experience in proposing roles as a fundamental concept, Trygve Reenskaug's answer is the cognitive difficulty which people experiences in conceptualizing both the notions of class and role. Witness the fallacy, made also in prominent books about OO, of saying that classes send or receive messages. Only objects send and receive messages and, if a more abstract notion is needed to precise a model, we should better say that roles send and receive messages. Instead, we keep teaching to students in programming language courses to think only in terms of classes and objects as the only elements when designing a program, thus perpetuating the difficulty of using roles.

He considers, however, a positive evolution in OO the recent debate about the notion of trait, which seems to be able to decompose a class into the different behaviors required by the specific roles that its instances can play.

Finally, Trygve Reenskaug gives us the explanation about the genesis of collaboration roles in UML. He was not directly involved in the standardization of this part, and he does not approve the idea of roles as classifiers in UML 1.0. He considers UML 2.0, where roles are properties through which the interaction between two objects takes place, an improvement with respect to UML 1.0.

4.2 Where Are the Relationships?

James Noble starts from a quotation about the programming language Smalltalk: "a program ... a community of communicating objects". Thus, the question of his talk becomes: "But where are the relationships?".

The need of introducing the notion of relationship as a first class citizen in Object Oriented programming, in the same way as this notion is used in OO modelling, has been argued by several authors, at least since Rumbaugh [17]: he claims that relationship are complementary to, and as important as, objects themselves. For this reason, they should be available in programming languages too, and not only in modelling languages, like UML or ER, either as primitives, or represented by means of suitable patterns. Noble [25] proposed two main alternatives for modelling relationships by mean of patterns: the relationship as attribute pattern, reducing the relationship to references, and the relationship object pattern, introducing a new class to represent the relationship. Each of these two solutions have pros and cons, as discussed by Noble [25].

However, we would like to have relationships as a real programming primitive. Many languages offer such primitives: Two-way Pointers, JavaFX, RelJ Relationships, RJ Relationships.

These solutions do not capture all the characteristics we would like to have in a relationship primitive; first, it should be abstract: its implementation is encapsulated. Second, participants and clients should be decoupled from implementation, so to have polymorphism and relationship interfaces. Third, to have reusability, relationships should not depend on participants and multiple instantiation of relationships and participants should be possible. Fourth, there should be compositionality, so to build new relationships from old ones. Finally, separation of concerns should hold: participants should be reusable without the relationship and reusable without each other.

These properties are satisfied by the Relationship Aspect Library proposed by Noble [26]. This proposal, however, does not satisfy some other requirements. For example, Balzer *et al.* [27] allows to add invariants to relationships, JQL and RAL allow to access the relationships of databases. In summary, the hypothesis is: Relationship = Tuples + Roles + Extents. Where, tuples are associations between participating objects, per-tuple data and behavior are classes, per-participant data and behavior are roles and collections of tuples are the extents.

This raises the question: what comes first? relationships or roles? Noble's hypothesis is that roles are relationship monopoles. A role provides behavior - perhaps with some state. But it makes sense only in the context of a relationship - where the object is playing that role. Thus, support for relationships should precede the support for roles.

5   Discussion

5.1   The Metarole Challenge

In his presentation titled "Towards a Role Manifesto", Friedrich Steimann made the point that if the attendees agreed on his position that the role concept deserves the status of an ontological primitive, roles should be found in the metamodel of any modelling formalism offering roles. According to Steimann's argumentation, this ruled out the role-as-adjunct-instance representation of roles, since this capture, like the Role Object Pattern, resorts to roles itself (namely the Role role and the Subject role), starting an infinite regress. In fact, so Steimann argued, any metamodel introducing the notion of roles (which a metamodel should do if role is to be regarded an ontological primitive) while at the same time resorting to the concept of role should use the very modelling construct it defines, or it raises doubts of the so defined role construct being the acclaimed primitive. Because roles are tied to relationships and metamodels without relationships seem unthinkable, any metamodel will also use roles, and the role concept the metamodel defines had better be (very similar to) the one it uses. Otherwise, the question why the one it uses is unsuitable for the modelling language it defines must be answered. Steimann conceded that this still leaves room for using the role-as-adjunct-instance approach to representing roles on the model level, but made clear that this capture cannot be the ontological primitive being sought for.

5.2   Group Discussion

Following Steimann's presentation, a discussion was started based on the following questions:

- Roles and state: Does each instance of role playing come with its own state? Or is this state part of the relationship? Does playing a role alone contribute to the state of an object?
- Role and relationship: Can roles be viewed independently from relationships?
- Composability of collaborations: Can a system be lumped together as a set of collaborations? If not, what else needs to be provided?
- Role interference: How can we deal with the fact that an object participating in several collaborations can change its state in unpredictable manners (as seen from each collaboration)?
- Why don't current programming languages come with a role construct?

To address these and other questions, the participants divided into four groups according to their different perspectives:

1. Ontology group (Kouji Kozaki, Frank Loebe, and Riichiro Mizoguchi): How are roles defined in ontologies? Which are their properties? Are roles an ontological primitive? In the ontology community there is an increasing consensus towards the idea that roles are entities (also called *qua entities*) which depend not only on the player of the role but also on a context. In fact, discussants agreed on the idea that the relationship of role to context is more prominent than that to role player and that roles can exist in some cases even without their players.

2. Multiagent systems group (Guido Boella and Thibaud Brocard): How are roles used in multiagent systems? Which is the relation between roles and organizations? Which are the properties attributed to roles in such field? The main debate in the multiagent community is whether to use roles as first class entities at runtime or only as a modelling concept. Recent works are leaning towards the first position. In this field, the concept of role is strictly related to the notion of organization which provides the context of the role. Roles are associated not only with a state and behavior but also with obligations, permissions, and institutional powers.

3. Roles and relationships group (Stefanie Balzer, Valerio Genovese, and Ulrik Schultz): Which is the relation between roles and relationships? Which of these notions come first? Can roles be reduced to relationships or vice versa? Roles are a promising abstraction when we have to understand the behavior of large systems. Roles are dependent on collaborations, and they are at the core of the answer to the question: how to compose collaborations safely? Roles belong to collaborations and players can be seen as a constellation of the roles they play. The interaction inside the collaboration happens via the roles played by objects. Roles, since they depend on the collaboration, can exist even detached from their players.

4. Roles in modelling and programming languages group (Uwe Assmann and Trygve Reenskaug): Which is the role of roles in modelling and programming systems? The result of the discussion goes against the position of the invited talk of James Noble: roles have priority over relationships. To summarize, roles can be seen from two different and opposite points of view, depending on how they are related with relationships. In the first view, roles are simply labels of their players in the relationship. Whereas, in the second view, roles identify a state of the particular interaction they describe, and they have an identity. In this approach, it is possible to extend the interaction capabilities of the players adding attributes and behavior, or also unifying the state of the interaction within a single entity (the relationship). Of course, with this approach some problems arise as concerns the coherence of the states of the two roles. The problem of roles and collaborations should be faced by studying respectively, the structure of the systems, its invariants and then its behavior, like proposed in the metamodel of roles of Genovese [13].

Friedrich Steimann as the moderator tried to reach a common agreement among the different groups, but the result was that the different communities are still on diverging positions. Moreover, the moderator had to accept that the discussants all insisted on roles having their identity separated from that of the player, that in fact roles can even exist without a player.

6   Conclusions

While relationship is a widely accepted notion, indeed one whose definition is (except perhaps for small variations) clear and generally agreed upon, role is still not. With this workshop, we tried to make the unequivocalness of the relationship concept carry over to the role concept, by putting the inherent relatedness of the two into focus. To a certain extent, this approach has failed: it seems that the traditional differences of the role conceptions created by the different disciplines are stronger than the commonalities suggested by the fact that the very concept of role is meaningless without that of counter role, and thus without relationship. To a certain extent, however, it has also succeeded: it showed that all application scenarios in which roles are identified and used are sufficiently similar to agree on its reason for existence and its general purpose (but not its representation!), and that there is a common vocabulary in which the differences can be formulated.

Acknowledgments

We first of all would like to thank the two invited speakers Trygve Reenskaug and James Noble for their stimulating talks, and all the participants of this workshop. Moreover, we would like to thank the organization of ECOOP'07 for the support offered to the invited speakers. We extend our thanks to all those who have participated in the organization of this workshop, in particular to the program committee, composed by: Uwe Assmann, Technische Universitaet Dresden; Colin Atkinson, Universitaet Mannheim; Matteo Baldoni, Università di Torino; Giancarlo Guizzardi, LOA-CNR Trento; Stephan Hermann, Technische Universitaet Berlin; Pierre Kelsen, University of Luxembourg; Claudio Masolo, LOA-CNR Trento; James Odell, Intelligent Automation, inc. Rockville MD; Andrea Omicini, DEIS Università di Bologna; Kasper Østerbye, IT University of Copenhagen; James Noble, Victoria University of Wellington; Daniel Oberle, SAP Research; Elke Pulvermueller, University of Luxembourg; Dirk Riehle, SAP Research, SAP Labs, LLC - Palo Alto, CA; Trygve Reenskaug, University of Oslo; Leendert van der Torre, University of Luxembourg; Harko Verhagen, DSV, KTH/SU.

References

1. Bachman, C., Daya, M.: The role concept in data models. In: Procs. of VLDB 1977, pp. 464–476 (1977)
2. Steimann, F.: The role data model revisited. Applied Ontology 2(2), 89–103 (2007)
3. Sandhu, R., Coyne, E., Feinstein, H., Youman, C.: Role-based access control models. IEEE Computer 2, 38–47 (1996)
4. Rumbaugh, J., Jacobson, I., Booch, G.: Unified Modeling Language Reference Manual. 2nd edn., Pearson Higher Education (2004)
5. Arbab, F.: Abstract behavior types: A foundation model for components and their composition. In: de Boer, F.S., Bonsangue, M.M., Graf, S., de Roever, W.-P. (eds.) FMCO 2002. LNCS, vol. 2852, pp. 33–70. Springer, Heidelberg (2003)
6. Kendall, E.A.: Role model designs and implementations with aspect-oriented programming. In: Proceedings of OOPSLA 1999, pp. 353–369. ACM Press, New York (1999)

7. Steimann, F.: On the representation of roles in object-oriented and conceptual modelling. Data and Knowledge Engineering 35, 83–848 (2000)
8. Masolo, C., Vieu, L., Bottazzi, E., Catenacci, C., Ferrario, R., Gangemi, A., Guarino, N.: Social roles and their descriptions. In: KR 2004. Procs. of Conference on the Principles of Knowledge Representation and Reasoning, pp. 267–277. AAAI Press, Menlo Park (2004)
9. Boella, G., Odell, J., van der Torre, L., Verhagen, H. (eds.): AAAI 2005 Fall Symposium on Roles, an interdisciplinary perspective (Roles 2005), Arlington, VA, 03/11/05-06/11/05. Volume FS-05-08 of AAAI Technical Report. AAAI, Menlo Park (2005)
10. Reengskaug, T.: Roles and classes in object oriented programming. In: Roles 2007. Proceedings of the 2nd Workshop on Roles and Relationship in Object Oriented Programming, Multiagent Systems, and Ontologies (2007)
11. Pinker, S.: How the Mind Works. Norton, New York (1997)
12. Dvinge, N., Schultz, U.P., Christensen, D.: Roles and self-reconfigurable robots. In: Roles 2007. Proceedings of the 2nd Workshop on Roles and Relationship in Object Oriented Programming, Multiagent Systems, and Ontologies (2007)
13. Genovese, V.: A meta-model for roles: Introducing sessions. In: Roles 2007. Proceedings of the 2nd Workshop on Roles and Relationship in Object Oriented Programming, Multiagent Systems, and Ontologies (2007)
14. Herrmann, S.: A precise model for contextual roles: The programming language Object-Teams/Java. Applied Ontology 2(2), 181–207 (2007)
15. Baldoni, M., Boella, G., van der Torre, L.: Interaction between Objects in powerJava. Journal of Object Technology 6, 7–12 (2007)
16. Balzer, S., Gross, T.R.: Member interposition: Defining classes. In: Roles 2007. Proceedings of the 2nd Workshop on Roles and Relationship in Object Oriented Programming, Multiagent Systems, and Ontologies (2007)
17. Rumbaugh, J.: Relations as semantic constructs in an object-oriented language. In: Procs. of the OOPSLA-87: Conference on Object-Oriented Programming Systems, Languages and Applications, Orlando, FL, pp. 466–481 (1987)
18. Baldoni, M., Boella, G., van der Torre, L.: Relationships define roles, objects offer them. In: Roles 2007. Proceedings of the 2nd Workshop on Roles and Relationship in Object Oriented Programming, Multiagent Systems, and Ontologies (2007)
19. Gibson, J.: The Ecological Approach to Visual Perception. Lawrence Erlabum Associates, New Jersey (1979)
20. Baldoni, M., Boella, G., van der Torre, L.: Relationships meet their roles in object oriented programming. In: Arbab, F., Sirjani, M. (eds.) FSEN 2007. LNCS, vol. 4767. Springer, Heidelberg (2007)
21. Kozaki, K., Sunagawa, E., Kitamura, Y., Mizoguchi, R.: Role representation model using owl and swrl. In: Roles 2007. Proceedings of the 2nd Workshop on Roles and Relationship in Object Oriented Programming, Multiagent Systems, and Ontologies (2007)
22. Loebe, F.: Abstract vs. social roles - towards a general theoretical account of roles. Applied Ontology 2(2), 127–158 (2007)
23. Mizoguchi, R., Sunagawa, E., Kozaki, K., Kitamura, Y.: A model of roles in ontology development tool: Hozo. Applied Ontology 2(2), 159–179 (2007)
24. Loebe, F.: Towards a definition of roles for software engineering and programming languages. In: Roles 2007. Proceedings of the 2nd Workshop on Roles and Relationship in Object Oriented Programming, Multiagent Systems, and Ontologies (2007)
25. Noble, J.: Basic relationship patterns. In: Procs. of EuroPLOP (1997)
26. Pearce, D., Noble, J.: Relationship aspects. In: Procs. of AOSD, pp. 75–86 (2006)
27. Balzer, S., Gross, T.R., Eugster, P.: A relational model of object collaborations and its use in reasoning about relationships. In: Ernst, E. (ed.) ECOOP 2007. LNCS, vol. 4609, pp. 323–346. Springer, Heidelberg (2007)

Component-Oriented Programming
Report on the 12th Workshop WCOP at ECOOP 2007

Wolfgang Weck[1], Ralf Reussner[2], and Clemens Szyperski[3]

[1] Independent Software Architect, Zürich, Switzerland
http://www.wolfgang-weck.ch
[2] Universität Karlsruhe (TH), Am Fasanengarten 5, D-76128 Karlsruhe, Germany
http://sdq.ipd.uka.de
[3] Microsoft, USA
http://research.microsoft.com/~cszypers

Abstract. This report covers the twelfth Workshop on Component-Oriented Programming (WCOP). WCOP has been affiliated with ECOOP since its inception in 1996. The report summarizes the contributions made by authors of accepted position papers as well as those made by all attendees of the workshop sessions.

1   Introduction

WCOP 2007, held in conjunction with ECOOP 2007 in Berlin, Germany, was the twelfth workshop in the successful series of workshops on component-oriented programming. The previous workshops were held in conjunction with earlier ECOOP conferences in Linz, Austria; Jyväskylä, Finland; Brussels, Belgium; Lisbon, Portugal; Sophia Antipolis, France; Budapest, Hungary; Málaga, Spain, Darmstadt, Germany, and Oslo Norway, Glasgow, Scotland, and Nantes, France.

The first workshop, in 1996, focused on the principal idea of software components and worked towards definitions of terms. In particular, a high-level definition of what a software component is was formulated. WCOP97 concentrated on compositional aspects, architecture and gluing, substitutability, interface evolution and non-functional requirements. In 1998, the workshop addressed industrial practice and developed a major focus on the issues of adaptation. The next year, the workshop moved on to address issues of structured software architecture and component frameworks, especially in the context of large systems. WCOP 2000 focused on component composition, validation and refinement and the use of component technology in the software industry. The year after, containers, dynamic reconfiguration, conformance and quality attributes were the main focus. WCOP 2002 had an explicit focus on dynamic reconfiguration of component systems, that is, the overlap between COP and dynamic architectures. 2003, the workshop addressed predictable assembly, model-driven architecture and separation of concerns. The 2004 instance of the workshop focused on various technical issues and also on issues of industrialization of component-orientation. WCOP 2005 revolved around different aspects of trustworthiness

M. Cebulla (Ed.): ECOOP 2007 Workshop Reader, LNCS 4906, pp. 123–131, 2008.
© Springer-Verlag Berlin Heidelberg 2008

with component-oriented programming. Considered were analyzing, asserting, and verifying functional and non-functional properties of individual components as well as of assembled systems. A central theme of WCOP 2006 was the composition and deployment of components, including component selection and adaption. A minor focus was the relation between components and aspects, that is between COP and AOP.

WCOP 2007 was reasoning on the nature of components, specifically its blackbox property. Talks and discussions argued on the blackbox property from a model-driven, performance, and aspects point of view.

WCOP 2007 had been announced as follows:

> WCOP seeks position papers on the important field of component-oriented programming (COP). WCOP 2007 is the twelfth event in a series of highly successful workshops, which took place in conjunction with every ECOOP since 1996.
>
> COP has been described as the natural extension of object-oriented programming to the realm of independently extensible systems. Several important approaches have emerged over the recent years, including component technology standards, such as CORBA/CCM, COM/COM+, J2EE/EJB,.NET, and most recently software services, but also the increasing appreciation of software architecture for component-based systems, as in SOA, and the consequent effects on organizational processes and structures as well as the software development business as a whole.
>
> COP aims at producing software components for a component market and for late composition. Composers are third parties, possibly the end users, who are not able or willing to change components. This requires standards to allow independently created components to interoperate, and specifications that put the composer into the position to decide what can be composed under which conditions. On these grounds, WCOP'96 led to the following definition:
>
>> A component is a unit of composition with contractually specified interfaces and explicit context dependencies only. Components can be deployed independently and are subject to composition by third parties.
>
> After WCOP'96 focused on the fundamental terminology of COP, the subsequent workshops expanded into the many related facets of component software.
>
> WCOP 2007 will discuss the black-box nature of components. On the one hand, for many, components became synonymously with the blackbox building blocks of software. Technically, this means a component is described by the interfaces it provides and requires. On the other hand, for many reasons, an abstract description of specific aspects of the component's behaviour in addition to the mere interface specification is needed. These reasons include architectural dependency analysis, the description of non-functional properties or the verification of the absence

of deadlocks. Therefore, in WCOP 2007 we explicitly ask for positions statements discussing work related to the question:

"How dark should a component blackbox be?"

This includes position statements dealing with components or component-based systems or component infrastructures, which explicitly make use of information on components beyond mere provides and requires interfaces.

Submitted papers circled around model-driven development and adaptation, component performance prediction, aspects for components and the nature of components.

Ten papers by authors were accepted for presentation at the workshop and publication in the workshop proceedings. Seventeen participants from around the world participated in the workshop. The workshop was organized into four morning sessions with presentations, one afternoon breakout session with three breakout groups, and one final afternoon session gathering reports from the breakout session and discussing future directions.

2   Presentations

This section summarizes briefly the contributions of the ten presenters, as grouped into four sessions, i.e. model-driven development and adaptation of components, component performance prediction, aspects and components, and component nature. The full papers of all presentations mentioned below are collected on the workshops web-page[1] and in the WCOP proceedings (Technical Report No. 2007-13 of the Faculty of Informatics of the University of Karlsruhe[2]).

2.1   Model-Driven Development and Adaptation of Components

The first session was concerned with model-driven development and component adaptation.

A case study on model-based adaptation in the area of the Windows workflow foundation by Javier Cubo, Gwen Salaün, Carlos Canal, Ernesto Pimentel, and Pascal Poizat opened WCOP 2007. In their presentation it was pointed out how to handle composition and adaptation of the Windows workflow foundation. The presented approach supports adaptation of behavioural interfaces, i.e. mismatches at an protocol level. After identifying such mismatches and mapping incompatible interfaces, the approach can generate adapters for protocol adaptation.

The second contribution by Eveline Kaboré and Antoine Beugnard dealt with an application of model transformations for enabling tracing design artifacts and

---

[1] http://research.microsoft.com/~cszypers/events/WCOP2007
[2] http://digbib.ubka.uni-karlsruhe.de/volltexte/1000007172

design decisions from a model. In a case study the approach is applied to the domain of "communication components". By intentionally limiting the application domain, code generation could be completely automated. The generated code includes static and behavioural aspects.

2.2   Component Performance Prediction

In the second session, presentations were dealing with the prediction of non-functional attributes, namely the performance of components.

The first presentation of this session was given by Klaus Krogmann. He presented a reverse engineering approach for models of software components, with special respect to performance attributes of behavioural component specifications. The proposed approach utilises a combination of static and dynamic analysis to construct a parameterised specification of component behaviour. For finding appropriate abstraction of the behavioural specification, machine learning algorithms are used.

Michael Kuperberg, giving the second presentation, discussed the relevance of parameters when performance-benchmarking Java bytecode or API. He pointed out that the execution time of bytecode and API largely depends on the parameters of its operations. Consequently, predictions methods must be capable of respecting operation parameters.

2.3   Aspects and Components

Bert Lagaisse and Wouter Joosen discussed a blackbox composition approach through aspect orientation in the third session. In their presentation they emphasized a need for pure blackboxes supporting components that make all bindings explicit. A case study showed the application of their aspect-oriented approach for expressing dependencies for a middleware.

Angel Núñez and Jacques Noyé used aspects to integrate models for protocols and components. They encapsulate components, not aware of certain protocols, into "aspect components", which are respecting modeled protocols. The non-intrusive aspect-driven approach keeps the blackbox nature of encapsulated components. Thereby, a specific adapated language is used for specifying component aspects.

The last aspect-related contribution was made by Guido Söldner and Rüdiger Kapitza. They contributed an approach enabling the runtime adaption of component middleware. In this approach, aspects are used to dynamically weave middleware component infrastructure. Extensions of their components (following a greybox view) are expressed within an ontology to ease adaptation.

2.4   Component Nature

The last session was dedicated to the nature of components.

Jakob Henriksson, Florian Heidenreich, Jendrik Johannes, Steffen Zschaler, and Uwe Aßmann argue for a greybox approach of components. Influenced by supporting declarative languages (such as XQuery or OWL) within their Reuse-ware approach, they claim for information beyond interfaces: Firstly, process-ing information is not available for declarative languages, secondly, Reuseware enables composition with techniques not being developed for reuse and compo-sition. That is why an intrusive approach is required from their point of view. Their greybox approach still aims at hiding as much information on component internals as possible.

In his talk, Franz Puntigam argued for a strict separation between black- and whitebox approaches, not allowing greyboxes. Component interfaces are usually used for specifying functional properties. Starting to specify non-functional as-pects like performance hinders substitutability as those details in general are specific to a certain implementation. Using the example of synchronisation, Puntigam proposed a possible solution for dealing with both functional and non-functional aspects in component interfaces, still maintaining the blackbox property of component in most cases.

Richard Rhinelander, giving his first international talk, discussed the relation between components and interfaces. He pointed out that components generally should not be specified by their interface. Instead, he proposes a strict distinction of component model and interface models. After presenting the up-to-date un-derstanding of interfaces and components in research, he proposed a converse and sophisticated understanding of both terms and their interrelation with special consideration of the differences between the available knowledge on components at design-, assembly-, and runtime.

3   Break-Out Sessions

In the afternoon the workshop participants were organized in break-out sessions addressing specific topics. Each group had a nominated scribe who, as named in the subsection titles below, took notes which were used by the authors to write the session summaries.

3.1   How Black Should a Component Be?

Scribe: Jakob Henriksson. The first breakout group was concerned with the major topic of the workshop: The blackbox principle of components. In their discussion the group defined the different shades:

- **Blackbox:** Only the interfaces of a component are known.
- **Greybox:** A component reveals interfaces and some selected component internals that are not part of the interface.
- **Whitebox:** Such components are available by their implementation only. All internals are known.

In this definitions, interfaces are an abstraction of the component: "technical" interfaces, behaviour specifications, informal descriptions, or other information to allow agreements on component usage.

How dark? The darkness (required level of abstraction) of a component depends on the component model a component is captured in. Each component model has specific requirements and application domains, hence the abstraction level cannot be fixed.

3.2 How Much Information/Metadata Can Be Expected from a Developer?

Scribe: Bert Lagaisse. The question for the required amount of information/metadata raised further questions – instead of finding many answers, plenty of new emerged:

- Who needs which information and why? What kinds of developers need to provide the data (web developer, business logic author, or expert developer)?
- How is the data specified?
- What kind of software is being developed? Is it safety critical or rapid/agile development?
- How much information is a developer willing to give?
- How much can be extracted from the source/other info? Is there an automation for collecting such data?

In the discussion, the participants were arguing whether it makes sense to use open source instead of specifications. Positions ranged from "don't specify, ship open source" to "it depends, source code can be used as fallback". Additionally, the benefit of specifications has to be seen from two viewpoints: Users vs. developer. While a certain amount of architectural/requirements documentation helps understanding, too much can lower comprehension.

3.3 Formalisms in Component-Oriented Software Engineering

Scribe: Michael Kuperberg. This breakout group was concerned with usage of formalisms in component-oriented software engineering. Following the question "How formal should we be?", the participants have identified and discussed the topic, focusing on state-of-the-art and on desirable use of formalisms in COP and software engineering in general.

- **"How"**: is there a metric or a measurement for degree of formalism? Can we state that "approach A is more formal than approach B" and justify such a statement?
- **"Formal"**
  - Is there a common understanding of "formal" beyond the origin of the word ("form", used here in the sense of shape)? Is there a catalogue of formal methods?
  - What is the relation of *formal* and *abstract*?
  - Can formalisms in component-oriented software engineering be grouped (for example, "behaviour-describing" vs. "structure-describing")? Is it useful to "tag" formalisms with attributes (for example, "works only for limited-scale models" or "is not realistic for highly parallel systems")?

- **"Should"**: Given increasing complexity of component-based software, better understanding can be gained by using models (i.e., formal abstractions). Model-driven development and architecting are currently gaining momentum and tool support is steadily increasing, so "should" is to be read "must" for the future.
- **"We"**: While we see the component-oriented programming from researchers' perspective, we understand that the end users of our research are software developers. Consequently, we should strive to hide the complexity of scientific formalisms from the tool developers and software end users to encourage promotion of formal concepts and models in component-based software development.

In fact, we believe that the *motivation* for using formalisms and models is comprised of several aspects, such as the pressure to develop quickly, effectively and in a cost-saving way, while remaining flexible and able to respond to design changes. In fact, achievement of these aspects can be used as success metrics for applying formalisms. Model-driven architecting and development rely on formal models and transformations help to ensure well-structured rapid software creation.

On the other hand, *understandability* is an important threat to formalisms, as these are often considered to be too complex to follow by practitioners and programmers. Yet a good counter-example of a formalism usage that abstracts away low-level details is UML and related technologies and tools.

Furthermore, *reasoning* on functional properties (correctness etc.) and extra-functional properties (performance, reliability etc.) of component-based software builds on the reasoning techniques from mathematics and logic, which themselves rely on formalisms.

Working examples of well-known formalisms suitable for above tasks include, among others,

- *ontologies* as semantical descriptions increasing the reuse of components and allowing semantic-level adaptation
- *protocol models* for allowing protocol checking and automated adaptation
- *process algebras*, *stochastic process algebras*, *stochastic regular expressions*, *timed* and *stochastic Petri nets* etc. for behaviour descriptions; some of these can be used for performance predictions and for proving correctness or reliability
- logic-based formalisms such as *Prolog* or *OCL* for model-checking and transformation-checking (especially w.r.t. correctness)

These examples show that formalisms have already gained strong foothold in every-day software engineering research. So if *practitioners* want to profit from research advantages, they need to accept using formalisms in a certain way. But unfortunately, it is almost impossible for one human to be professional in all formalisms and low-level technologies.

So we can conclude that to bridge the understanding gap between researchers and developers/designers, formalisms should be further developed toward inclusion into real-world tools. Resulting *encapsulation* in tool chains must happen in such a way that end users are exposed only to input, output and a few understandable tool settings, while the researchers keep the freedom to "plug in" their formalisms into the tool chains.

4   Final Words

We, the organizers, look back on a more than eleven years' series of very successful workshops on component-oriented programming. It is good to see, how over the years the range of topics constantly evolves, while the increasing importance of the aspects trust, quality attributes, architecture, and industrial engineering is well recognized. In particular, we see that the notion of a component got more refined: today we see, that the blackbox principle that a component should not make assumptions on the implementation it does not necessarily follow that no additional information on a component besides the interfaces should be specified. Much more, it turns out that to make component based systems applicable in critical application domains, one need information beyond the interface to perform analysis on the system's quality properties, such as safety, reliability of performance. Such information needed for analysis forms an abstraction of the component's behavior, and, in this way, links to the provided and required interfaces. However, ti keep the benefits of information hiding, users should not base assumptions on this abstract component behavior specification, i.e., they should not use this information implicitly in their implementation using the component.

The field of component orientation is now well connected to many other research areas, such as prediction of extra-functional properties, software architecture modeling and even aspect orientation. We have traveled a long way from the first WCOP in 1996 in Linz and look forward to the continuing journey.

With respect to WCOP 2007, we would like to thank all participants and contributors. In particular, we would like to thank the scribes of the breakout groups Jakob Henriksson, Bert Lagaisse and Michael Kuperberg and Klaus Krogmann for his support in preparing this report.

5   Accepted Papers

The full papers of all presentations are collected on the workshops web-page[3] and in the WCOP proceedings (Technical Report No. 2007-13 of the Faculty of Informatics of the University of Karlsruhe[4]).

The following list of accepted and presented papers is sorted by the order of the presentation.

1. Javier Cubo, Gwen Salaün, Carlos Canal, Ernesto Pimentel, University of Malaga, Spain; Pascal Poizat, Université d'Evry Val d'Essonne, France and INRIA Rocquencourt, France. *Relating Model-Based Adaptation and Implementation Platforms: A Case Study with WF/.NET 3.0?*

---

[3] http://research.microsoft.com/~cszypers/events/WCOP2007
[4] http://digbib.ubka.uni-karlsruhe.de/volltexte/1000007172

2. Eveline Kaboré and Antoine Beugnard, ENST Bretagne, France. *On the benefits of using model transformations to describe components design process*
3. Klaus Krogmann, Universität Karlsruhe (TH), Germany. *Reengineering of Software Component Models to Enable Architectural Quality of Service Predictions*
4. Michael Kuperberg and Steffen Becker, Universität Karlsruhe (TH), Germany. *Predicting Software Component Performance: On the Relevance of Parameters for Benchmarking Bytecode and APIs*
5. Bert Lagaisse and Wouter Joosen, K.U.Leuven, Belgium. *Aspectual Dependencies: Towards Pure Black-Box Aspect-Oriented Composition in Component Models*
6. Angel Núñez and Jacques Noyé. *A Seamless Extension of Components with Aspects using Protocols*
7. Guido Söldner and Rüdiger Kapitza, University of Erlangen-Nürnberg, Germany. *AOCI: An Aspect-Oriented Component Infrastructure*
8. Jakob Henriksson, Florian Heidenreich, Jendrik Johannes, Steffen Zschaler, and Uwe Aßmann, Technische Universität Dresden, Germany. *How dark should a component black-box be? The Reuseware Answer*
9. Franz Puntigam, Technische Universität Wien, Austria. *Black & White, Never Grey: On Interfaces, Synchronization, Pragmatics, and Responsibilities*
10. Richard Rhinelander, University of Kitara, Australia. *Components have no Interfaces!*

List of Participants

Name	Affiliation, Country
Javier Cubo	University of Malaga, Spain
Guillaume Dufrêne	INRIA, France
Jakob Henriksson	TU Dresden, Germany
Jendrik Johannes	TU Dresden, Germany
Klaus Krogmann	Universität Karlsruhe (TH), Germany
Michael Kuperberg	Universität Karlsruhe (TH), Germany
Bert Lagaisse	K. U. Leuven, Belgium
Anne Martens	Universität Karlsruhe (TH), Germany
Angel Núñez	EMN / INRIA, France
Aleš Plešek	INRIA, France
Cristian Prisacariv	University of Oslo, Norway
Franz Puntigam	TU Wien, Austria
Holger Schmidt	University Ulm, Germany
Ralf Reussner	Universität Karlsruhe (TH) / FZI, Germany
Richard Rhinelander	University of Kitara, Australia
Guido Söldner	University Erlangen, Germany
Clemens Szyperski	Microsoft, Redmond, USA

Model-Driven Software Adaptation

Report on the Workshop M-ADAPT at ECOOP 2007

Nelly Bencomo[1], Gordon Blair[1], and Robert France[2]

[1] Computing Department, InfoLab21, Lancaster University,
Lancaster, LA1 4WA, UK
{nelly,gordon}@comp.lancs.ac.uk
[2] Computer Science Department, Colorado State University,
Fort Collins, 80523-1873, USA
france@cs.colostate.edu

Abstract. This first edition of the workshop Model-driven Software Adaptation (M-ADAPT'07) took place in the Technische Universität Berlin with the International Conference ECOOP'07 in the beautiful and buzzing city of Berlin, on the 30th of July, 2007. The workshop was organized by Gordon Blair, Nelly Bencomo, and Robert France. Participants explored how to develop appropriate model-driven approaches to model, analyze, and validate the volatile properties of the behaviour of adaptive systems and its environments. This report gives an overview of the presentations as well as an account of the fruitful discussions that took place at M-ADAPT'07.

1 Introduction

Adaptability is emerging as a critical enabling capability for many applications, particularly for environment monitoring, disaster management and other applications deployed in dynamically changing environments. Such applications have to reconfigure themselves according to fluctuations in their environment. The unpredictability of changes in the environments and their requirements pose new challenges to Software Engineering. Current software development approaches specify the functionality of the system at design-time. Such approaches are not sufficiently expressive to develop systems that dynamically adapt to environment fluctuations. As a result, alternative approaches are required that take into account the specification of behaviour and functionality during the execution. However, dynamic adaptation can lead to emergent and unpredictable behaviour. The workshop aimed to start the establishment of a sound foundation for the use of model-driven techniques for software adaptation.

Research and industry efforts focused on model-driven technologies have proved the value of the use of models during the design, implementation, and deployment stages of development. However, the use of model-driven techniques for validating and monitoring run-time behaviour can also yield significant benefits. In particular, models can be used to provide a richer semantic base for

M. Cebulla (Ed.): ECOOP 2007 Workshop Reader, LNCS 4906, pp. 132–141, 2008.

runtime decision-making related to system adaptation and other runtime concerns. For example, models can be used to help determine when a system should move from a consistent architecture to another consistent architecture.

This workshop builds on a sister event, Models@runtime 2006, held at MODELS 2006 in Italy [2]. Models@runtime 2007 was also held at MoDELS 2007 in Nasville, USA. Bringing the workshop to an ECOOP audience helped broaden the discussions to cover issues related to the integration of modelling techniques with other techniques typically covered at ECOOP (e.g. component-based and reflection techniques).

The call for submissions mainly focused on the following research topics:

- Formal notations for modeling, analyzing, and validating adaptive systems
- Management and modelling the dynamic variability intrinsic in the structure and behaviour of adaptive systems and their environments
- The relevance and suitability of different model-driven approaches to monitoring and managing systems during runtime
- Compatibility (or tension) between different model-driven approaches
- Experience related to the use of run-time models to adapt software systems
- Model-driven design for adaptability

The workshop placed strong emphasis on the cross-pollination of ideas from different researchers from diverse research fields including model-driven engineering, product lines and system families, software architectures, computational reflection, embedded systems, and autonomous and self-adaptive systems. The programme committee of M-ADAPT'07 reflected this diversity; thirteen international researchers from different areas were tasked with the reviewing process of the papers submitted.

In response to the call for papers, 15 papers were submitted, of which 10 were accepted for presentation and discussion in Berlin: 6 long papers and 4 short papers. Long papers identified clear research challenges and offered clear contributions and answers to the workshop. Short papers identified research challenges and specific working examples during the discussions of the workshop. The number of papers submitted represented a healthy interest in M-ADAPT. Each submitted paper was reviewed by at least 3 programm committee members who suggested detailed improvements to the accepted papers. The papers can be found in the proceedings of the workshop [1] and on the associated web pages [3].

The workshop was opened to attendees who were not co-authors of any of presented papers; Twenty two people in total registered for the event from Brazil, France, Germany, Spain, UK, and USA.

2   Workshop Structure

The workshop was structured in two parts: presentations during the morning and discussions during the afternoon. During the first 15 minutes of the morning, Gordon Blair and Nelly Bencomo introduced the goals of the workshop and proposed a roadmap of the rest of the day. On the basis of the suggested research topics in the Call for Papers and on the contents of the accepted papers, the presentation part was organized in 3 sessions. The first two sessions were devoted to *Autonomic and Embedded Systems* and *Specific Techniques* and were dedicated to the long papers. The third session *Stated Problems* included the 4 short papers.

Long papers were presented by two speakers, the first speaker was an author of the paper and the second speaker was an independent reader. Second readers provided a second view on the contents of the paper, placing it in relation to the workshop topics and research questions. Authors of short papers presented their research work and stated research challenges identified from their research.

To ensure effectiveness in trems of time, each long paper presentation was limited to 15 minutes of presentation by the main author and 5 minutes for the second reader followed by 5 minutes of questions. Short paper were limited to 5 minutes of presentation

The afternoon was dedicated to focused debates. The workshop was closed by a general discussion, including an evaluation of the workshop itself by the participants. Details of the sessions are provided in Sections 3 and 4. The proposed format worked well, with all attendees contributing to the workshop through constructive and friendly discussion.

3   Paper Presentations

In this session we summarize the presentations, contributions, and the discussions raised from the talks.

Session 1: Autonomic and Embedded Systems

The workshop opened with three papers on Autonomic and Embedded Systems issues. The first paper *"On Run-time Behavioural Adaptation in Context-Aware Systems"* by Javier Cámara [1], Gwen Salan, and Carlos Canal. The second reader of the paper was Franck Barbier. The authors reported on their experiences tackling the problem of runtime modifiable adaptation policies dependent on the current state of the context of the system. Instead of creating an appropriate adaptor to compose the different components at design time, it was explained how their approach aims at dynamically creating this adaptor. Javier described a way to model externally visible communication behavior of components as well as (context-dependent) valid inter-communications between the different components. Javier also explained how their research could be used as the basis for dynamic adaptor generation using dynamic aspect weaving. Javier's work was well received as a good technique for adaptation of software. This presentation provided a crosslink with another ECOOP Workshop, the 4th workshop on Coordination and Adaptation Techniques for Software Entities (WCAT'07) [6]. The co-authors of the paper presented by Javier were organizers of WCAT'07 making valuable contributions to M-ADAPT.

---

[1] We use underline to denote the name of the author presenting the paper at the workshop.

The second paper, "*A Model-driven Approach to the Development of Autonomous Control Applications*" by Helge Parzyjegla, Michael Jaeger, and Gero Muehl and discussed by Mario Trapp as a second reader. Helge presented a model-driven approach for the development of Autonomous Control applications in sensor networks. Helge explained how their work was motivated by the need to relieve the developer from the inherently high complexity of such development. The authors proposed the encapsulation of the necessary expert knowledge in a model transformation. In order to facilitate runtime adaptation, knowledge from the model is made available at runtime. The research is partially based on the MDA philosophy [4]; a multi-step transformation process from application models to code generation for target platforms was presented. The authors focus on basic role deployment (i.e., a kind of impersonating behaviors that nodes/devices can perform). Participating nodes are equipped with self-stabilizing algorithms for inter-role communication and dynamic role assignment that are the basis of reconfiguration at runtime. It was praised how the approach proposed by Helge and his colleagues offer simple initial ideas on the use of a model information to drive adaptation and auto-organization.

The last paper in the session was "*Development of Safe and Reliable embedded systems using dynamic adaptation*" by Rasmus Adler, Daniel Schneider, and Mario Trapp with Helge Parzyjegla as the second reader. Rasmus presented a classification of approaches to implementing dynamically adapting systems. Such systems were classified in four categories from 'no dynamic adaptation' via 'implicit dynamic adaptation' all the way through to 'systematically engineered dynamic adaptation'. Rasmus talked about the project MARS. This project aims at providing a seamless engineering approach from the requirements to running systems. Starting from a feature model the system architecture is defined using their own Architecture Description Language (ADL). After specifying the adaptation behavior, a design model in Matlab/Simulink is generated that combines adaptation and functionality in an integrated model. They use validation and verification techniques of the adaptation behavior include simulation, verification, and probabilistic analysis. A major contribution of the presentation was Rasmus' comments on the state of the art and future research requirements for the field of dynamic adaptation. The classification presented a systematic approach to the development of dynamically adapting systems. The thoughts on future research directions led to healthy discussion about the need to study the impact of dynamic adaptation on safety and reliability. From the discussions, it was concluded and highlighted by Heldge that common understanding of terms (as for example, adaptivity) is essential when developing the right model-driven techniques for adaptive systems.

Session 2: Specific Techniques[2]

The second session was dedicated to more specific techniques for software adaptation. The session was introduced by the paper on *Applying Architectural*

---

[2] This session had originally three papers; however one of the papers could not be presented as the speaker could not attend the workshop.

Constraints in the Modeling of Self-adaptive Component based Applications by Mohammad Ullah Khan, Roland Reichle, and Kurt Geihs, with Ethan Hadar as the second reader. Mohammad described an approach for model-based development of dynamically reconfigurable systems. The modeling technique enables developers to model the variabilities of a system with respect to runtime adaptation. The above may result in a large combinatorial number of alternative configurations (or variants). Mohammad emphasized the fact that many of these variants are usually not feasible, as some component realizations may require or exclude realizations for other components. Hence, he showed how the authors adopted an approach that builds on architectural constraints specified as part of the application model. They assumed that component realizations may have some features (properties) that have to correspond to the features of other component realizations or exclude some components realizations. Features are associated with a simple constraint. These constrains (invariants) are checked by the adaptation management when creating the application variants. Examples of constrains are (i) a feature which is common to all involved components or (ii) a feature exclusively provided by only one component. The modeling framework follows the MDA paradigm to transform the application UML model [5], including the architectural constraints, to appropriate source code. The final application is deployed to a middleware platform supporting adaptive applications. The middleware supporting the adaptive applications uses the generated source code for filtering out all infeasible combinations at runtime, based on the feature names and the constraints. During discussion, it was highlighted that the role of MDA in the proposed idea was not crucial for the adaptation concerns of the approach. The use of MDA was not different from the traditional use. The main contribution identified is the way how Mohammad and his co-authors have tackled the unforeseen conditions that appear at runtime. The identification is based on the architectural constrains using the features identified. Architectural constrains has a crucial role when addressing the scalability problem of the number of variants.

The second session was closed by the paper *"Modeling Software Adaptation Patterns"* by Hassan Gomaa. The second reader was Mohammad Ullah Khan. Hassan talked about the importance of being able to dynamically adapt software architectures at run-time. Hassan also described his research on software adaptation patterns and their role in software system adaptation. It was shown how a software adaptation pattern could define the way a set of components (as an architecture or design pattern) dynamically cooperate to change the software configuration to a new configuration. Four patterns were presented and discussed: Master-Slave Centralized control Client/Server Decentralized control. Hassan pointed out that for every software architectural or design pattern, there is a corresponding software adaptation pattern, which models how the software components and interconnections should be changed. Using his premise, it is possible to think of automatic evolution of software architectures using software adaptation patterns. A research challenged identified by Hassan and acknowledged by other participant is the automatic selection of the appropriate adaptation pattern to maintain a partial service while adaptation is taking place, and QoS issues during software adaptation, for example. Mohammad and other participants raised the fact that the work presented was heavily based on UML highlighting that there was no use of domain-specific languages, for example.

Session 3: **Stated Problems**
Four short papers were presented in the third and last session.

- *"Experiments with a Runtime Component Model"* by Jo Ueyama, Geoff Coulson, Edmundo Madeira, Thais Batista, and Paul Grace

- *"SELF-*: Endowing Software Components with Autonomic Capabilities Based on Modeling Language Executability"* by Cyril Ballagny, Nabil Hameurlain, and Franck Barbier

- *"Modelling Adaptation Policies for Self-Adaptive Component Architectures"* by Franck Chauvel and Olivier Barais

- *"A Reconfiguration Mechanism for Statechart Based Components"* by Xabier Elkorobarrutia, Gaiuria Sagardui, and Xabier Aretxandieta

These presentations identified different problems where model-driven techniques can be useful to provide sound solutions. Model-driven techniques seem to be useful to drive software composition during runtime. Models also have a role in guiding and generating component reconfiguration in different domains. However, it was highlighted that the potential value of models is (i) their capability to represent the dynamic reconfiguration of sets of components (i.e. during execution), (ii) its use in conjunction with reflection. adaptation policies, autonomous (self-adaptive) application , and (iii) validation and verification. Models can be used to predict and analyze the quality of the adaptation behavior to enable systematic control of the software development as highlighted by Rasmus et all.

4   Discussion Sessions

4.1   Preamble

As a preamble to the general discussion, Gordon Blair wrapped up the morning sessions summarizing what he had observed and learned so far from the workshop.

The most striking aspect of the morning for him was the universal recognition of the pressing need for Software Engineering (SE) methodologies, and specifically model-driven techniques, for adaptive systems. However, it was clear that the research field is currently in an embryonic stage, with no clear consensus about approaches or even a common terminology. It is essential to use the experience from existing approaches and acknowledge the contributions already offered by different communities. These contributions provide building blocks and the base knowledge required to answer the open questions and research challenges tackled in this workshop. Crucially, there are also very few opportunities to bring together the required communities and hence this workshop was viewed as timely.

He commented that the papers from the morning actually provided a strong and complementary representation of such existing work under the headings techniques and methods, and methodologies:

Techniques and Methods

- The use of Components, context, composition, and adaptation techniques [Javier Cámara et al]
- Context and policies [Franck Chauvel et al]
- State-based models (at run-time) [Cyril Ballagny et al]
- Real-time (reflective) component models [Jo Ueyama et al]
- daptation patterns, adaptation taxonomy [Hassan Gomaa]

Methodologies

- Modelling of adaptation for embedded systems [Rasmus Adler et al]
- Models, roles and self-stabilizing algorithms [Helge Parzyjegla et al]
- Models and architectural constraints [Mohammad Ullah Khan et all]

He then presented a set of key challenges that have to be tackled before the area can mature. The first was the lack of a common terminology which makes it difficult to have meaningful dialogue across the various contributing communities. The second was then embracing the full complexity of real world distributed applications where there is typically a very large design space of components and features, where you have to deal with both anticipated and unanticipated events, where you may need distributed and/ or decentralised solutions for scalability, and where you need to address whether to seek domain specific or generic solutions. He also highlighted the key distinction between adaptive and autonomic systems (the latter embracing self-* management and inevitably emergent properties), and the subsequent need to have model-driven techniques that embrace what is in effect a spectrum of adaptive or autonomic solutions.

He then concluded with a set of open questions for the audience to consider in the afternoon [2]:

- What is an appropriate MDE methodology for adaptive and/ or autonomic (distributed) systems
- What are the appropriate constituent models?
- What is an appropriate transformational process?
- Where is adaptation folded into such a process?
- Is there a role for models@run-time?
- What do we know (useful building blocks)?
- What do we not know (towards a roadmap)?
- and, of course, what should we do next!

The attendees then submitted a number of questions that they saw as important based on the discussions so far. From this, two key areas were identified for further discussion in the afternoon:

- Overall (model-driven) methodologies for adaptive and/ or autonomic distributed systems
- Specific focus on the role of models at execution time (cf. Models@Runtime)

4.2   Summary of Ensuing Discussion

As mentioned above, the discussion in the afternoon focused on overall methodologies and also on the concept of Models@Runtime.

The discussion on overall methodologies was facilitated by Hassan Gomaa and build on the considerable expertise in the group on different aspects of adaptive systems. The discussion focused mainly on identifying common terminology and synergy between the different approaches. Particular attention was given to the complementary roles of *triggers, adaptation actions,* and *adaptation rules* as defined below:

trigger: an event or condition that causes the need of adaptation, e.g. user-related actions and changes in the environment.

action: which realizes the actual adaptation, e.g. architecture, algorithms, and parameters.

adaptation rule: a rule that defines which triggers cause which adaptation actions. Rules also describe the conditions that should be met to carry out an action.

This provided a common framework to then seek more comprehensive solutions for adaptive distributed systems.

The other group focused exclusively on the emerging concept of maintaining a model of a system at runtime. This is very much a new idea and initial discussion concentrated on motivation for such an approach, highlighting the role that such models can have in informing and constraining the adaptation process. There was also a view that such models can raise the level of abstraction in discourse about such adaptive processes. The rest of the discussion then considered the key question of what a model at runtime would look like, what level of abstraction should this offer, and what (meta-) information should be maintained in such models? Should their also be one model or are we looking at a series of orthogonal models.

The two groups then came back together and discussed their collective results. The participants agreed that the workshop had raised many very valuable questions and that this is potentially a very important area for research. Some insights emerged during the workshop. For example, as explained in Hassan's work, models can be used to represent adaptation patterns that would be automatically selected during runtime. The paper presented by Mohammad showed initial ideas on how to use constrains in architecture-based models as a way to deal with the unanticipated conditions often found in adaptive systems. Furthermore, given the potential impact of dynamic adaptation on reliability and safety properties of systems, a major concern highlighted was the need to predict and analyze the level of quality of adaptive behaviour. In this sense, models used during runtime should represent information that makes explicit the use of QoS during adaptation.

5   Final Remarks

The main goal of the workshop was to bring together researchers from different communities interested in the field to get them to know about each other's work. The workshop lived up to its expectations with high-quality papers, presentations, and discussions. The fact that there are actually very few forums where the constituent researchers from different communities can get together was highlighted. For these reasons the opportunity to held the workshop M-ADAPT was timely. However, it was concluded that next steps should include clarification of the terminology to help come to a common understanding of adaptive systems. This common understanding would help to concentrate rather than dilute efforts. The concept of models at runtime was also flagged as a crucial area for further investigation.

Three papers were selected to be published (in extended versions) in IEEE Distributed Systems online [7]. These were the papers presented by Rasmus Adler et all, Mohammad Ullah Khan et all, and Helge Parzyjegla et all.

The workshop was closed with a warm "thank you" from the organizers to all participants for a successful workshop. After the workshop finished, participants headed to the workshop reception at ECOOP to continue sharing ideas and enjoy each other's company.

6   List of Attendees

Javier Camara, Universidad de Malaga, Spain
Pascal Poizat, INRIA/ARLES, University of Evry, France
Javier Cubo, Universidad de Malaga, Spain
Carlos Canal, Universidad de Malaga, Spain
Hassan Gomaa, George Mason university
Jó Ueyama, University of Campinas, Brazil
Bassein Elkarablich, University of Texas, Austin, USA
Ethan Hada, CA Labcs, USA
Rasmus Adler, IESE, Fraunhofer, Germany
Daniel Schider, IESE, Fraunhofer, Germany
Mario Trapp, IESE, Fraunhofer, Germany
Anne Martens, Universitt Karlsruhe (TH), Germany
Xabier Elkorobarrutia, Mondragon Unibertsitatea ,Spain
Mohammad Ullah Khan, University of Kassel, Germany
Franck Barbier, University of Pau, France
Antoine Beugnard, GET/ENST Bretagne, France
Nabil Hameurlain, University of Pau
Cyril Ballagny, University of Pau
Helge Parzyjegla, Berlin University of Technology
Franck Chauvel, IRISA, Universit de Rennes, France
Nelly Bencomo, Lancaster University, UK
Gordon Blair, Lancaster University, UK

Acknowledgments. First of all, we would like to thank the members of the program committee who acted as anonymous reviewers and provided valuable feedback to the authors: *Franck Barbier, Benoit Baudry, Fabio M. Costa, Eli Gjrven, Gang Huang, Rui Silva Moreira, Klaus Pohl, Marten van Sinderen, Arnor Solberg, Mario Trapp, Thaís Vasconcelos Batista, Steffen Zschaler, Lus Ferreira-Pires,* and *Bedir Tekinerdogan.* We also thank to the Workshop Chairs P*eter Pepper Arnd* and *Poetzsch-Heff* and specially *Michael Cebulla* for the organization and patience dealing with the organization of the workshops. Last but not least, the participants and authors of all submitted papers are thanked for helping us making this workshop possible.

References

1. Blair, G., Bencomo, N., France, R., Cebulla, M.: Proceedings of the First Workshop on Model-driven Adaptation (M-ADAPT 2007) at ECOOP 2007, Bericht Nr. 2007–10 (2007)
2. Blair, G., Bencomo, N., France, R.: Summary of the Workshop Models@run.time at MoDELS 2006. In: Nierstrasz, O., Whittle, J., Harel, D., Reggio, G. (eds.) MoDELS 2006. LNCS, vol. 4199, pp. 226–230. Springer, Heidelberg (2006)
3. http://www.comp.lancs.ac.uk/~bencomo/M-ADAPT07/index.html (2007)
4. Kleppe, A., Warmer, J., Bast, W.: MDA Explained The Model Driven Architecture: Practise and Promise. Addison-Wesley, London (2003)
5. Fowler, M., Scott, K.: UML Distilled Addison Wesley (1999)
6. Canal, C., Murillo, J., Poizat, P.: WCAT 2007. Proceedings of the Fourth International Workshop on Coordination and Adaptation Techniques for Software Entities (2007)
7. http://dsonline.computer.org (2007)

Object-Oriented Reengineering

Report on the Workshop WOOR'07 at ECOOP 2007
10th Anniversary Edition

Serge Demeyer[1], Yann-Gaël Guéhéneuc[2], Anne Keller[1], Christian F.J. Lange[3],
Kim Mens[4], Adrian Kuhn[5], and Martin Kuhlemann[6]

[1] Department of Mathematics and Computer Science,
University of Antwerp — Belgium
[2] Department of Computer Science and Operations Research,
Université de Montréal — Canada
[3] Engineering and Technology Group,
Eindhoven University of Technology — Netherlands
[4] Département d'Ingénierie Informatique,
Université catholique de Louvain — Belgium
[5] Software Software Composition Group,
University of Berne —Switzerland
[6] School of Computer Science,
University of Magdeburg — Germany

Abstract. The ability to reengineer object-oriented legacy systems has become a vital matter in today's software industry. Early adopters of the object-oriented programming paradigm are now facing the problem of transforming their object-oriented "legacy" systems into full-fledged frameworks. To address this problem, a series of workshops has been organised to set up a forum for exchanging experiences, discussing solutions, and exploring new ideas. Typically, these workshops were organised as satellite events of major software engineering conferences, such as ECOOP [1,2,3,4,5,6,7,8,9,10,11] and ESEC/FSE [12,13,14]. During the past 10 years, participants of this workshop series have been actively contributing to the state-of-the-art on reengineering of object-oriented systems. This special 10th anniversary edition was no exception and this report summarises the key discussions and outcome of that workshop.

1   Introduction

In preparation to the workshop, participants were asked to submit a position paper that would help in steering the workshop discussions. Five position papers were accepted, of which eight authors were present during the workshop. Together with a number of organisers and participants without position paper, the workshop attracted eighteen participants. The position papers and other information about the workshop are available on the workshop web-site at http://smallwiki.unibe.ch/woor2007/ [15].

A format for the workshop day was chosen that balanced presentation of position papers and time for discussions, using the morning for presentations of position papers and the afternoon for discussions in working groups. The workshop was concluded

M. Cebulla (Ed.): ECOOP 2007 Workshop Reader, LNCS 4906, pp. 142–153, 2008.
© Springer-Verlag Berlin Heidelberg 2008

with a plenary session during which the results of the working groups were exposed and discussed by *all* workshop participants in the larger group.

2   Position Papers

Taking into account positive feedback from participants from the previous years, we decided to require that each paper be presented by the authors of another paper. We have observed over the years that this system ensures that participants read the position papers of one another and are able to discuss them from different viewpoints. For the authors, it is also interesting to hear what another researcher in the field has understood from the submission and thinks about the approach. As in previous years, this format resulted in vivid discussions during the presentations, which formed a good foundation for the afternoon discussions. We now give a short summary of each of the five position papers that were presented at the workshop.

Discussion on the Results of the Detection of Design Defects [16]. In this paper, the authors present validation results of their design defect detection method (DECOR), which allows the systematic specification of design defects and subsequently the automatic generation of design defect detection algorithms from these specifications. The specification language is based on high-level key concepts identified from textual design defect descriptions. The validation is based on evaluating of 4 design defects together with their 15 smells in terms of precision and recall.

nMARPLE: .NET Reverse Engineering with MARPLE [17]. Detecting design pattern in a system is an aspect of reverse engineering that may contribute to the understanding of the overall system design. The authors of this paper present a tool (nMARPLE) that is an extension of the existing design pattern detection tool MARPLE. nMarple is specifically designed to reverse engineer .Net executables and the authors discuss peculiarities of reverse engineering in a .Net context.

Challenges in Model Refactoring [18]. While refactoring of source code is a well-known technique to improve maintainability, refactoring of models is a largely unexplored territory. The authors of this paper discuss nine challenges in model refactoring that they identified as the most important ones. The discussed challenges include traditional refactoring issues—such as (model) quality and behaviour preservation—and modelling-specific issues—such as model synchronisation and defining refactorings for domain specific languages.

Must Tool Building Remain a Craft? [19]. In the reverse-engineering community, tool building plays an important role for validating research results. In this position paper, the author argues that despite its importance as validation instrument and its cost, tool building is approached as a craft rather than as an engineering discipline. On the basis of an extensive study of research literature, the author identifies shortcomings in academic tool building in the fields of requirements engineering, design-related issues, and development process.

A Meta-model Approach to Inconsistency Management [20]. As models become increasingly important software development artefacts, consistency between models, *i.e.*, between different views, different versions, and different abstraction levels, also gains importance. Consistency between models however should be managed rather than enforced. The authors of this paper introduce the idea of an inconsistency meta-model to support inconsistency management.

3 Working Groups

Taking into account the presented position papers and the discussions that followed them, we split up in three working groups for the afternoon. The next three subsections report on the discussions that were held in each of these working groups.

3.1 Working Group 1: Model Reengineering

The topic of the first working group was *modelling*. The main objective of the working group was to discuss how the interests of the WOOR workshop such as reengineering and refactoring relate to modelling. Originally, models were used in software engineering to describe and communicate about a system. However, in recent techniques, such as Model Driven Architecture (MDA [21]), automated transformations are performed on models to create new models. The target model is based on the source model, but it contains more details, *i.e.*, it is more specific than the source model. The transformation is called *code generation* in case the target model is a representation of the original model in the form of source code. An overall result of the discussion is that, in the context of modelling, there are three areas of interest for reengineering research. We present the three areas of interest together with open questions that were raised during the discussions:

- **Source model.** Which flaws exist in a model? What are the quality requirements for the model to be useful to its audience or to be 'transformable'?
- **Target model.** Which flaws exist in a model? To what extent do flaws in the source model lead to flaws in the target model?
- **Transformation.** Is 'reengineering-by-transformation' possible (*i.e.*, can source model flaws be resolved by transformations)? Can transformations be improved by means of reengineering?

The discussions were divided into two parts that are summarised below. The major part of the discussion addressed *model smells*, similar to code smells (as proposed by Fowler [22]). A smaller part of the discussion was devoted to *code generation*.

Model Smells. Model smells are flaws in a model. To distinguish model smells from bugs or errors in general, the working group defined model smells as being specific for models, *i.e.*, they are caused by characteristics that are inherent to models. Additionally, it was agreed upon that model smells can be distinguished from "simple errors" by the amount of human effort that is involved in dealing with them. Usually the amount of human effort involved in detecting, analysing, prioritising, and resolving model smells is rather important, in comparison to simple errors, where automated techniques reduce the amount of human effort involved in dealing with them.

Furthermore the discussion addressed the resolution of model smells. The following set of basic model operations was identified, that can be used to resolve model smells: *add, remove, delete, merge, collapse, flatten,* and *split*. Depending on the type of a model smell and its location, its resolution consists of applying a subset of these operations. Future work should relate model smell types to particular resolution strategies based on these operations.

Two substantial questions regarding resolution were addressed:

- *Can* all smells be resolved?
- *Must* all smells be resolved?

The first question could not be answered at all in the discussion, because there did not exist an exhaustive list of model smells and because there exists only little work in the area of model smell resolution. The working group formed an opinion about the latter question. It is assumed that for automated processing of models (*e.g.,* model transformation) "small errors" must be resolved, and model smells should be resolved. However, for a human-only use of the models, errors and smells could remain unresolved, depending on the purpose of the model usage. More research is required to investigate which types of model smells must be resolved for particular purposes and which ones do not necessarily need to be resolved.

Besides these observations concerning model smells, the main outcome of the discussion was a list of types of model smells:

- *Inconsistency.* Inconsistencies are contradictions between different parts of the models, *e.g.,* between diagrams.
- *Incompleteness.* Incompleteness is the absence of necessary model elements. Typically, a model is incomplete with respect to some other artefacts, for example with respect to the requirements, *i.e.,* not all functionalities are modelled, or with respect to the information needed by a stake-holder.
- *Imbalance.* Imbalance refers to differences between parts of a model with respect to their properties, such as level of abstraction or completeness.
- *Redundancy.* Redundancy is present if a concept is described in different parts of a model. Redundant parts can be inconsistent, they can differ with one another, *e.g.,* with respect to their levels of abstraction or versions.
- *Violations of Modelling Conventions.* Modelling conventions [23] are a means to assure a uniform style of modelling amongst several modellers. Violations of these conventions are considered model smells.
- *(Too high) Complexity.* In modelling, usually different ways of modelling can be used to describe the same system. If a complex way of modelling is chosen while a simpler model would be possible, the high complexity is regarded as a model smell. This complexity differs from the complexity that is inherent to a problem, which cannot be reduced by a particular way of modelling.
- *Too abstract–Too detailed.* The appropriate level of abstraction depends on the goal of a model. A wrong choice in the abstraction level is regarded as a model smell.
- *Dead model parts.* Dead model parts are parts of a model that are outdated or that are not used anymore.

– *Layout flaws.* Several models offer diagrams as graphical representations. In case the layout of the diagrams does not follow established layout guidelines (*e.g.,* Sun et al. [24]), the flaw is regarded as a model smell.

Code Generators. A smaller part of the discussion was devoted to code generators. It was noticed that implementations that are based on the same source model can have different behaviours, depending on the code generator that was used. Additionally, participants reported that the choice of a particular code generator would strongly affect whether model refactorings are behaviour preserving. Therefore the comparison with respect to differences in behaviour between code generators, such as AndroMDA or GMF, was identified as an area for future research.

3.2 Working Group 2: Tool Building Issues

The second working group discussed a number of issues relevant to builders of reengineering tools. First of all, based on Kienle's position paper "Must tool building remain a craft?" [19], which was presented in the morning session, the group discussed whether or not tool building should remain a craft and highlighted some points in favour and against. Next they discussed what lessons could be learned from experienced tool builders: what are the success stories and what are the pitfalls to avoid? Finally, they briefly discussed the issue of how to compare and benchmark tools.

Should tool building remain a craft? Several arguments in favour of considering tool building as a craft were put forward. One of the strongest arguments is that building research tools is often an exploratory process. In many cases, neither the requirements nor the solution space of the problem at hand are known completely up front. Flexibility in research is needed. In such a situation, the process of building a tool can actually help researchers to shape the way they think about the problem and to discover what their tool can and should do. Exploratory modelling is often a key task in research tool building.

On the other hand, sometimes making just a proof of concept is not enough and there are some strong reasons for tool building not to be an ad-hoc process. First of all, having a more rigid process can increase the productivity of tool builders and may lead to better quality tools. It may even allow to automate part of the process. Also, if you do not want a tool that is just built for one occasion or experiment but rather a tool or a tool framework that remains for many years, then maybe following an ad-hoc process is not the right choice.

In conclusion, there seems to be a kind of trade-off to be made by the tool builders. But maybe these two alternative ways of building tools should not be regarded as two independent and separate approaches, but rather as complementary. Maybe the best process to follow is to first make a "quick and dirty" prototype of the tool that you would like to develop, possibly reusing some existing building blocks or parts of other tools built earlier. Having made such a prototype allows you to evaluate it and improve on it. This process can be repeated until you are happy with the developed tool or until some important limitations are encountered. At that point, it is probably wise to start adopting a more rigourous tool building process.

Positive lessons learned in building tools. There was a consensus among tool builders present at the workshop that, in the long run, it pays off to invest into shared infrastructure and common exchange formats. This facilitates both reuse of existing work and co-operation between researchers and research groups.

A well-known example of such a *common exchange format* in the domain of object-oriented reengineering is the FAMIX exchange model [25,26]. This model allows reengineering tools or prototypes to exchange information concerning object-oriented source code. Building a common exchange format has the advantage that it is easier to get accepted than a common tool infrastructure, yet might lead to a common infrastructure once everyone starts using that common format.

To avoid reinvestigating effort in earlier tools, it is often better to build a bridge (like for instance mentioned in the reengineering pattern "build a bridge to the new town" [27]) to prior tools rather than reimplement them whenever you want to apply them in a new context or port them to a new environment. A noteworthy example hereof is the IntensiVE tool-suite [28], implemented in the Smalltalk language, which was originally built to manage and reason about evolution of Smalltalk programs. Since the underlying ideas of the tool were applicable to any object-oriented language, the decision was taken to extend the tool-suite to deal with Java programs as well. One way of doing so would have been to reimplement from scratch the entire tool in Java. However, this would have lead to a major implementation effort and two separate branches of the tool to be maintained: one for Smalltalk and one for Java. Instead, a bridge was implemented to allow the Smalltalk tool to access Java programs in an Eclipse workspace. Although implementing this bridge was not a trivial endeavour; in the end, it allowed having one tool that can deal with several languages. In addition, the bridge itself could be reused for similar Smalltalk programs that reason over Java programs.

A third proven recipe for success in reverse engineering tools is to make a common framework or tool that can serve as a backbone for several other tools. We can mention several examples of such a common backbone:

- The MOOSE platform that implements the language-independent FAMIX model mentioned above.
- The SOUL declarative meta-programming language [29] that was used as a backbone for the IntensiVE tool-suite [28] and many other tools that require reasoning over the structure of object-oriented source code.
- The (ASF+SDF) Meta-Environment [30] that is a framework for language development, source code analysis, and source code transformation. It has been successfully used in a wide variety of analysis, transformation, and renovation projects.
- the PADL meta-model of the Ptidej tool suite that is a language-independent meta-model to describe object-oriented systems and patterns, and that has been used in several research work, see for example [31].

Pitfalls in tool building. Tool development in research differs from tool building in industrial environments. The main difference is that research tools are mainly built as proofs of concept of techniques, solutions, and algorithms, rather than for commercial use. That particular set-up gives rise to several pitfalls and drawbacks, some of which are listed below.

- Research tools are usually built by Ph.D. candidates, and when the original tool builder leaves the research group, the tool often dies.
- Researchers often implement their tools from scratch, rather than building on prior tools or frameworks.
- Researchers tend to reimplement algorithms and tools that have already been implemented earlier. We have to remember that we are tool builders and not algorithm implementers.
- To be dependent on tools maintained by other researchers can be dangerous, as there is no guaranteed maintenance of research tools (see the first item above). This is a trade-off with the previous item: to avoid such dependencies, researchers often prefer to reimplement things themselves.
- We should use the right tool for the job. Some tools and environments are better for achieving your goal than others (try to make the right choice up front). For example, every so many years, a new language or environment hype appears in research or industry. As researchers, we should not switch to those new languages or environments when there is no real need to. On the one hand, remember that we are not commercial tool builders: techniques, solutions, and algorithms can also be proven and verified in more dynamic and lightweight environments. On the other hand, a good reason for jumping on the mainstream could be to have a large user base for conducting empirical studies.

Tool building patterns. We identified the need to distil recurring patterns from these pitfalls and positive lessons. There have been some interesting approaches in that direction recently. For example, to overcome the tendency of building monolithic, single-purpose software development tools, Vainsencher and Black [32] proposed a pattern language that would enable the integration of multiple analyses and tools in a more modular fashion.

An example that was discussed in the working group was the "tool bridge pattern". Many tool builders use a bridge pattern to reuse existing subtools with an "ad-hoc" bridge (for example, a bridge from your tool to the Eclipse API to access the right data in the Eclipse UI, or a bridge to a dedicated program like Mathematica to do some advanced calculations). Advantages of such a bridge are that it becomes much faster to implement the tool (because you do not have to reimplement the subtools) and that it is easy to replace the subtools you rely on by other ones later on. Disadvantages are that the tool(s) may be considered as less coupled from a user point of view (you need two or more subtools rather than having one homogeneous tool) and that the bridge may bring some runtime overhead. Implementing such a bridge may also require quite some hacks and technicalities, thus leading to a more complex maintenance process.

Good practices. From the above discussions, we then distilled some "good practices" for tool builders to take into account:

- Probably a good strategy is to start by implementing an ad-hoc prototype first, to get the ideas straight, and then gradually adhere to a more rigourous development process.
- Developing a backbone tool infrastructure, or at least a common exchange format, is generally a good idea.

- Give the tool an extensible (data) architecture, to make it easy to extend or reuse later on.
- Overcome the "not invented here" syndrome and try to avoid reinventing or reimplementing existing tools. Rather, reuse or extend (mature) existing ones.
- Avoid "cowboy coding" where tools are implemented from scratch in an ad-hoc fashion.
- Create a community of researchers that use or work on the tool (either a single research group or bigger).

In addition to these good practices the importance of publishing scientific articles on the tool itself (and not only on the results that were obtained with it) was stressed. In spite of what is generally believed, there do exist several journals where such articles can be published, such as Elsevier's "Experimental Software and Toolkits" (EST) or Wiley's "Software—Practice and Experience" (SPE). There exist several workshops in domains related to object-oriented reengineering, where tool papers can be presented and published, sometimes as a special issue of some journal.

How to compare/benchmark tools? To conclude our working group session a final discussion was held on how to compare and benchmark tools. Although many articles and books have been written on "evaluation", tool builders do not seem to be sufficiently aware of that literature. They should get acquainted with that literature and use it in their articles, mentioning clearly what kind of evaluation was conducted (just some argumentation, benchmarks, prototypical examples, interviews and surveys, case studies, user studies, ...). Part of the problem is the lack of background of many researchers in empirical studies. Ideally, every researcher should have had a course on doing good formal empirical studies during his studies (statistics, null hypothesis, independent variables...). Unfortunately, often this is not the case.

3.3   Working Group 3: Language Independence for Reverse Engineering Tools

The subject of this working group was language independence for reverse engineering tools. The problem is that reverse engineering tools must accommodate many existing programming languages in (as well as making room for the new ones that appear) without having the need to "reinvent the wheel". This problem was raised during the morning session and in previous WOOR workshops and there was some overlap between this working group on the previous working group on tool building. Nevertheless, it was felt that language independence deserved dedicated focus because it is a problem that exists for many years and no solution, to the best of our knowledge, is yet within grasp. The discussions attempted to formalise the problem and to provide guidelines for future research on language independence. The discussions, although intense, led to a smaller body of knowledge than other working sessions because of the reduced number of participants and of the need for further research.

Conclusion of the discussions. During the discussions of this working group four main points came out.

- Language independent representations of source code need an agreed-upon level of abstraction, which could be an intermediate representation or bytecode.

- Language independence depends on the kind of analyses that will be performed on the program representations. Indeed, to define a language independent representation, we need to know what kind of analyses will be performed, because these analyses may *not* be language independent, possible only on a subset of major languages. In any case, there must exist mechanisms to extend the language independent representation of a program with language-dependent data, some context.
- The representation must be fit both for representing programs and for being queried. It is possible that a true language independent representation will be defined only as a set of low-level queries, which results can then be aggregated. Queries allow the integration of the concept of views.
- Language independent representation must itself be language independent. The use of XML Schema seems like promising to define such a representation, if used Schema must be instantiated/implemented in different programming languages according to the needs of its users.

Future directions of research. Future work includes studying existing program representations (whether they claim to be language independent or not) to compare them with one another and possibly identify common primitives. A representation must include a mechanism to allow new data to be included incrementally but applying successive analyses. A first list of existing representations includes (but is certainly *not* limited to):

- Basic elements, for example Elemental Design Pattern, inheritance, method calls...
- ASTs but one for each version of each language.
- MOF-based meta-model for Java in the process of combining with C++ (cf. Helmut)
- Queries-based, SOUL (Smalltalk, Java)
- UML.
- PADL.
- Rigi Standard Format but maybe language dependent because does not carry any semantics.
- FAMIX.
- AOL.

Future work also includes researching all known analyses developed or performed on a regular basis by researchers and practitioners to identify common and opposing requirements with respect to language independence. Then, among all possible candidates, a choice should be made based on the decision whether to support an analysis in the representation or not. A first list of existing analyses includes (but is certainly *not* limited to):

- Design pattern detection.
- Code smell detection.
- Association/aggregation/composition (but may be too low level).
- Point-to analysis.
- Clustering.
- Metric computations (which might enrich a representation).
- Slicing (dynamic and static).
- Test suite generation.
- Type inference (tagging nodes, refining nodes, instantiating new nodes).

4 Conclusion: What Next ?

In this report, we have listed the main ideas that were generated during the workshop on object-oriented reengineering organised in conjunction with ECOOP 2007. After this tenth anniversary edition, the main question was whether it was worthwhile to continue working on reengineering, or whether it was better to continue on a new topic. The question remained open, but some participants suggested to organise a tool builders workshop, because tool building (integration, exchange formats, benchmarks...) has been an active topic of discussions that appeared throughout the whole WOOR series.

Acknowledgements

This workshop was sponsored by the Interuniversity Attraction Poles Programme (IUAP) on "Modeling, Verification, and Evolution of Software" (MOVES), financed by the *Belgian State – Belgian Science Policy* from January 2007 to December 2011.

References

1. Casais, E., Jaaksi, A., Lindner, T.: FAMOOS workshop on object-oriented software evolution and re-engineering. In: Bosch, J., Mitchell, S. (eds.) ECOOP 1997 Workshops. LNCS, vol. 1357, pp. 256–288. Springer, Heidelberg (1998)
2. Ducasse, S., Weisbrod, J. (eds.): Proceedings of the ECOOP Workshop on Experiences in Object-Oriented Re-engineering. FZI report 6/7/98, FZI Forschungszentrum Informatik (July 1998)
3. Ducasse, S., Weisbrod, J.: Experiences in object-oriented reengineering. In: Demeyer, S., Bosch, J. (eds.) ECOOP 1998 Workshops. LNCS, vol. 1543, pp. 72–98. Springer, Heidelberg (1998)
4. Ducasse, S., Ciupke, O. (eds.): Proceedings of the ECOOP Workshop on Experiences in Object-Oriented Re-engineering. FZI report 2-6-6/99, FZI Forschungszentrum Informatik (June 1999)
5. Ducasse, S., Ciupke, O.: Experiences in object-oriented re-engineering. In: Moreira, A.M.D., Demeyer, S. (eds.) ECOOP 1999 Workshops. LNCS, vol. 1743, pp. 164–183. Springer, Heidelberg (1999)
6. Demeyer, S., Ducasse, S., Mens, K. (eds.): Proceedings of the ECOOP 2003 Workshop on Object-Oriented Re-engineering (WOOR 2003). Technical Report, University of Antwerp - Department of Mathematics and Computer Science (June 2003)
7. Demeyer, S., Ducasse, S., Mens, K.: Workshop on object-oriented re-engineering WOOR 2003. In: Buschmann, F., Buchmann, A., Cilia, M.A. (eds.) ECCV-WS 2003. LNCS, vol. 3013, pp. 72–85. Springer, Heidelberg (2004)
8. Wuyts, R., Ducasse, S., Demeyer, S., Mens, K. (eds.): Proceedings of the ECOOP 2004 Workshop on Object-Oriented Re-engineering (WOOR 2004). Technical Report, University of Antwerp - Department of Mathematics and Computer Science (June 2004)
9. Wuyts, R., Ducasse, S., Demeyer, S., Mens, K.: Workshop on object-oriented re-engineering (WOOR 2004). In: Malenfant, J., Østvold, B.M. (eds.) ECOOP 2004. LNCS, vol. 3344, pp. 177–186. Springer, Heidelberg (2005)
10. Wuyts, R., Ducasse, S., Demeyer, S., Mens, K.: Workshop on object-oriented re-engineering (WOOR 2005). In: Black, A.P. (ed.) ECOOP 2005. LNCS, vol. 3586. Springer, Heidelberg (2005)

11. Wuyts, R., Ducasse, S., Demeyer, S., Mens, K.: Workshop on object-oriented re-engineering (WOOR 2006). In: Thomas, D. (ed.) ECOOP 2006. LNCS, vol. 4067. Springer, Heidelberg (2006)
12. Demeyer, S., Gall, H. (eds.): Proceedings of the ESEC/FSE Workshop on Object-Oriented Re-engineering. TUV-1841-97-10, Technical University of Vienna - Information Systems Institute - Distributed Systems Group (September 1997)
13. Demeyer, S., Gall, H.: Report: Workshop on object-oriented re-engineering (WOOR 1997). ACM SIGSOFT Software Engineering Notes 23(1), 28–29 (1998)
14. Demeyer, S., Gall, H. (eds.): Proceedings of the ESEC/FSE 1999 Workshop on Object-Oriented Re-engineering (WOOR 1999). TUV-1841-99-13, Technical University of Vienna - Information Systems Institute - Distributed Systems Group (September 1999)
15. Demeyer, S., Guéhéneuc, Y.G., Mens, K., Wuyts, R., Ducasse, S., Gall, H. (eds.): Proceedings of the ECOOP 2007 Workshop on Object-Oriented Re-engineering (WOOR'07) – 10th anniversary edition (June 2007), http://smallwiki.unibe.ch/woor2007/
16. Moha, N., Guéhéneuc, Y.G., Duchien, L., Meur, A.F.L.: Discussion on the results of the detection of design defects. In: Demeyer, S., Guéhéneuc, Y.G., Mens, K., Wuyts, R., Ducasse, S., Gall, H. (eds.) Proceedings of the ECOOP 2007 Workshop on Object-Oriented Re-engineering (WOOR 2007) – 10th anniversary edition (2007)
17. Arcelli, F., Cristina, L., Franzosi, D.: nMARPLE:NET reverse engineering with MARPLE. In: Demeyer, S., Guéhéneuc, Y.G., Mens, K., Wuyts, R., Ducasse, S., Gall, H. (eds.) Proceedings of the ECOOP 2007 Workshop on Object-Oriented Re-engineering (WOOR 2007) – 10th anniversary edition (2007)
18. Mens, T., Taentzer, G., Müller, D.: Challenges in model refactoring. In: Demeyer, S., Guéhéneuc, Y.G., Mens, K., Wuyts, R., Ducasse, S., Gall, H. (eds.) Proceedings of the ECOOP 2007 Workshop on Object-Oriented Re-engineering (WOOR 2007) – 10th anniversary edition (2007)
19. Kienle, H.M.: Must tool building remain a craft? In: Demeyer, S., Guéhéneuc, Y.G., Mens, K., Wuyts, R., Ducasse, S., Gall, H. (eds.) Proceedings of the ECOOP 2007 Workshop on Object-Oriented Re-engineering (WOOR 2007) – 10th anniversary edition (2007)
20. Keller, A., Demeyer, S.: A meta-model approach to inconsistency management. In: Demeyer, S., Guéhéneuc, Y.G., Mens, K., Wuyts, R., Ducasse, S., Gall, H. (eds.) Proceedings of the ECOOP 2007 Workshop on Object-Oriented Re-engineering (WOOR 2007) – 10th anniversary edition (2007)
21. Object Management Group: MDA Guide, Version 1.0.1. omg/03-06-01 edn. (June 2003)
22. Fowler, M.: Refactoring: Improving the Design of Existing Code. Addison-Wesley Co., Inc. (November 1999)
23. Lange, C.F.J., DuBois, B., Chaudron, M.R.V., Demeyer, S.: An experimental investigation of UML modeling conventions. In: Nierstrasz, O., Whittle, J., Harel, D., Reggio, G. (eds.) MoDELS 2006. LNCS, vol. 4199, pp. 27–41. Springer, Heidelberg (2006)
24. Wong, K., Sun, D.: On evaluating the layout of UML diagrams for program comprehension. Software Quality Journal 14(3), 233–259 (2006)
25. Demeyer, S.T.S., Steyaert, P.: FAMIX 2.0 - the FAMOOS information exchange model, Technical report, University of Berne (August 1999)
26. Tichelaar, S., Ducasse, S., Demeyer, S.: FAMIX and XMI. In: Proceedings of the Seventh Working Conference of Reverse Engineering, pp. 296–298. IEEE Computer Society Press, Los Alamitos (2000)
27. Demeyer, S., Ducasse, S., Nierstrasz, O.: Object-Oriented Reengineering Patterns. Morgan Kaufmann, San Francisco (2002)
28. Mens, K., Kellens, A., Pluquet, F., Wuyts, R.: Co-evolving code and design with intensional views — a case study. Journal on Computer Languages, Systems and Structures 32(2–3), 140–156 (2006)

29. Mens, K., Michiels, I., Wuyts, R.: Supporting software development through declaratively codified programming patterns. Journal on Expert Systems with Applications (23), 405–431 (2002)
30. Klint, P.: A meta-environment for generating programming environments. ACM Transactions on Software Engineering nd Methodology 2(2), 176–201 (1993)
31. Antoniol, G., Guéhéneuc, Y.G.: Feature identification: An epidemiological metaphor. Transactions on Software Engineering 32(9), 627–641 (2006)
32. Vainsencher, D., Black, A.P.: A pattern language for extensible program representation. In: Pattern Languages of Programming Confernce (PLoP2006) (2006)

Practical Approaches for Software Adaptation
Report on the 4th Workshop WCAT at ECOOP 2007

Carlos Canal[1], Juan Manuel Murillo[2], and Pascal Poizat[3,4]

[1] Universidad de Málaga, GISUM Software Engineering Group
canal@lcc.uma.es
[2] Universidad de Extremadura, Quercus Software Engineering Group
juanmamu@unex.es
[3] IBISC FRE 2873 CNRS - Université d'Évry Val d'Essonne
[4] INRIA / ARLES project-team
pascal.poizat@inria.fr

Abstract. Coordination and Adaptation are two key issues when developing complex distributed systems. Coordination focuses on the interaction among software entities. Adaptation focuses on solving the problems that arise when the interacting entities do not match properly. This is the report of the fourth edition of the WCAT workshop, that took place in Berlin jointly with ECOOP 2007. Previous editions the workshop dealt with general issues which mainly served for a better characterization of Software Adaptation as an emerging discipline within the field of Software Engineering. For this edition, we wanted to put the focus on practical approaches for software adaptation, in order to show how this discipline helps in the construction of current software systems.

1 Introduction

The development of distributed systems requires means to structure them in order to leverage their complexity. This has led to different structuring means, such as modules and objects, and more recently, components and services. Systems are then built as assemblies of these smaller and reusable parts, and during system construction the focus is shifted towards interaction issues: how to combine the different entities that form the system, how to coordinate them in order to achieve the desired goals, and how to adapt them when there is some kind of mismatch that avoids their proper composition.

These new challenges have promoted the development of specific fields of Software Engineering such as Coordination [1] and Adaptation [2,3]. Coordination addresses the description of the interactions between entities and provides expressive and effective means to compose them. Coordination is a hot topic in Component-Based Software Engineering (CBSE) [4] and Service Oriented Architecture (SOA) [5], for instance, or for Web Services, where choreography and orchestration mechanisms are instances of the coordination concept [6].

On the other hand, Software Adaptation aims at automatically deriving adaptors, pieces of software specifically designed for solving interaction mismatch.

M. Cebulla (Ed.): ECOOP 2007 Workshop Reader, LNCS 4906, pp. 154–165, 2008.

Adaptation procedures must combine solutions from different research domains, namely (i) model-based or formal approaches to develop mismatch detection and adaptor generation algorithms, (ii) middleware technology to support the detection of mismatch at runtime and the implementation of adaptor models, (iii) QoS and prediction models to assess the effect of adaptation on running systems.

A serious limitation of currently available interface descriptions is that they provide too little information about the entities described, preventing any kind of reasoning about what could be expected from their interaction. Indeed, while the notations commonly used provide convenient ways to describe the typed signatures of software elements, they offer a quite limited support to describe their interactive behaviour, non-functional properties (time, QoS), and semantics. To avoid these limitations, different kinds of extensions to interface languages have been proposed, and some of them are already reaching industrial maturity, such as WSBPEL, for describing the orchestration of composite Web Services.

In this context, the goal of Software Adaptation is to take these extended interface specifications of the components that are being combined to form a system, together with a generated or end-user specified composition contract of the desired connection among them, and generate automatically an adaptor —a specific computational entity with the main goal of guaranteeing that software components will interact in the right way not only at the signature level, but also at the protocol, Quality of Service, and semantic levels. In particular, Adaptation focuses on the dynamic and automatic generation of adaptors. In this sense, models for software adaptation can be considered as a new generation of coordination models. An introduction to Software Adaptation, its state-of-the-art, the description of the main research lines in the field, and some of its open issues can be found in [2].

This report summarizes the fourth edition of the WCAT workshop [7], that took place in Berlin jointly with ECOOP 2007. The WCAT workshop series provides a venue where researchers and practitioners on these topics can meet, exchange ideas and problems, identify some of the key issues related to coordination and adaptation, and explore together and disseminate possible solutions. The successive WCAT editions tried to address different issues related to coordination and adaptation. The 2007 edition was focused on more specific practical approaches related to coordination and adaptation at runtime, the implementation of coordinators and adaptors, context-aware and dynamically evolving coordination or adaptation contracts, and relations between service composition and adaptation in pervasive computing. The list of topics of interest of the workshop was:

- interfaces, types and contracts supporting coordination and adaptation;
- identification and specification of interaction requirements and problems;
- behavioural interfaces, extra-functional properties;
- automatic generation of compositions of adaptors;
- formal/rigorous approaches to Software Adaptation;
- coordination and adaptation of services;

- coordination and adaptation in pervasive computing;
- relations between adaptation and the software life-cycle;
- relations between adaptation and MDE;
- relations between adaptation and AOSD;
- metrics and prediction models for software coordination and adaptation;
- prediction of the coordination and adaptation impact on Quality of Service;
- surveys, case studies, industrial and experience reports.

The rest of this report is organized as follows. In Section 2 we enumerate the contributions received, and also the participants of the workshop. Then, Section 3, presents a comparative outline of these contributions. Finally, Section 4 presents the conclusions of the workshop, and identifies several open issues in the field to be addressed in future editions.

2   Contributions and Workshop Participants

In order to enable lively and productive discussions, prospective participants were required to submit in advance a short position paper, describing their work in the field, open issues, and their expectations for the workshop. From the contributions received, we decided to invite ten position papers. These papers have been published in the proceedings of the workshop [7], as a technical report of the Universities of the organizers. They are also available online at the website of the workshop:

$$\text{http://wcat.unex.es}$$

where also information about past editions can be found.

The list of accepted papers, together with the names and affiliations of their authors is as follows:

- A Model of Self-Adaptive Distributed Components
  An Phung-Khac, Antoine Beugnard, Jean-Marie Gilliot,
  and Maria-Teresa Segarra*
  {an.phungkhac,antoine.beugnard,jm.gilliot,mt.segarra}@enst-bretagne.fr
  ENST Bretagne, France

- A Framework for Automatic Generation of Verified Business Process
  Orchestrations
  Faisal Abouzaid
  mohamed-faical.abouzaid@polymtl.ca
  École Polytechnique de Montreal, Canada

- Automatic Refactoring-Based Adaptation
  Ilie Savga*, and Michael Rudolf
  {is13, s0600108}@inf.tu-dresden.de
  Technische Universität Dresden, Germany

Authors that were in fact present at the workshop are marked with and asterisk in the relation above. Apart from those, also attended the workshop, without presenting a paper:

- *Cyril Ballagny* (cyril.ballagny@univ-pau.fr)
  University of Pau, France
- *Michael Cebulla* (mce@cs.tu-berlin.de)
  Technical University Berlin, Germany
- *Fabricio Fernandes* (fabricio.fernandes@emn.fr)
  École des Mines de Nantes, France
- *Ethan Hadar* (ethan.hadar@ca.com)
  CA Labs, Israel
- *Nabil Hameurlain* (nabil.hameurlain@univ-pau.fr)
  University of Pau, France

In total, eighteen participants coming from five different countries attended the workshop.

3   Comparative Summary of the Presentations

The position papers presented in the workshop covered a wide number of issues related to coordination and adaptation, but mainly focused on practical adaptation issues, as it was demanded in the call for papers of the 2007 edition. The contributions can be classified into three different categories:

- adaptation techniques for specific software engineering approaches;
- adaptation techniques for specific structural elements;
- adaptation techniques and tools for specific platforms.

In the sequel, these works are briefly summarized and they are classified according to the taxonomy of software adaptation techniques [8], which was one of the main results of the first edition of the WCAT workshop series.

3.1   Adaptation Techniques for Specific Software Engineering Approaches

The first group of works was concerned with how software adaptation can be managed when a specific software engineering approach is chosen to build software systems. Three papers fall in this category, dealing respectively with adaptation in distributed component systems (CBSE), Web 2.0 engineering, and Aspect Oriented Software Development.

The work by An Phung-Khac and his colleagues from ENTS Bretagne (*A model of Self Adaptive Distributed Components*) tackles the problem in the context of distributed component systems, where adaptation must be performed in the different nodes hosting the components of the system. In such a situation, the coordination between the adaptation procedures performed at each node is critical to ensure the correctness of the whole system. For that, the authors propose a self-adaptive distributed component model. The model is based on the separated specification of communication and adaptation. At runtime, each functional component is associated to a composite manager which contains a manager variant connected to an adaptation manager. Such managers are in charge of detecting adaptation at other sites and triggering the convenient adaptations in the associated functional component. In this way, self-adaptive adaptation is handled.

The authors propose extending their work by going into the implementation of coordination protocols to support node connection and disconnection for open systems and providing optimizers for the composite managers.

Since the composite managers detect the adaptation at runtime this approach can be classified as runtime adaptation. Moreover, the adaptation is performed by the adaptation manager, so it can be considered as automatic adaptation.

Juan Carlos Preciado presented his work on *Adapting Web 1.0 User Interfaces to Web 2.0 User Interfaces through RIAs*, jointly developed with his colleagues from the University of Extremadura. Their proposal deals with adaptation in the context of Web 2.0 User Interfaces (UIs) using Rich Internet Applications (RIAs) [9]. The authors claim that it is not only important to have methodologies for developing applications for Web 2.0 from the scratch, but it is also necessary to have methods for adapting existing Web 1.0 applications to Web 2.0 UIs. With this problem in mind, they have developed the RUX-Model, a model driven method for user interface adaptation. RUX provides a component library in charge of specifying the correspondences between the elements in the old interface and the elements in the new one. The method works by first extracting the connections rules from the legated Web 1.0 application (connections between pages, data used by the web application, and the existing hypertext element groupings), and then obtaining an abstract model of the application. In the two subsequent steps a concrete (new) interface, and a final Web 2.0 user interface are obtained applying transformation rules supported by the components library.

The methodology is supported by the RUX-Tool which currently works together with WebRatio, a tool suite for the WebML modeling language [10], but there is also work in progress with other similar case tools such as UWE and OO-H CASE.

The approach presented in this work can be considered as static time adaptation supporting both manual and automatic adaptation.

The last work in this first group —*Safe Dynamic Adaptation using Aspect-Oriented Programming*— was presented by Miguel A. Pérez-Toledano, also from the University of Extremadura, and developed jointly with the University of Málaga. The work focuses on adaptation using the Aspect-Oriented Software Development paradigm (AOSD) [11]. AOSD adaptation approaches make use of aspects to facilitate the dynamic adaptation of the components, but are unable to derive automatically the correct composition of the corresponding aspectual adaptors, since they may interfere with each other. It is hence necessary to verify the behaviour of the resulting system in order to ensure the correctness of the adaptation process. This is precisely the issue addressed in their work. The approach starts from the specification using the Unified Modeling Language (UML) of both the initial system and the aspects that will be in charge of the different facets of the adaptation required. These specifications are validated by transforming them into an algebraic description of the system in the Calculus of Communicating Systems (CCS) [12]. Next, extended finite state machines are automatically generated to verify, simulate, and test the modeled system's behaviour. The result of this process can then be compared with the actual behaviour of the running system. To optimize this task, the authors propose grouping components so as to center the study on the points actually affected by the behaviour introduced by the aspects.

Since the new aspects are added to the software system in a dynamic way this approach falls in the category of runtime adaptation approaches. Also, aspects are written by a programmer, so it can be considered as manual adaptation. Finally, as aspects can modify the behaviour of the system they are applied to, the approach deals with behavioural adaptation.

3.2   Adaptation Techniques for Specific Structural Elements

The works in this group are concerned with how adaptation can be managed when the software development is based on using some specific structural elements such as frameworks, product lines, or virtual machines.

In the presentation of his work *Automatic Refactoring-Based Adaptation*, Ilie Savga, from the Technische Universität Dresden, focused on the mismatch problems that can appear when changes are introduced in the frameworks on which an application is based. For example, a version update of a framework could produce mismatches between the new version and the components using the previous one. The authors argued that most of the changes causing signature mismatch can be automatically detected and solved by using the information about the changes in the code. More specifically, their work focuses on refactoring techniques [13], preserving behaviour but changing the signature representation of the components.

To cope with this problem the authors propose the definition of a problem/solution library of transformations, where a problem is the occurrence of a framework refactoring and its solution is a comeback (a behaviour-preserving transformation that defines how a compensating adaptor can be constructed). Such comebacks are executed on an adaptation layer that makes components inquiries adapt to the refactoring performed.

The approach builds automatically binary (component-to-component) adaptors, so it can be classified as runtime, automatic adaptation.

The work *Feature Dependent Coordination and Adaptation of Component-Based Software Architectures* was presented by his author Hassan Gomaa from the George Mason University. It addresses software adaptation in the field of product lines. Feature modeling is an important aspect of product line engineering since it captures the product line variability in terms of common, optional and alternative features [14]. Common features are mandatory in all product line members, optional features are mandatory only for some specific product line members, and alternative features denote that a choice of features is available. There can be also dependencies between features, such as mutual exclusion. Deriving new elements of a product line can be conceived as adapting an existing element for supporting a different set of features. The paper describes how feature-dependent coordination is well suited to coordinate and adapt distributed component based software architectures. Hence, it can be considered as manual and design time adaptation.

Finally, Michael Haupt from the University of Postdam presented his work *Disentangling Virtual Machine Architecture* developed with his colleagues from the University of Victoria. The work faces the problems derived from the code and feature tangling in the implementation of virtual machines. The authors have analysed the design and implementation of several virtual machines verifying the existence of many crosscutting concerns which create dependencies between modules that usually are hardwired inside the modules involved [15]. This fact leads to virtual machines which are not easily evolvable and adaptable making difficult the adaptation of the applications running on them. To solve this problem, the work proposes organizing virtual machines architecture based on service modules, which are modules constituting well-defined services provided by the virtual machine to the applications being run on it. The interaction and the coordination between modules as well as the crosscutting concerns are implemented using aspect-oriented programming techniques.

In this approach aspects are generated manually, too, so it can be considered as non-automatic adaptation. Aspects can be applied both at compile and runtime.

3.3 Adaptation Techniques and Tools for Specific Platforms

The last group of papers presented tools and techniques for practical adaptation for some specific implementation platforms such as JBoss, or .NET, and for context-aware systems.

The first paper in this category (*Invasive Patterns: Aspect-Based Adaptation of Distributed Applications*) came from École de Mines de Nantes, and was presented by Luis Daniel Benavides Navarro. He argued that in contrast with sequential or parallel software systems, in massively distributed systems software patterns are not frequently used due to the lack of flexibility in their definition. Dealing with this problem the authors propose their model of Invasive Patterns that support the modular definition and adaptation of distributed applications. The need for Invasive Patterns is motivated in the context of the JBoss Cache, a software product for caching frequently accessed Java objects in order to improve the performance of e-business applications. The language support for Invasive Patterns, and an implementation of such language based on AWED [16] —an aspect-oriented programming language explicitly addressing distribution issues— are also sketched in the paper. The authors are currently extending their work by augmenting the expressive power of the patterns, optimizing their implementation and exploring their formal properties.

Invasive Patterns are conceived at design time. Consequently this approach can be classified as design time manual adaptation.

The next paper in this group —*On Run-time Behavioural Adaptation in Context-Aware Systems*— came from the University of Málaga, and was presented by Javier Cámara. This work was accepted for the ECOOP'2007 workshop on Model-Driven Adaptation (M-ADAPT), but since it fell in the scope of both workshops we found interesting to have it presented also at WCAT, and decided jointly with the organizers of M-ADAPT the double submission of the work. For this reason, only a short abstract appears in the proceedings of WCAT07, but the full paper can be found in the website of the workshop.

Context-Aware computing [17] studies the development of systems which exploit context information (e.g., user location, network resources, time, etc.), which is of special relevance in mobile systems and pervasive computing, where the execution environment of the system is likely to change at runtime. Hence, an appropriate adaptation of the components does need to reflect all these environmental changes which might affect system behaviour. In order to support these unpredictable changes, the authors advocate for the use of variable adaptation policies between an arbitrary number of components, depending on the current execution state of the system. The work considers additional policies which may depend exclusively on context changes (i.e., context-triggered actions).

The approach simplifies the complexity of mapping specification relying on the principle of separation of concerns, and avoids the costly off-line generation of adaptors, adapting components at runtime by means of a composition engine which manages dynamically communications within the system. A composition/adaptation model was presented, sketching some general implementation questions. The proposal was illustrated by a case study: a wireless medical information system. The main perspective of the work is to implement the whole proposal in a middleware using dynamic AOP. This enables to shape up the composition engine as aspects able to: (i) intercept service invocations between components; (ii) apply the composition process with respect to the adaptation mapping in order to make the right message substitutions, and (iii) forward the substituted messages to their recipients transparently. From this point of view, the approach can be considered as an automatic and dynamic software adaptation technique.

Finally, the last presentation was a joint work from the University of Málaga and INRIA, presented by Carlos Canal. Its title was *Relating Model-Based Adaptation and Implementation Platforms: a case study with WF/.NET 3.0*, and again was a double submission presented both at WCAT07 and WCOP07, the workshop on Component-Oriented Programming, whose proceedings contain the full text of the work. As many current software adaptation proposals, it deals with the behavioural interoperability level, but in this case the focus is put in relating the proposal with an existing implementation platform, in this case Microsoft's Windows Workflow Foundation (WF) [18], which allows most of the code of the adaptor to be automatically generated.

This work presents an adaptation procedure starting from the extraction of behavioural interfaces from WF workflows and their representation using labelled transition systems (LTS). By comparing the LTSs of the components, signature and behavioural mismatch can be detected, and a mapping solving the mismatch is (manually) given. Then, an adaptor LTS is generated following an automated procedure [19], and from that, the skeleton of the WF orchestrator solving the mismatch is generated. The proposal was illustrated by means of a case study: an on-line computer sale system.

The proposal can be classified as a semi-automatic approach to behavioural adaptation, performed at design time.

4 Conclusions of the Workshop

After the presentations, the participants were divided into groups in order to discuss the different issues raised during the workshop. As a summary of the discussions, we identified the following open issues, that can be considered as a road map for future research work in software adaptation, and as hot topics to be addressed in future editions of the WCAT workshop:

- **Domains of adaptation.** Coordination and adaptation are always related to software interaction. The way in which software components interact is closely related to the structuring technique chosen for the system, used both as a mix of divide-to-conquer, in order to rule complexity out, and for promoting component reuse. Hence, it must be analyzed which are the structuring techniques and paradigms of coordinated/adapted systems that software engineering researchers and developers are currently dealing with. The papers presented in the workshop dealt with component-based systems, service-oriented systems, user interfaces, etc. It should be determined what is specific to these paradigms and what are generic issues in Software Adaptation. New trends, like Autonomic Computing [20], or the use of Model Driven Architecture/Engineering (MDA/MDE) [21] must also be considered.
- **Adaptation viewpoints.** Which are the problems solved and at which interface level? In addition to the four interoperability/adaptation levels (signature, behavioural, service, semantics) detected and characterized in [8], some other adaptation problems (user interfaces, software refactoring, etc.) have been addressed by the papers presented at the workshop. What are the possible solutions to these new adaptation problems and how the different solutions may be combined? An idea would be to define "modules" of model-based adaptation and coordination at the different levels, and then combine them, but the latter remains an important open issue in the field of Software Adaptation.
- **Adaptation time.** Should mismatch detection, adaptor model generation, and adaptor implementation be performed at design time, deployment time, or runtime? Which are the points in favor and against the time chosen for making the adaptation?

The works presented during the WCAT07 workshop give a broad view of current practical adaptation techniques for solving the different problems that appear during the composition of different kinds of systems. These approaches are summarized in this workshop report. As a result of the workshop, a special issue in the Journal of Universal Computer Science (JUCS) is being prepared. The participants of the workshop were invited to submit extended technical versions of their papers to the special issue, and a public call for papers has also been launched in order to attract contributions out of these presented in the WCAT07 edition. The special issue is scheduled to be published in the September 2008 issue of JUCS.

References

1. Arbab, F.: What Do You Mean Coordination? In: Bulletin of the Dutch Association for Theoretical Computer Science (NVTI) (1998)
2. Canal, C., Murillo, J.M., Poizat, P.: Software adaptation. L'Objet 12(1), 9–31 (2006)
3. Becker, S., Canal, C., Diakov, N., Murillo, J.M., Poizat, P., Tivoli, M.: Coordination and Adaptation Techniques: Bridging the Gap Between Design and Implementation. Report on the Third WCAT Workshop. In: Südholt, M., Consel, C. (eds.) ECOOP 2006 Ws. LNCS, vol. 4379, pp. 72–86. Springer, Heidelberg (2007)
4. Szyperski, C.: Component Software: Beyond Object-Oriented Programming. Addison-Wesley, London (1998)
5. Bieberstein, N., et al.: Service-Oriented Architecture (SOA) Compass. Pearson, London (2006)
6. World-Wide Web Consortium (W3C): Web Services Architecture. Technical Report (2004), available at, http://www.w3.org
7. Canal, C., Murillo, J.M., Poizat, P. (eds.): WCAT 2007. Fourth International Workshop on Coordination and Adaptation Techniques for Software Entities (2007), Available at http://wcat.unex.es/
8. Canal, C., Murillo, J.M., Poizat, P.: Coordination and Adaptation Techniques for Software Entities. Report on the First WCAT Workshop. In: Malenfant, J., Østvold, B.M. (eds.) ECOOP 2004. LNCS, vol. 3344, pp. 133–147. Springer, Heidelberg (2005)
9. OpenLaszlo: An Open architecture Framework for Advance Ajax Applications (white paper). Technical Report (2006), available at, http://www.openlaszlo.org
10. Ceri, S., et al.: Designing Data-Intensive Web Applications. Morgan Kaufmann, San Francisco (2002)
11. Fillman, R., et al. (eds.): Aspect-Oriented Software Development. Addison-Wesley, London (2005)
12. Milner, R.: Communication and Concurrency. Prentice-Hall, Englewood Cliffs (1989)
13. Fowler, M.: Refactoring: improving the design of existing code. Addison-Wesley, London (1999)
14. Gomaa, H.: Designing Software Product Lines with UML: from Use Cases to Pattern-based Software Architectures. Addison-Wesley, London (2005)
15. Griswold, W., et al.: Modular sofware design with crosscutting interfaces. IEEE Software 23, 51–60 (2006)

16. Benavides-Navarro, L.D., Südholt, M., Vanderperren, W., Fraine, B.D., Suvée, D.: Explicitly distributed AOP using AWED. In: AOSD 2006. Proc. 5th Int. ACM Conf. on Aspect-Oriented Software Development, pp. 51–62. ACM Press, New York (2006)
17. Schilit, B., Adams, N., Want, R.: Context-aware computing applications. In: IEEE Workshop on Mobile Computing Systems and Applications. IEEE Computer Society Press, Los Alamitos (1994)
18. Scribner, K.: Microsoft Windows Workflow Foundation: Step by Step. Microsoft Press (2007)
19. Canal, C., Poizat, P., Salaün, G.: Synchronizing behavioural mismatch in software composition. In: Gorrieri, R., Wehrheim, H. (eds.) FMOODS 2006. LNCS, vol. 4037. Springer, Heidelberg (2006)
20. Kephart, J.O., Chess, D.M.: The vision of autonomic computing. IEEE Computer 36, 41–51 (2003)
21. Schmidt, D.: Model-driven engineering. IEEE Computer 39, 25–31 (2006)

Quantitative Approaches in Object-Oriented Software Engineering

Report on the 11th Workshop QAOOSE at ECOOP 2007

Yann-Gaël Guéhéneuc[1], Christian F.J. Lange[2], Houari A. Sahraoui[1],
Giovanni Falcone[3], Michele Lanza[4], Coral Calero[5], and Fernando Brito e Abreu[6]

[1] Department of Computer Science and Operations Research,
Université de Montréal — Canada
[2] Software Engineering and Technology Group,
Eindhoven University of Technology — The Netherlands
[3] Lehrstuhl für Softwaretechnik
Universität Mannheim — Germany
[4] Faculty of informatics,
University of Lugano — Switzerland
[5] Department of Computer Science,
Escuela Superior de Informatica of the Castilla-La Mancha University — Spain
[6] Department of Computer Science,
Lisbon New University — Portugal

Abstract. The QAOOSE 2007 workshop brought together, for half day, researchers working on several aspects related to quantitative evaluation of software artifacts developed with the object-oriented paradigm and related technologies. Ideas and experiences were shared and discussed. This report includes a summary of the technical presentations and subsequent discussions raised by them. Exceptionally this year, one of the founders of the workshop, Horst Zuse, gave a keynote on the Theoretical Foundations of Object-Oriented Measurement. Three out of the four submitted position papers were presented, covering different aspects such as measuring inconsistencies, visualizing metric values, and assessing the subjective quality of systems. In the closing session, the participants discussed open issues and challenges arising from researching in this area and tried to forecast what will be hot research topics in the short and medium terms.

1 Introduction

Measures of software internal attributes have been extensively used to help software managers, customers, and users to characterize, assess, and improve the quality of software products. Many software companies have intensively adopted software measures to increase their understandability of how (and how much) software internal attributes affect the overall software quality. Estimation models based on software measures have successfully been used to perform risk analysis and to assess software maintainability, reusability, and reliability. Although most of known work applies to object-oriented software, it is also desirable to find measures for component-based software (CBS) and

M. Cebulla (Ed.): ECOOP 2007 Workshop Reader, LNCS 4906, pp. 166–170, 2008.

aspect-oriented development, and for web-based software (WBS), model-based development, in general.

Submissions were invited, but not limited, to the following topics, organized in four areas:

- Metrics collection, including support and standards for sharing research hypotheses, data and results; evaluation of metric collection tools; metric values visualization; evolutionary software metrics collection and validation.
- Quality assessment, including Measuring non-functional requirements of OO systems; metric-based reengineering; quantitative assessment of OO analysis/design patterns, frameworks, aspect-oriented systems, agent-based Web services.
- Metrics validation, including meta-level metrics; formal and empirical validation; measurement Theory; validation techniques and their limits.
- Process management, including reliability and rework effort estimates based on design measures; quantitative tracking of OO, web services, and CBS development; empirical studies on the use of measures for process management.

The workshop was specifically scheduled to increase fruitful interactions and discussions. Participants were requested to submit a contribution in advance. Each participant was expected to read the material submitted by the other participants, so that all participants are acquainted with the ideas that exist within the group and that the workshop could be devoted to discussions instead of presentations. After a short welcome session during which participants introduced themselves, Horst Zuse gave a one-hour keynote on the theoretical foundations of object-oriented measurement [1]. Then, three position papers were presented. The position papers are published in the workshop proceedings [2]. Finally, all participants discussed the presented work and future work.

2 Keynote: Horst Zuse

Theoretical concepts behind software measures and software measurement are necessary in order to have a precise qualitative interpretation of the numbers [3]. In this presentation it was shown, that the properties of software measures for imperative and object-oriented measurement are different. While measures for imperative languages very often assume the extensive structure, object-oriented measures do not assume this measurement structure. This shows, that behind the object-oriented concept of software development another paradigm is hidden than behind imperative languages. Software measures reflect these different paradigms.

3 Keynote: Giovanni Falcone

The goal of developing an ordering technique for a large scale software component search engine is mainly comprised of two majors steps. In a first step a search request is defined by a user. Several techniques are used in practice, reaching from the simple definition of keywords toward the definition of interfaces a particular component should fulfill. In general, the similarity of the components to the given search request are calculated and used as a primary step in the ordering of the components in the results list. In the literature several solutions for measuring a similarity are given. However, depending on the level of abstraction a given request is made, two extremes are found:

- The result set is comprised of components where all of them have a different similarity and the primary ordering technique is sufficient.
- The result set is comprised of one large subset where all of the entities within have the same similarity measure.

Even if in practice the abstract view on the constitution of the result set lies somewhere in between, it shows that the primary ordering based on a similarity measure is not sufficient. By mainly using an interface driven driven search, where an interface is used as basis for the search request, the first step of ordering the results is given by measuring the conformance of the functional properties of the components to the ones of the defined interface. In a second step non-functional properties need to be taken into account, where software measures seem to be the most valuable ones. Therefore a set of software measures have been calculated for more than 3 million Java based source code components and the results have been further investigated.

In the literature criticism that several software measures show a correlation to other measures is found. In general, the results described in the literature are mainly based on small to medium sized projects. For the purpose of building a second level ordering technique in a software component search we further investigated the behavior of the correlation between some basic software measures.

We presented an overview of the correlation coefficients of a set of about 30 software measures and have shown that a strong correlation between mostly all of the complexity measures investigated has been found (LOC, cyclomatic complexity, number of statements, number of executable statements, number of branch statements, and the number of methods) using the Brevais-Pearson as well as the Spearman rank correlation coefficient. The same results have been found for all of the measures of the Halstead suite where the Breavis-Pearson correlation coefficient was slightly below the Spearman correlation coefficient, except the Effort measure indicating a very weak correlation for the Breavis-Pearson turning in a strong correlation for the rank based correlation.

Based on the presented results, further steps of analyzing the data have been discussed comprising the dimensional reduction using a principal component and a clustering analysis based on the principal components. Next steps have be identified, one of them including a mapping of responsibilities to the clusters found.

4   Position Papers

4.1   Paper: Inconsistencies of Metrics in C++ Standard Template Library

Authors: by *Zoltán Porkoláb, Ádám Sipos, and Norbert* Pataki. Since McCabe's cyclometric measure, structural complexity have been playing an important role measuring the complexity of programs. Complexity metrics are used to achieve more maintainable code with the least bugs possible. C++ Standard Template Library (STL) is the most popular library based on the generic programming paradigm. This paradigm allows implementation of algorithms and containers in an abstract way to ensure the configurability and collaboration of the abstract components. STL is widely used in industrial softwares because STL's appropriate application decreases the complexity of the code significantly. Many new potential errors arise by the usage of the generic programming paradigm, including invalid iterators, notation of functors, etc. In this position paper, the authors present many complexity inconsistencies in the application of STL that a precise metric must take into account, but the existing measures ignore the characteristics of STL.

4.2   Paper: Automatic Generation of Strategies for Visual Anomaly Detection

Authors: Salima Hassaine, Karim Dhambri, Houari Sahraoui, and Pierre Poulin. An important subset of design anomalies is difficult to detect automatically in the code because of the required knowledge. Fortunately, software visualization offers an efficient and flexible tool to inspect software data searching for such anomalies. However, as maintainers typically do not have a background in visualization, they often must seek assistance from visualization expert. This position paper proposes an approach based on taxonomies of low-level analytic tasks, interactive tasks, and perceptual rules to design an assistant that helps analysts to effectively use a visualization tool to accomplish detection tasks.

4.3   Paper: Perception and Reality: What Are Design Patterns Good for?

Authors: Foutse Khomh and Yann-Gaël Guéhéneuc This position paper presents a study of the impact of design patterns [4] on quality attributes. An empirical study was performed by asking respondents their evaluations of the impact of all design patterns on several quality attributes. Additionally, detailed results for three design patterns (Abstract Factory, Composite, and Flyweight) and three quality attributes (reusability, understandability, and expendability) were presented. The authors reported on a Null hypothesis test and concluded that, contrary to popular beliefs, design patterns do not always improve reusability and understandability, but that they do improve expendability.

5   Discussions

The informal discussions focused on the following subjects:

– Semantics of measures and how to take semantics of programs into account.
– In metrics visualization, mapping between graphical attributes and some measures, such as DIT.
– Study of community-based preferences that go against "common" sense and validation.
– Taking into account participants' experience and the languages used.

Future directions of research. The participants concluded on the need to perform an extensive survey of the literature on the use of metrics and how validation evolve over time. The agreed to divide the work among the participants to create tooling to identify the relevant papers (in PDF) and extract automatically pertinent information from these papers. This work is currently being pursued.

References

1. Zuse, H.: A Framework of Software Measurement. Walter de Gruyter, Berlin (1998)
2. e Abreu, F.B., Calero, C., Guéhéneuc, Y.G., Lange, C.F.J., Lanza, M., Sahraoui, H.A., Cebulla, M. (eds.): QAOOSE 2007. Proceedings of the 11the ECOOP Workshop on Quantitative Approaches in Object-Oriented Software Engineering Forschungsberichte der Fakultät IV – Elektrotechnik und Informatik. Technische Universität Berlin (2007)
3. Zuse, H.: Foundations of object-oriented software measures. In: METRICS 1996. Proceedings of the 3rd International Symposium on Software Metrics, p. 75. IEEE Computer Society Press, Los Alamitos (1996)
4. Gamma, E., Helm, R., Johnson, R., Vlissides, J.: Design Patterns: Elements of reusable Object-Oriented Software. Addison-Wesley, London (1994)

Object Technology for Ambient Intelligence and Pervasive Computing

Report on the OT4AmI-Workshop at ECOOP 2007

Jessie Dedecker[1,2,*], Éric Tanter[2,**], Holger Mügge[3],
Cristina Videira Lopes[4], and Pascal Cherrier[5]

[1] PROG Lab, Vrije Universiteit Brussel, Belgium
[2] PLEIAD Lab, Computer Science Dept (DCC), University of Chile, Chile
[3] University of Bonn, Germany
[4] University of California, USA
[5] France Telecom, France

Abstract. This report summarizes the main activities held during the third workshop on object-technology for Ambient Intelligence and Pervasive Computing. The goals of this workshop series are to identify and discuss the impact of Ambient Intelligence on object-oriented technologies and vice versa. This report summarizes the scope of the workshop as well as the contents of the presented position papers, the discussions provoked by these papers and the brainstorm sessions that followed the presentations. In particular, groups of participants actively discussed issues such as context volatility, development process, and user involvement in adaptable applications.

1 Introduction

Computing technology is no longer uniquely associated with mainframes or desktop computers. Due to the technological advances computing technology has become so small and cheap that it can be embedded in everyday devices such as cars, toys, furniture and even clothes. This integration of technology with everyday devices, which is also known as "ubiquitous computing", "pervasive computing" and "ambient intelligence", enables new types of applications and requires a model of interaction that is less intrusive than the traditional desktop model of computing. The idea is that everybody will be surrounded by a dynamically-defined processor cloud, of which the applications are expected to cooperate smoothly. This technological setting puts new challenges on the software. Software should take into account the context in which it operates and adjust its behavior as its ambient context changes over time. Context changes are provoked due to the mobility of the users and the devices. Devices form a large-scale distributed system that communicates using wireless technology.

* J. Dedecker is partially funded by FONDECYT project 3080020.
** É. Tanter is partially financed by the Millennium Nucleus Center for Web Research, Grant P04-067-F, Mideplan, Chile, and FONDECYT Project 11060493.

M. Cebulla (Ed.): ECOOP 2007 Workshop Reader, LNCS 4906, pp. 171–181, 2008.
© Springer-Verlag Berlin Heidelberg 2008

The use of wireless technology and limited energy resources implies that the distributed software system will be subject to a higher rate of failures as compared to a traditional distributed system. Other issues such as security, privacy, new interaction models, limited resources and others also have a high impact on the design and implementation of software.

2   Scope of the Workshop

2.1   Goals

Important goals of the workshop were to identify and discuss the impact of Ambient Intelligence on object-oriented technologies and vice versa, and to outline fruitful paths for future research concerning the connection between Ambient Intelligence and object-oriented programming languages and systems. In this context, we understand the term "object technology" to cover the whole range of topics that have evolved around the notion of object-orientation in the past decades, starting from programming language design and implementation, ranging over software architectures, frameworks and components, up to design approaches and software development processes.

2.2   Topics

In the call for participation, the following non-exhaustive list of potential topics was included: programming models, reflection, security, software adaptation, context modeling, engineering of autonomous systems, biologically-inspired concepts, human-device and device-device interaction. We accepted eight workshop papers discussing various topics such as distributed memory management, mobile agents, and rule-based systems to support the development of ambient intelligent systems.

2.3   Workshop Organization

The workshop format was chosen to promote discussions on the topics set for the workshop. In order to accommodate this format we asked the authors to prepare short (with a maximum of ten minutes) presentations where they would defend the position of their paper. Hence, the goal was not to elaborate on the technical details of their work but rather defend their vision on how software for ambient intelligence should be developed. In preparation of the workshop we asked all participants to read the accepted papers. The positions of the accepted papers were presented in the morning. The afternoon session was used to brainstorm on emerging topics resulting from the paper discussions.

3   Summary of Position Paper Discussions

In the paper session each principal author defended the position of his paper in a short (under ten minutes) presentation. After the presentation there were two discussion rounds. In the first round of discussions two participants were selected:

one participant had to argue in favor of the position whereas the other participant had to argue against the position. In this process the presenter was not allowed to intervene and could only act as an observer. The second discussion round enabled participants to ask questions to the presenter and gave the presenter the opportunity to react to remarks made in the first discussion round. This section presents the abstracts of the submitted position papers and summarizes the discussions that followed the presentations. These papers are included in the workshop proceedings [4], and can be downloaded from the workshop's home page at http://sam.iai.uni-bonn.de/ot4ami2007/

3.1 Introducing Context-Awareness in Applications by Transforming High-Level Rules [5]

In the last years, we have witnessed the increase in the popularity and capabilities of mobile technologies. This evolution has enforced the idea of smart environments, in which devices are aware and able to react to changes in their environment. In this position paper we describe a specific approach for the development of context-aware software. We propose to make existing applications context-aware by means of three main components: context models, high-level rules and code-generation processors. We present each component and analyze the issues related to the development of context-aware software following this strategy.

Arguments Pro. A generational approach has advantages because it enables separation of concerns: the context specific behavior is generated and compiled into the application. Also, the rules that determine when the context specific behavior should be enabled are separated from the base application. The rules encapsulate the adaptations to the base applications.

Arguments Contra. Is it possible to use a generational approach without the requirement that the application has to be refactored? The quality of the base application code affects the efforts that will be required to adapt the code with context information. The proposed use of annotations seems to conflict with the base application developer being unaware of the context adaptations that will be required. Conflicts can arise when different context adaptations affect the same application behavior.

3.2 Reasoning about Past Events in Context-Aware Middleware [6]

The miniaturization of computational devices like for instance mobile phones have caused a revolution in every day life. With the use of a variety of standard technologies like infrared, bluetooth and wifi, we are able to interconnect these devices in a mobile ad hoc network. These technologies bring us closer to the vision of Weiser where persons are surrounded by a cloud of small devices cooperating with each-other and adapting themselves to their context. As these small devices can go out of earshot at any moment in time, these disconnections cause important changes in the perceived contextual information. The Fact Space Model is a coordination model which gives the user fine-grained control over the effects of disconnection and thus over changes in the perceived context. However, this model does not incorporate the loss of useful information from the past. For example when we have used a service in the past, this information might even be relevant when this service is currently not available. In order to overcome the loss of useful information we have extended our Fact Space Model with temporal operators capturing exactly this relevant information an application might need in the future. In order to let applications better adapt their behaviour to the current context, we advocate the use of this logic coordination language incorporated with temporal operators.

Arguments Pro. Looking back at history is fundamentally a good idea. Looking back at what one has done is important to understand what is relevant for taking the decision of what to do now. Problems such as circular triggering of rules can be easily addressed by preprocessing/analyzing the temporal logic statements.

Arguments Contra. Using logic programming is confusing for end users because they must be able to understand how to describe the behavior of their application. The current approach generates too much mental overhead on the user that defines the rules. Finding a manner to express the rules in a more convenient way is needed. Especially the temporal operators seem unintuitive to interpret.

3.3 Context-Aware Leasing for Mobile Ad Hoc Networks [3]

Distributed memory management is substantially complicated in mobile ad hoc networks due to the fact that nodes in the network only have intermittent connectivity and often lack any kind of centralized coordination facility. Leasing provides a robust mechanism to manage reclamation of remote objects in mobile ad hoc networks. However, leasing techniques limits the lifetime of remote objects based on timeouts. In mobile networks, we also observe that devices need to continuously adapt to changes in their context. In this position paper, we argue that changes in context not only require adaptation in the behaviour of the application but also permeate to distributed memory management, leading to the concept of context-aware leasing.

Arguments Pro. The presented approach contributes to a field that has been mainly focussing on the use of timeouts. Involving context information in the memory reclamation process is interesting because it enables memory management to not only be guided by non-functional concerns but also application-specific details. Another interesting approach is to involve the user in the process of determining which remote objects may be reclaimed.

Arguments Contra. The expressiveness of the presented approach seems limited. Is it possible to use more expressive formalisms to determine whether objects can be reclaimed? The problem is that time is not an expressive means to define memory reclamation rules. Also, manual memory management strategies have been abandoned in many popular programming languages today. In this regard it seems odd that one is interested to introduce it again because it's an extra burden for the developer.

3.4 AmI: The Future Is Now [2]

Because of the unique nature of the AmI domain, specifically the high amount of industrial involvement in this area, we fear that a classical long-term scenario for the use of academic research is no longer valid. In this paper we argue that the AmI research community should adapt to this context. To do this, we consider a short-term approach, and raise some points for discussion.

Arguments Pro. It is true that in the domain of Ambient Intelligence we are not fast enough to do relevant contributions. The available manpower in academic institutes is limited compared to the available manpower in industrial projects. Another advantage found in industry is that they are focussed on "real world" problems whereas academics sometimes do not have such a focus.

Arguments Contra. The presented perspective of what happens in industrial context is too pragmatic. There are no criteria for evaluating the manner in which problems are solved. It is difficult to compare industrial to academic approaches because in an industrial approach the main goal is make things work whereas the main focus in academic research is to find better methods to make things work.

3.5 Ambient-Oriented Programming in Fractal [7]

Ambient-Oriented Programming (AmOP) comprises a suite of challenges that are hard to meet by current software development techniques. Although Component-Oriented Programming (COP) represents promising approach, the state-of-the-art component models do not provide sufficient adaptability towards specific constraints of the Ambient field. In this position paper we argue that merging AmOP and COP can be achieved by introducing the Fractal component model and its new feature: Component-Based Controlling Membranes. The proposed solution allows dynamical adaptation of component systems towards the challenges of the Ambient world.

Arguments Pro. The approach promotes separation of concerns: adaptation of the component is separated from the business code. As a consequence both the adaptation and the business code can evolve independently from one another. The adaptations are encapsulated at the membrane level. The manner in which the membrane controls the business code and how it can hook into the business code can be based on quantitative approaches found in AOP.

Arguments Contra. It is hard to support independent evolution of the business code and the adaptations because there can be composition conflicts. Furthermore, easy composition of the adaptations with the business code depends on the quality of the code. Code that has been well structured will be more easy to compose vs. code that lacks the right structures. Another issue is where to put the code that deals with multiple conflicting adaptations. This is a hard problem because of the separation of the business code and the adaptations.

3.6 Dealing with Ambient Intelligence Requirements [8]

Ambient Intelligence is characterized by a heterogeneous and highly dynamic infrastructure. In this paper we present requirements that we identified for developing applications for Ambient Intelligence scenarios. We sketch our own approach based on self-adaptive mobile processes that makes application development a manageable task and fulfills parts of these requirements.

Arguments Pro. The presented work is pragmatic because it combines several established methods to solve problems in a new field. Furthermore, the solution proposes to automate many of the individual steps. For example, the BPEL code that is being generated. Another advantage of this approach is that the code generator can be "trusted" as opposed to individual developers deploying their component in the system.

Arguments Contra. It is not clear whether it is possible to really address the intricacies of such applications at a higher level. For example, where is the development taking place? It is impossible to automate all steps in the development process. Furthermore, it is unclear how the presented model supports evolution of the code. In order to support such a system it is important to have a good mapping between high-level (models) and low-level (code) artifacts. This is especially important in the debugging phase of the application. In the debugging process it needs to be clear whether the cause of the problem is related to the code or the models.

3.7 Proximity Is in the Eye of the Beholder [1]

The notion of proximity is a key to scalable interactions in distributed systems of any kind, both natural and artificial, and in particular in pervasive computing environments. However, proximity as such is a vague notion that can be considered both in a very factual manner (spatial distance) and in a very subjective manner (user affinity). We claim that an adequate system or programming language for ambient intelligence applications ought to support an open notion of proximity, making it possible to rely on different, possibly subjective, understandings of proximity, as well as their combinations.

Arguments Pro. It is good to have a more general notion of proximity. Perhaps physical proximity can be used as a starting point for the objective dimension because physical proximity can rely on a metric system that is widely accepted. Starting from this definition the middleware or language can then support further customization and enable the introduction of other such notions.

Arguments Contra. The dimension of physical proximity is merely one case. One could argue that physical proximity is encompassed in the abstract proximity. The distinction objective vs. subjective definitions of proximity seems good. However, it is unclear whether it is possible to integrate subjective definitions and it seems much more convenient to choose one shared definition.

4   Discussion on Emerging Topics

During the afternoon brainstorm sessions three subjects were selected based on an iterative agreement process. Each participant proposed three subjects. After that three groups of three participants were formed and within these groups the participants had to agree on a single topic. The selected topics and the following breakout discussions are briefly summarized below:

4.1   Context Volatility

Group: Elisa Gonzalez Boix, Christophe Scholliers, Eline Philips, Peter Barron, Jessie Dedecker

The goal of this brainstorm session was to identify the different types of context volatility and to discuss how the software system should deal with its consequences.

Types of Context Volatility

Accuracy. Every sensor has a fault margin and can provide inaccurate readings. Ideally, readings with an unacceptable error margin should be filtered or weighed with the other readings.

Timeliness and Freshness. The frequency by which a sensor is read is important w.r.t. the freshness of the data. Some sensors require a substantial amount of time to be read and can require a substantial amount of energy. As a consequence, continuously reading the sensor is not always possible such that a tradeoff has to be made between the frequency at which a sensor is being read and the timeliness of the sensor data.

Source of Information/Trust. Sensor data delivered from third party components in a distributed context brings the risk that the data can be forged.

Concurrent Transactions in Context. Determining context based on multiple sensor sources that are not necessarily read at the same point in time implies that the determined context can be inaccurate.

Impact of Context Volatility on Software

Where is the volatility exposed? An important consideration is at what level to expose the volatility of context. A first option is to expose it at the lowest level, where the context is being derived. At this level inaccuracies and faulty readings could be filtered away by weighing the results. However, there is probably no common strategy that fits all application requirements. Another manner to deal with context volatility is to introduce context as a first-class concept in the middleware and provide hooks such that an application is exposed to the context volatility. Regarding context volatility as a first-class concept would involve exposing details such as the sensor specifications w.r.t. accuracy, the sources that were used to derive the detected context information and the sensor and the freshness of the sensor data.

How to deal with concurrent transitions in context? While context-dependent code is executing it is possible that a change in context is detected. Dealing with such concurrent adaptations is not trivial. One option is to introduce the concept of atomic adaptations and process context-dependent actions as non-interruptible events. Another option is to consider context-dependent actions from a transactional perspective. Whenever the context changes during a context-dependent action a roll back could undo previous computations before adapting to the new context.

Approaches to deal with Volatility. When dealing with context volatility at a lower level the history of sensor data becomes an important resource. The history is important because it is useful to determine what sensor data should be considered as faulty and also as a way to improve sensor readings (i.e. by weighing them against previous results). Dealing with context volatility at a higher level could be done with meta -or aspect architectures to separate the context-specific code from the base level. Other options are to use rule-based systems such as logic programming to consider multiple possible context derivations. Fuzzy logic programming could be used to explicitly consider uncertainty in the context rules.

4.2   Responsibilities for AmI Concerns in Development Chain

Group: Carlos Parra, Ales Plsek, Guillaume Dufrene, Philip Mayer

The goal of this brainstorm session was to identify the layers found in AmI infrastructure and to determine the responsibilities of each layer. For the brainstorm session a number of assumptions were made: the AmI system is a distributed system that is based on an event-messaging model and there is an established ontology for context information. The group identified five responsibility layers, which are listed below in a bottom-up order:

Communication in Ambient Environments. At the lowest level, devices are communicating via events. These events disperse observed information about the ambient environment to other devices in proximity of one another. These low-level events contain information that is retrieved from sensors deployed in the ambient environment.

Context Construction. At the next level the events containing low-level sensor information are picked up and combined into context events that are more meaningful and better match the domain of the application. At this level sensor resolution techniques can also be employed to deal with inaccurate sensor readings.

Context Reason. After the establishment of meaningful context events it becomes possible to further reason about this context information and derive the context semantics of the ambient environment.

Application (business logic). The application layer expresses the core semantics of the AmI systems and is influenced by the context reasoning engine that feeds facts about the physical environment to the application.

User. The user layer is responsible for tracking the user's preferences. This information can be either explicit or implicit. Explicit preferences are unambiguously chosen by the user whereas implicit preferences can be derived by observing a user's behavior.

4.3 On User Involvement in Adaptable Applications

Group: Carlos Noguera, Guido Sölduer, Holger Schmidt, Éric Tanter, Ellen Van Paesschen

This group discussed the issue of user involvement in adaptable applications. A lot of work is dedicated to build adaptable programs, but most of the time, this adaptation is foreseen and/or specified by the programmers. How can actual end users be involved in the adaptation process? What consequences does this have on the techniques to adopt for developing the system?

Spectrum of Involvement. User involvement in adaptation can be seen as a spectrum, with fully transparent and oblivious adaptation on one extreme, and at the other extreme, the user has to configure every adaptation explicitly. The first extreme has the disadvantage of being *obscure* for the user, while the latter is *obstrusive.* What is needed is to address a middle ground in this spectrum.

Learning. The group discussed the idea of learning in the adaptation process. First of all, when does learning actually start? It seems that just inference is not enough. From a user perspective, it is interesting that a system can learn by examples and counter-examples. This means using feedback on decisions, in order to determine whether a particular adaptation was well received by the end user. To this end, it is necessary to be able to support explicit declarations by the user. Of course, there is a tradeoff in determining what parts of adaptations can be scripted by the user, and which are not accessible.

Profiles. The group agreed that the profiles, i.e. archetypes, are a good way to abstract away minor variability scenarios by providing a set of possible coarse-grained alternatives. It was recognized that it is important to support both *user*

profiles and *application profiles*. The adaptation process then consists in matching a user profile to an application profile. Problems include: who is the best indicated to find the relevant profiles of real users of a system? how can we define archetypes in complex environments? Also, since all this is about ambient intelligence, there is a need for group-wide, collective, adaptations; in other words, *ambiental profiles*, describing typical ambiental scenarios.

Engineering. Creating adaptable systems therefore requires to consider profiles from the start. Profiles are (or are associated to) sets of transformations or extensions to apply to the system. This clearly refers to variability management, such as product line architectures, with a particular focus on runtime variability. But there are also additional engineering challenges if one wants to deliver system that are capable of "offshore learning", that is, learn new adaptations (and discover new profiles?) once they have been delivered and are used by clients in unforeseen ways and contexts.

5   Conclusion

This third edition of the OT4AmI workshop was particularly lively due to the format including group work sessions. We can see that beyond the particular details of each technical contribution discussed in the presented articles, there is a growing concern for engineering and usability issues, such as how to distribute responsibilities in the process of developing ambient applications, and how to help the user drive context adaptation. As a matter of fact, users are at the center of the ambient intelligence vision, so it is time to develop software that lets the knowledge of end users pervade through the whole system, driving adaptations in a consistent manner. This undoubtedly raises a huge number of challenges, of which only a few have been briefly touched upon during the workshop.

References

1. Barron, P., Dedecker, J., Tanter, É.: Proximity is in the eye of the beholder. In: Mügge, et al. (eds.) [4], pp. 1–6
2. Fabry, J., Noguera, C.: AmI: The future is now – a position paper. In: Mügge, et al. (eds.) [4], pp. 13–18
3. Boix, E.G., Vallejos, J., Von Cutsem, T., Dedecker, J., De Meuter, W.: Context-aware leasing for mobile ad hoc networks. In: Mügge, et al. (eds.) [4], pp. 7–12.
4. Mügge, H., Tanter, É., Cherrier, P., Dedecker, J., Lopes, C., Cebulla, M. (eds.): Proceedings of the 3rd ECOOP workshop on Object Technology for Ambient Intelligence and Pervasive Computing (OT4AmI 2007), Berlin, Germany, Technical Report 2007-12, Technische Universität Berlin (July 2007)
5. Parra, C.A., D'Hondt, M., Noguera, C., Paesschen, E.V.: Introducing context-awareness in applications by transforming high-level rules. In: Mügge, et al. (eds.) [4], pp. 19–25

6. Philips, E., Scholliers, C., Herzeel, C., Mostinckx, S.: Reasoning about past events in context-aware middleware. In: Mügge, et al. (eds.) [4], pp. 27–32
7. Plsek, A., Merle, P., Seinturier, L.: Ambient-oriented programming in Fractal. In: Mügge, et al. (eds.) [4], pp. 33–38
8. Schmidt, F., Kapitza, R., Franz, J.H.: Dealing with ambient intelligence requirements – are self-adaptive mobile processes a feasible approach? In: Mügge, et al. (eds.) [4], pp. 39–44

Pedagogies and Tools for the Teaching and Learning of Object Oriented Concepts

Report on the 11th Workshop TLOOC at ECOOP 2007

Jürgen Börstler[1] and Irit Hadar[2]

[1] Umeå University, Sweden
jubo@cs.umu.se
[2] University of Haifa, Israel
hadari@mis.haifa.ac.il

Abstract. This report summarizes the results of the eleventh workshop on pedagogies and tools for the teaching and learning of object-oriented concepts. The focus of this year's workshop was on desirable properties of examples and the usage of simple tools. The workshop gathered 17 participants, all from academia, from 7 different countries.

1 Introduction

It is generally accepted that transitioning to object-oriented development implies a paradigm shift. Compared to procedural development it requires different ways of thinking and different ways of approaching problems. Very likely, it therefore also requires a different way of teaching. Although the object-oriented paradigm has become mainstream long ago, approaches for teaching introductory programming courses are still heavily discussed [8].

Traditionally, programming concepts have been systematically introduced one after one, each building nicely on the concepts already learned. Abstract and advanced concepts, like for example modules and abstract data types, could be handled in later courses. In the object-oriented paradigm, on the other hand, the basic concepts are tightly interrelated and cannot easily be taught and learned in isolation. Furthermore, the basic object-oriented concepts are on a higher level of abstraction. Together this results in a higher threshold for the learner.

The complexity of common languages, libraries and tools add to this problem [1]. It is therefore important to share experiences and explore ideas that can help us to improve the teaching and learning of object technology.

This was the eleventh in a series of workshops on issues related to the teaching and learning of object technology. Reports from previous workshops and links to the accepted contributions of most workshops can be found at the workshop series home page[1].

The workshop format makes it possible to present and discuss actual results as well as early ideas for approaches and tools to support the teaching and learning

---

[1] http://www.cs.umu.se/research/education/ooEduWS.html

M. Cebulla (Ed.): ECOOP 2007 Workshop Reader, LNCS 4906, pp. 182–192, 2008.

of object-oriented concepts. For this year's workshop, we particularly invited submissions on the following topics:

- successfully used exercises, examples, and metaphors;
- approaches and tools for teaching (basic) object-oriented concepts;
- approaches and tools for teaching analysis and design;
- teaching analysis and design early;
- teaching outside the CS curriculum;
- experiences with innovative CS1 curricula and didactic concepts;
- learning theories and pedagogical approaches / methods;
- misconceptions related to object technology; and
- learners' views on object technology education.

2   Workshop Organization

Participation at the workshop was by invitation only. The number of participants was limited to encourage lively discussions. Potential attendees were required to submit either a full research paper or experience report, or a position paper or vision statement.

Of the contributions submitted to the workshop, seven where selected for presentation at the workshop; three for full formal presentation (30 minutes each) and four for short presentations. All accepted contributions were made available on the workshop's home page some weeks before the workshop, to give attendees the opportunity to prepare for the discussions.

All formal presentation activities were scheduled for the morning sessions to get enough time for discussions around particular questions. The full workshop program can be found in table 1.

The workshop gathered 17 participants from 7 different countries, all of them from academia. A complete list of participants together with their affiliations and e-mail addresses can be found in table 2.

3   Summary of Presentations

This section summarizes the main points of the presented papers and the main issues raised during the morning discussions. Copies of the presented papers can be obtained from the workshop's home page[2].

3.1   Short Papers

Jesse Heines (University of Masachusetts Lowell, USA) presented a GUI Programming course that focuses on the object-oriented aspects of building user and application programmer interfaces (APIs). Jesse suggested that OOP is best taught within a context of an application or software framework. Since the

---

[2] http://www.cs.umu.se/~jubo/Meetings/ECOOP07

Table 1. Workshop program

```
 9:00   Welcome and introduction
 9:15   SHORT PAPERS
        – Teaching Object-Oriented Concepts Through GUI Program-
          ming,
          Jesse Heines and Martin Schedlbauer, USA
        – Leave out the Modeling when Teaching Object-Orientation
          to Beginners,
          Axel Schmolitzky, Germany
        – "Consuming before Producing" as a Helpful Metaphor in
          Teaching Object-Oriented Concepts,
          Christian Späh and Axel Schmolitzky, Germany
        – Learners' Views on Objects-First and Objects-Later—
          Results of an Exploratory Study,
          Albrecht Ehlert and Carsten Schulte, Germany

10:30   Coffee break
11:00   FULL PAPERS
        – Teaching Classes' Relations: A Walkthrough Using UML Ar-
          row Methodology,
          Irit Hadar and Ethan Hadar, Israel
        – COINED—Collaborative Object INteraction in EDucation,
          Till Schümmer and Petra Kösters, Germany
        – Improving the Viability of Mental Models Held by Novice
          Programmers,
          Linxiao Ma, John Ferguson, Marc Roper, Murray Wood, Scotland

12:30   Lunch break
14:00   Parallel working groups
15:30   Coffee break
16:00   Parallel working groups contd.
16:30   Working group summaries and discussion
17:20   Wrap-up
17:30   Closing
```

strengths of object-orientation are not apparent in small applications, students should write relatively large programs very early to get first-hand experience of the advantages the paradigm offers. GUI programming provides a particularly effective vehicle for this purpose, because fairly large and meaningful applications can be developed by (re-)using software from various libraries or toolkits. GUI programs also offer the advantage of immediate feedback through tangible, visual results.

Axel Schmolitzky (University of Hamburg, Germany) claimed that object-oriented modeling (OOM) and object-oriented programming (OOP) should be kept clearly separate. The first year should only deal with OOP. He based his position on several observations of teaching OOP to novices over the last six years. Although programming is modeling, as seen by the teacher, for the students programming is "just" the construction of a program out of building blocks. According to Axel, modeling in any paradigm requires a basic knowledge of the building blocks and their relations in this paradigm. They therefore provide all necessary models in the first semester and let students "just" implement those models, which seems difficult enough.

Christian Späh (University of Hamburg, Germany) discussed the metaphor of "Consuming before Producing" that helped his group structuring the contents of CS1&2 courses. The basic premise of this approach is that consuming (e.g., sending a message) is much easier than producing (e.g., implementing a method), in particular when producing something for the first time. Consuming or using is an effective way to gather information, since it involves learning (this process can be unconscious). To implement this approach, Christian and colleagues have carefully defined consuming and producing "patterns" for most object-oriented concepts. By investigating relations and interactions between these patterns, more or less effective orderings of topics might be found. Experience from the University of Hamburg shows that students can more easily access topics in courses that are structured according to these ideas.

Carsten Schulte (Freie Universität Berlin, Germany) presented first results from an empirical study investigating the differences of topic order in introductory OOP courses; objects-first versus objects-later. Two courses with identical learning goals, but different sequencing of topics, were taught in parallel. Results indicate differences between the two groups regarding motivation, perception of difficulty and of relevance of different topics. Surprisingly, the objects-later group outperformed the objects-first group in the topics related to object-orientation. Few differences are, however, statistically significant.

3.2   Full Papers

Irit Hadar (University of Haifa, Israel) presented the "UML arrow methodology" for supporting the selection of the most appropriate relationships between classes in UML. The methodology defines a relationship selection process consisting of a checklist together with a list of nine guiding questions. The answer to each question (Y/N) is marked in the checklist. Depending on the answer pattern, one or more relationships are appropriate. The methodology was practised in university courses with 142 participants. Results showed that students could identify inappropriate relationships as well as required refactoring actions using the methodology. This helped students to gradually improve their designs.

Till Schümmer and Petra Kösters (FernUniversität Hagen, Germany) presented a role-based approach to foster object-oriented thinking. In particular they wanted to refrain students from developing a "centralized mindset" (see, e.g., [13]). After analyzing different approaches for teaching object interaction, they developed a tool (COINED) for engaging students in virtual object-interaction role plays. COINED is a groupware application where each student directs a set of objects and thereby reacts to messages sent to these objects. This idea very much resembles CRC-card roleplays, except that COINED supports distributed roleplays in a structured way. COINED furthermore visualizes interactions between objects. Students can even create shared artifacts. Initial experience shows that using the system helps students to better understand the roles of objects, in particular in the early stages of analysis/design.

Murray Wood (University of Strathclyde, Scotland) presented a study on a constructivist-based teaching model targeting students' mental models of reference assignment (see also [18]). Results of the study show that tight integration of program visualization with a cognitive conflict event, that highlights a student's inappropriate understanding of assignment, can help students improving their understanding of the concept. Most participants of the study (14 out of 18) successfully changed their mental model after using the proposed teaching model.

4   Working Group Discussions

For the afternoon sessions participants formed two working groups to discuss specific topics in more detail. Topic selection was done before the workshop by interacting with the participants through email to maximize the time available for discussion during the workshop.

The following subsections summarise the results of the working group discussions.

4.1   Simple Tools for the Teaching of Basic Object Oriented Concepts

This group started with dissecting the title of the topic into various aspects that where then discussed separately; simplicity, teaching, tools, and concepts.

Simplicity. What is simple and what makes a tool simple? Participants suggested that simple tools should be intuitive. The users of such a tool should not need to invest a lot conscious effort for using it. Simple tools should serve as an extension of human capabilities and act as intellectual bridges. Tools for teaching target users with initially very little or even no knowledge and skills in the particular subject. Simple tools should therefore not add unnecessary cognitive overhead, which might hinder learning. Instead, they should enable their users to achieve goals (understanding concepts, solving problems) that they would have found more difficult to achieve without these tools.

Some challenges and risks need to be considered when talking about simplicity. First, the evaluation of the degree of simplicity is subjective and highly dependent on the audience, the learning stage, and the context. There is also a risk of oversimplifying. Particularly difficult or complex content must be handled very carefully. Simply deferring or even ignoring it, may lead to misconceptions which can be difficult to resolve later [9].

The following questions should be taken into account regarding the usage of simple teaching tools: Who requires simplicity (students, teachers or tool developers)? Why do we want simplicity, i.e. what are the expected benefits? Will a simple(r) tool really make it easier to achieve the learning goals?

Teaching. With respect to teaching the group had quite different preferences and expectations regarding teaching-related characteristics of (simple) tools. An ideal teaching tool should be

- tangible and physical (Schmolitzky),
- visual (Hadar),
- enable the development of large and meaningful applications (Schedlbauer),
- create cognitive conflict to lead students from understanding to applying (Wood),
- foster discovery-based learning.

Summarizing, a "good" teaching tool should help students to solve problems or to work with concepts in a way they would not be able to without the tool.

An interesting question emerged regarding learning for understanding (focusing on knowledge) versus learning for applying (focusing on skill); which of them do we teach? Which of them should a tool support? Participants agreed that a good tool should support both. However, in reality, many teaching tools seem to focus only on one of these aspects.

Tools. One general problem with using tools for teaching and learning is distinguishing between teaching the tools and teaching with the tools. For example, a simple UML tool might support the teaching and learning of some object-oriented concepts (e.g., the different kinds of relationships between classes). However, while knowing how to work with UML is an important skill, it may not necessarily help students learning the most basic concepts. It may even interfere with learning, if taught too early (Schmolitzky).

The group concluded that different tools need to be used for different stages in the learning process. A tool that is very adequate for the introduction phase due to its simplicity, could be inappropriate later when more complex concepts are discussed. On the other hand, a tool that is very beneficial in later stages, like for example Eclipse with its many special-purpose plug-ins, may very well interfere with learning in early stages, in case its unnecessary complexity cannot be suppressed. A teaching tool must therefore always be chosen for a particular teaching/learning context. The teacher needs to make sure that the user knowledge required and the tool's complexity and level of abstraction are adequate for the specific learning environment or situation.

Concepts. One of the main problems of novices is their difficulty to think and argue at high levels of abstraction [2,5,7,16,11]. However, abstraction is a very important concept in computer science, and even more so in object-orientation. Understanding concepts, such as "object", "class", "abstract class", "encapsulation", etc. requires high abstraction skills [3]. In this discussion the group struggled with the question of how to teach object-oriented concepts given their abstract nature. To alleviate problems with high levels of abstraction, we need to find ways to make abstract concepts more concrete, for example by examples or metaphors the students can relate to, or by carefully comparing the concepts to things they already have learned.

Looking for ways to make concepts concrete, thus keeping them simple, spawned several discussion threads. The first was the question *should we teach concepts first and languages later or vice versa?* Teaching a (concrete) language first will make general concepts more concrete, at least in the sense of their applicability. For each new concept, the students will immediately implement and use it. However, this brought us back to the discussions of understanding versus applying (see subsection Teaching) and consuming before producing (see Christian's presentation). It can be doubted that learning the concrete syntax of a particular programming language really leads to a true understanding of the underlying abstract concepts; it probably leads to mere instrumental understanding of programming [22]?

Teaching (abstract) concepts first focuses on the "spirit" of concepts and its relations to other concepts, before restricting the view to limitations and approaches of a specific language. On the other hand, teaching concepts first, without a concrete language, has its own difficulties and challenges. Abstract understanding is built on the basis of vast concrete understanding and experience (see, e.g., [10,17]), which novices don't have. Taking this into consideration, how can we expect our students to really understand (abstract) concepts when they don't know how to (concretely) implement and manipulate them?

Another direction for "keeping it simple" is to reduce the number of concepts to be taught at the first stages. This requires some kind of linear ordering and prioritization of the concepts. However, most basic object-oriented concepts are highly interrelated and students have problems even with the most basic ones, like for example the differences between objects and classes [20].

4.2   Properties of "Good" Examples

The second working group approached the problem of defining desirable properties for examples from two angles; (1) by investigating possible meanings of "good" and (2) by analysing actual examples that work well according to first-hand experience of working group participants.

For the context of our discussion, we accepted a quite general interpretation of example. An example need not be an object-oriented program; it can be any problem, model, technique or metaphor that helps to support the teaching and learning of object-oriented concepts (or computer science concepts in general). We furthermore agreed, after some discussion that there are no bad examples, as long as you make clear what's bad about them [19]. Jesse pointed out that what many people call a bad example actually might be a good counter example.

Definitions of "good". Participants proposed many desirable properties of examples that, in large, did not cause any controversies (see listing below).

- An example must take care of the particular target group.
  - It must build on the student's existing knowledge [14].
  - It must be taken from a familiar application domain. An example requiring some background in Mathematics might for example work well for

Computer Science majors, but fail when teaching students with a Social Sciences background.

– An example must take care of the particular teaching and learning environment.

  • It must challenge the students, but not to a degree leading to cognitive overload (c.f. cognitive load theory [23]).
  • At least its core features must be easy to understand. This includes, in particular, sufficient and meaningful documentation.
  • The level of abstraction must be appropriate (c.f. the abstract versus concrete discussion in section 4.1).
  • It must serve a clear focus that is clear to the students and the teacher(s).

– An example must be faithful to the object-oriented paradigm.

  • Objects and classes must exemplify the ideal case, i.e. objects should actually be instantiated dynamically, actually send messages and have (non-trivial) states that can change depending on the messages they receive. If we only show exceptions to the general "rules", we cannot expect students to pick up these rules (see [6,15]).
  • An example must not violate general object-oriented guidelines, principles, or rules. Students should not be invited to acquire bad habits, when they could be avoided (see for example [12,21]).

– An example must fulfil certain general didactical criteria.

  • The example, or some story behind it, must stay in the students' minds (so they remember more easily).
  • It must always work. Since the students use examples as role models (templates) it is important that they can be reused and extended easily.
  • Examples should have some "external effect". A program with a tangible or visual effect is easier to grasp and remember than a program where all effects of computations are kept internal and invisible.

Although most properties or criteria were well understood, it was much more difficult to describe, in general terms, how examples should be constructed according to these properties or criteria. After some time, the group came to the conclusion that finding further properties does not seem meaningful, as long as they cannot be accompanied by rules that help enforcing them (as for example in [12,15,21]).

More controversies raised the discussion regarding the use and misuse of comments. Strategic comments were generally welcomed by all participants, but excessive and early use of JavaDoc (which seems to become more and more popular in introductory textbooks), should be discouraged. In some textbook examples the amount of comments makes it very difficult to "see the forest for the trees".

Examples that work. Several working group participants shared their experience with particular examples. Jesse, for example, described the "women's handbag" metaphor, which he has used successfully for many years to explain the difference between public and private. A women's most private thing is her handbag, but how do you get something out of it then? Suppose you want to borrow your mother's car, but she has her key in her handbag. How do you get it out of the handbag? According to Jesse it usually does not take long until a student comes up with the solution of taking the handbag to his or her mother and asking her to take out the key for him or her.

An example of a small application favoured by several working group participants was the Ticket-Machine example from a popular textbook [4]. This example comprises only a single class and is simple enough to be used very early in an introductory programming course. It is also faithful to the object-oriented paradigm as described in the previous subsection. Since ticket machines is a familiar domain, the example does not require any particular student background.

Axel shared a nice example for how information on the Internet can be used to compare various kinds of data types and algorithms. He uses book texts that are available on-line to demonstrate the usage of sets, for example for counting the number of words and the number of unique words in a text, respectively. Doing this in front of his class, with data from real books (e.g., Moby Dick), gives a memorable lesson for the differences in efficiency for various set implementations.

Axel and Jesse also suggested the usage of media databases. They are very familiar applications and can be used to exemplify the semantics of references and all kinds of aliasing problems. There is however one caveat when using such, more complex, examples; the larger or more complex an example, the more time must be spent introducing the the the example domain. This will take away time from the actual learning goals. Choosing a familiar example domain is therefore very important.

5   Summary and Conclusions

This was the eleventh workshop in a series of workshops on pedagogies and tools for the teaching and learning of object-oriented concepts. It gathered 17 participants, who shared experiences from a wide range of teaching contexts.

The presentations revealed that, in certain contexts, a good idea can be sufficient to solve a particular teaching/learning problem. On the other hand, huge efforts can be necessary to solve more basic problems in more general ways.

Our discussions focused mainly on "simple" tools and "good" examples and the conclusions can be summarized as follows.

- *Keep it simple.* Tools and examples should be as simple as possible, but still powerful or complex enough to facilitate doing or understanding things that would otherwise have been too difficult for the students.
- *Make it sufficiently complex.* Examples should be as simple as possible, but not simplistic. Many advantages of the object-orientation paradigm require a certain amount of complexity to become apparent. Example programs need therefore be sufficiently complex to reveal these advantages.
- *Make sure it suits your students.* There are no "one size fits all" tools and examples; they must be carefully chosen with respect to student background and prerequisite knowledge.

- *Make abstract concepts concrete, but don't stay at the concrete level.* Abstract concepts are easier to understand when they are made concrete. However, when staying at a concrete level throughout, students will only get an instrumental understanding of the subject.
- *Don't reinvent the wheel.* There are numerous tools and examples "out there" that have been successfully applied in a wide range of settings. However, when reusing a tool or example make sure to evaluate the context of its use (see 'make sure it fits your students').

Table 2. List of workshop participants

Name	Affiliation	E-mail Address
Jürgen Börstler	*Umeå University, Sweden*	jubo@cs.umu.se
Albrecht Ehlert	*Oberstufenzentrum Informationstechnik Berlin, Germany*	ehlert@oszimt.de
Irit Hadar	*University of Haifa, Israel*	hadari@mis.haifa.ac.il
Jesse Heines	*University of Masachusetts Lowell, USA*	heines@cs.uml.edu
Petra Kösters	*FernUniversität Hagen, Germany*	petra.koesters@fernuni-hagen.de
Boriss Mejass	*Université Catholique de Louvain, Belgium*	boriss.mejas@uclouvain.be
Peter Osburg	*Hasso-Platter-Institute, Germany*	peter.osburg@hpi.uni-potsdam.de
Michael Perscheid	*Hasso-Platter-Institute, Germany*	michael.perscheid@hpi.uni-potsdam.de
Daniela Rose	*TU Berlin, Germany*	dani.rose@web.de
Wilfried Rupflin	*University of Dortmund, Germany*	wr@irb.cs.uni-dortmund.de
Martin Schedlbauer	*University of Masachusetts Lowell, USA*	mschedlb@cs.uml.edu
Axel Schmolitzky	*University of Hamburg, Germany*	schmolitzky@acm.org
Carsten Schulte	*Freie Universität Berlin, Germany*	schulte@inf.fu-berlin.de
Till Schümmer	*FernUniversitat Hagen, Germany*	till.schuemmer@fernuni-hagen.de
Christian Späh	*University of Hamburg, Germany*	christian.spaeh@blue-flat.de
Mariann Unterluggauer	*ORF, Austria*	unterluggauer@orf.at
Murray Wood	*University of Strathclyde, Scotland*	murray.wood@cis.strath.ac.uk

References

1. ACM Java Task Force: Java Task Force materials, Version 1.0 (2006) (accessed 2006-10-05), http://jtf.acm.org/index.html
2. Aharoni, D., Leron, U.: Abstraction is Hard in Computer-Science too. In: Proceedings of the 21st Conference of the International Group for the Psychology of Mathematics Education, vol. 3, pp. 2-9–2-16 (1997)
3. Armstrong, D.J.: The Quarks of Object-Oriented Development. Communications of the ACM 49(2), 123–128 (2006)
4. Barnes, D.J., Kölling, M.: Objects First with Java ŨA Practical Introduction using BlueJ. Prentice-Hall, Englewood Cliffs (2006)
5. Berge, O., Borge, R.E., Fjuk, A., Kaasbøll, J., Samuelsen, T.: Learning Object-Oriented Programming. In: Proceeding Norsk Informatikkonferanse (NIK), pp. 37–47 (2003)
6. Börstler, J.: Improving CRC-Card Role Play with Role-Play Diagrams. In: Companion to the 20th Conference on Object-Oriented Programming Systems, Languages, and Applications, pp. 356–364 (2005)

7. Bucci, P., Long, T.J., Weide, B.W.: Do We Really Teach Abstraction. In: Proceedings of the 32nd SIGCSE Technical Symposium on Computer Science Education, pp. 26–30 (2001)
8. Bruce, K.: Controversy on How to Teach CS 1: A Discussion on the SIGCSE-members Mailing List. SIGCSE Bulletin – Inroads 36(4), 29–35 (2004)
9. Clancy, M.: Misconceptions and attitudes that infere with learning to program. In: Fincher, S., Petre, M. (eds.) Computer Science Education Research, pp. 85–100. Taylor & Francis, Abington (2004)
10. Dubinsky, E.: Reflective Abstraction in Advanced Mathematical Thinking. In: Tall, D. (ed.) Advanced Mathematical Thinking, pp. 95–123. Kluwer, Netherlands (2001)
11. Fleury, A.E.: Encapsulation and Reuse as Viewed by Java Students. In: Proceedings of the 32nd SIGCSE Technical Symposium on Computer Science Education, pp. 189–194 (2001)
12. Fowler, M.: Refactoring: Improving the Design of Existing Code. Addison-Wesley, Reading (1999)
13. Guzdial, M.: Centralized Mindset: A Student Problem with Object-Oriented Programming. In: Proceedings of the 26th SIGCSE Technical Symposium on Computer Science Education, pp. 182–185 (1995)
14. Hadjerrouit, S.: A Constructivist Approach to Object-Oriented Design and Programming. In: Proceedings of the 4th Conference on Innovation and Technology in Computer Science Education, pp. 171–174 (1999)
15. Holland, S., Griffiths, R., Woodman, M.: Avoiding Object Misconceptions. In: Proceedings of the 28th SIGCSE Technical Symposium on Computer Science Education, pp. 131–134 (1997)
16. Holmboe, C.: A cognitive framework for knowledge in informatics: The case of Object-Orientation. In: Proceedings of the 4th Conference on Innovation and Technology in Computer Science Education, pp. 17–20 (1999)
17. Leron, U.: Abstraction Barriers in Mathematics and Computer Science. In: Proceedings of the 3rd International Conference for Logo and Mathematics Education (1987)
18. Ma, L., Ferguson, J., Roper, M., Wood, M.: Investigating the Viability of Mental Models Held by Novice Programmers. In: Proceedings of the 38th SIGCSE Technical Symposium on Computer Science Education, pp. 499–503 (2007)
19. Malan, K., Halland, K.: Examples that Can do Harm in Learning Programming. In: Companion to the 19th Conference on Object-Oriented Programming Systems, Languages, and Applications, pp. 83–87 (2004)
20. Ragonis, N., Ben Ari, M.: A long-term investigation of the comprehension of OOP concepts by novices. Computer Science Education 15(3), 203–221 (2005)
21. Riel, A.: Object-Oriented Design Heuristics. Addison-Wesley, Reading (1996)
22. Skemp, R.R.: Relational Understanding and Instrumental Understanding. Mathematics Teaching 77, 20–26 (1976)
23. Sweller, J., van Merriënboer, J., Paas, F.: Cognitive Architecture and Instructional Design. Educational Psychology Review 10(3), 251–296 (1998)

Refactoring Tools
Report on the 1st Workshop WRT at ECOOP 2007

Danny Dig[1], Ralph Johnson[1], Frank Tip[2], Oege De Moor[3], Jan Becicka[4],
William G. Griswold[5], and Markus Keller[6]

[1] Department of Computer Science,
University of Illinois at Urbana-Champaign
{dig,johnson}@cs.uiuc.edu
https://netfiles.uiuc.edu/dig/www
[2] IBM T.J. Watson Research Center
ftip@us.ibm.com
[3] Oxford University Computing Laboratory
oege@comlab.ox.ac.uk
[4] Sun Microsystems
Jan.Becicka@sun.com
[5] Department of Computer Science and Engineering
University of California - San Diego
wgg@cs.ucsd.edu
[6] Rational Zurich Research Lab
markus.keller@ch.ibm.com

Abstract. WRT'07 was the first instance of the Workshop on Refactoring Tools. It was held in Berlin, Germany, on July 31st, in conjunction with ECOOP'07. The workshop brought together over 50 participants from both academia and industry. Participants include the lead developers of two widely used refactoring engines (Eclipse and NetBeans), researchers that work on refactoring tools and techniques, and others generally interested in refactoring. WRT'07 accepted 32 submissions, however, it was impossible to present all these submissions in one single day. Instead, in the morning session we started with a few technical presentations, followed by large group discussions around noon, a poster session and small group discussions in the afternoon. WRT'07 ended with a retrospective session and unanimous consensus to organize another session in the future.

1 Objectives and Call for Participation

Refactoring is the process of applying behavior-preserving transformations to a program with the objective of improving the programs design [5]. A specific refactoring is identified by a name (e.g., Extract Method), a set of preconditions, and a set of specific transformations that need to be performed. Tool support for refactoring is highly desirable because checking the preconditions for a given refactoring often requires nontrivial program analysis, and applying the transformations may affect many locations in the program. In recent years, the emergence

M. Cebulla (Ed.): ECOOP 2007 Workshop Reader, LNCS 4906, pp. 193–202, 2008.
© Springer-Verlag Berlin Heidelberg 2008

of light-weight programming methodologies such as Extreme Programming has generated a great amount of interest in refactoring, and refactoring support has become a required feature in modern-day IDEs. Until now, there has not been a suitable forum for discussions among researchers and developers of such tools. Therefore, we propose to organize a full-day workshop at ECOOP07 on refactoring tools with a strongly practical focus. We plan to invite developers and researchers in the field of refactoring to submit presentations and demonstration proposals about practical refactoring tools.

1.1   Call for Papers

There is a great deal of interest in the development of tool support for refactoring. However, researchers and tool vendors rarely work together. This forum will enable the transfer of ideas and expertise in both ways: researchers can show the state-of-the-art analyses they are using in developing tool support for refactoring while tool vendors can offer valuable insights on the challenges of scaling such analyses for realistic applications. By bringing together the researchers and tool vendors, we can shorten the time to embody ideas into production systems. In addition, by making researchers aware of what others are working on, the potential for reinventing the wheel is greatly reduced while the potential for creative collaboration is greatly enhanced. This workshop is the next step in our effort to create such a community, the first step being the creation of a refactoring research web portal (http://refactoring.info).

Potential topics are those related to refactoring tools including, but not restricted to:

- refactoring engines
- improving the usability of existing refactoring engines
- program analyses for refactoring tools
- tools for detecting applied refactorings
- tools for suggesting refactorings (e.g., detecting code-smells)
- testing and verification of refactoring tools
- language-independent refactoring tools
- refactoring tools for non-OO languages (e.g., functional languages, aspect-oriented, etc.)

2   Organizers, Participants, and Accepted Papers

2.1   Organizers

- Danny Dig (chair and primary organizer), University of Illinois at Urbana-Champaign, dig@cs.uiuc.edu
- Ralph Johnson, University of Illinois at Urbana-Champaign, johnson@cs.uiuc.edu
- Frank Tip, IBM T.J. Watson Research Center, ftip@us.ibm.com
- Oege de Moor, Oxford University Computing Laboratory, oege@comlab.ox.ac.uk

- Jan Becicka, NetBeans Refactoring Engine, Sun Microsystems, Jan.Becicka@sun.com
- William G. Griswold, University of California at San Diego, wgg@cs.ucsd.edu
- Markus Keller, Eclipse Refactoring Engine, IBM, markus.keller@ch.ibm.com

2.2   Participants

- Malte Appeltauer
- Thomas Baar
- Jan Becicka
- Andrew P. Black
- Serge Demeyer
- Danny Dig
- Bassem Elkarablieh
- Yishai Feldman
- Tammo Freese
- Robert Fuhrer
- Christian Hammer
- Zoltn Horvth
- Petr Hrebejk
- Maha Idrissi Aouad
- Ralph Johnson
- Nicolas Juillerat
- Douglas Kirk
- Ondrej Lhotak
- Chuan-kai Lin
- Carlos Lpez
- Laszlo Lovei
- Slavisa Markovic
- Ral Marticorena
- Philip Mayer
- Andreas Meissner
- Tom Mens
- Kim Mens
- Dirk Mller
- Helmut Neukirchen
- Carlos Noguera
- Javier Perez
- Jürgen Reuter
- Romain Robbes
- Wilfried Rupflin
- Gregor Snelting
- Sergio Soares
- Gabriele Taentzer
- Frank Tip
- Luigi Troiano

- Shmuel Tyszberowicz
- Guido Wachsmuth
- Dietmar Winkler
- Petr Zalac
- Benjamin Zeiss

2.3 Accepted Papers

WRT'07 asked for short position papers (2-pages). The interested reader can find the 32 accepted papers published as a technical report [3] or on the workshop's webpage [9].

3 Organization

Due to the large number of accepted submissions (32), the Program Committee decided not to have a traditional technical paper presentation, but rather to engage the participants in several discussions. The PC selected a few papers for presentation in the plenary session. These are papers that are representative and have the potential to steer discussions among participants. The interested reader can find the slides of these talks on the workshop's webpage [9].

To engage the participants, we designed two sessions for large group discussions. These sessions took place immediately before, respectively after, the lunch break.

In the afternoon session, we designed a poster session, followed by small group discussions based on common topics of interest. We concluded the event with a retrospective of the day.

3.1 Short Presentations

The presenters in this category had 15 minutes for presentation followed by 5 minutes of Q&A. The developers of Eclipse and NetBeans refactoring engines were allowed 25 minutes for presentation and 10 minutes for discussion with the audience. Next we give a short summary of each presentation, the * symbol denotes the presenter.

Presentations by developers of Eclipse and NetBeans refactoring engines

Advanced Refactoring in Eclipse: Past, Present, and Future. Adam Kiezun, Robert M. Fuhrer*, Markus Keller. The Eclipse developers led us through the history of the development and maturity of the refactoring APIs in Eclipse. The first refactorings in Eclipse were implemented as text manipulation transformations. The refactoring infrastructure evolved into the AST rewriter framework, while the program analyses used for checking preconditions became more sophisticated (e.g., using type-constraints analysis [6]). The next step was the inclusion of refactoring infrastructure in the Language Toolkit (LTK) which allows others to write their own refactorings. The infrastructure was further refactored to allow others to extend the existing refactorings in the engine using the processor-participants architecture. The more recent development efforts were focused toward supporting the new language features in Java 1.5, supporting collaboration among large teams (e.g., through recording-and-replaying refactorings across different workspaces). The developers of the Eclipse refactoring engine outlined some directions for future development: *composable* refactorings opening the road for user-defined refactorings, new classes of refactorings, and supporting the increasing mixture of languages.

Using Java 6 Compiler as a Refactoring and an Analysis Engine. Jan Becicka*, Petr Hrebejk*, Petr Zajac. The NetBeans developers presented the refactoring APIs in NetBeans refactoring engine. Since the NetBeans IDE and the Java language is developed by the same company (Sun Microsystems, Inc), the refactoring APIs in NetBeans use exactly the same program elements that the 'javac' compiler uses. The NetBeans APIs complement the javac APIs with utility methods for searching and manipulating the AST program elements. The NetBeans developers concluded with presenting the Codeviation project. The Codeviation project has many goals: to assist the developers by suggesting what should be refactored, to asses whether a refactoring initiative was successful, to inspect arbitrary builds by combining a suite of metrics and analysis tools, and to integrate refactorings with Version Control Systems and Bug-tracking systems.

Research Presentations

Code Analyses for Refactoring by Source Code Patterns and Logical Queries. Daniel Speicher, Malte Appeltauer*, Gnter Kniesel. The authors are addressing a well known problem in the refactoring community: the program analysis for refactoring needs to be based on solid formalism, therefore, it can be complex. Currently, there is a big gap between the formalism and its implementation. The authors advocate that logic-based program analysis bridges this gap between specification and implementation of refactoring preconditions. However, the developers that want to implement new refactorings need to learn a new meta-level program representation which does not resemble the familiar program abstractions. The authors propose a new language, *GenTL*, which is a generic language for transformations; it has a concrete syntax resembling the program abstractions that a Java developer is already familiar with. The authors concluded by showing how they used GenTL to express the analysis for a complex refactoring, namely the one that replaces concrete types of method arguments with the most general supertypes [7].

Refactoring Functional Programs at the University of Kent. Huiqing Li, Simon Thompson*, Chris Brown, Claus Reinke. Refactoring became popular as a topic of research and as a practice within the OO community (first in Smalltalk, then in Java). Thompson's presentation was interesting because it presented the design and implementation of two refactoring engines for functional languages, Haskell and Erlang. The presenter focused on some of the unique challenges that stem from the differences between functional languages and OO languages: values not variables, expressions not assignments, functions as data, rich data and types, controlled side-effects, the semantics of a program are sensitive to the layout of the program (in Haskell), declarative descriptions of refactorings. The presenter quickly described HaRE, a refactoring engine for Haskell, and Wrangler, a refactoring engine for Erlang. Both these engines are integrated with emacs and gvim. The presenter concluded by talking about various design decisions regarding the integration of their refactoring engines with the IDEs and with other tools (e.g., makefiles, test generation tools).

Visual interface for type-related refactorings. Philip Mayer*, Andreas Meibner, Friedrich Steimann. The authors classify the type-related refactorings into 'lightweight' refactorings (e.g., the 'extract interface' refactoring) that do not require much input from the user, and 'heavyweight' refactorings (e.g., the 'use supertype where possible' refactoring) where the analysis is very involved, requires some help from the user, and can produce unpredictable results. Developers have a tendency to avoid the heavyweight refactorings because these refactorings are hard to control/parameterize, and the developers do not feel 'in control'. The authors propose to separate the analysis part from the transformation part and to bring the user back in control. Their tool allows the user to visualize the resulting type hierarchy obtained as the outcomes of different type-related refactorings. In addition, the tool might suggest some other type-related refactorings.

3.2 Large Group Discussions

To 'break the ice' for some large group brainstorming, we used two short presentations.

LAN Simulation: A refactoring teaching example. Serge Demeyer*. The author presented a Software Engineering lab session designed to teach refactoring principles. The author uses a pre-cooked LAN simulation implementation [1] to introduce the notion of 'bad smells' and the ever changing requirements for new features.

This presentation was followed by a large group brainstorming on **How to teach refactoring effectively**. Several participants agreed that students are not likely to learn refactoring unless they were 'forced' in a situation where the code grew as a clumsy codebase. Students are more likely to learn when they 'feel the pain' of poorly written code. Ralph Johnson suggested that students should start their Software Engineering education not with a brand new project, but rather by continuing a project that somebody else developed. This forces the student to refactor the code in order to understand it.

Several other topics were raised: when is the right time to teach refactoring principles (in the introductory programming courses vs. advanced software engineering courses), how to teach refactoring in industry, etc.

Why Don't People Use Refactoring Tools. Andrew Black*, Emerson Murphy-Hill.
The author's main thesis is that there are two kinds of refactoring processes: the
'floss refactoring' and the 'root canal refactoring'. The floss refactorings refer
to a state where programmers refactor constantly to maintain healthy software;
refactoring is interleaved with other programming tasks. The root canal refactoring refers to the state where programmers refactor in clumps to fix unhealthy
software; programming and refactoring are two distinct activities. The authors
suggest that the reason why not everybody uses refactoring tools is because the
current research on refactoring is favoring the root canal refactorings, rather
than the floss refactorings. By observing hundreds of software developers, the
authors conclude that most refactorings were performed in the floss process.

This presentation was followed by a large group discussion on **Why aren't
refactoring engines used more often**. Several answers were given to this
question: obscure textual error messages in case that a refactoring precondition
fails, hard to select code as input to the tools, poorly designed user interfaces,
users not trusting the correctness of the refactoring engine. For the providers of
the refactoring engines it still remains an open question on how much analysis
should a refactoring engine perform: too much analysis is slow and disrupts the
user, too little analysis is fast but can produce unsafe results.

3.3   Small Group Discussions

After the poster presentation session, the large audience was split into small
groups based on common interests. Each small group delegated a presenter that
summarized the findings of the group: what are the main problems/challenges
within their topic area, what is the state of the art solutions, and what needs to
be done next.

Refactoring and API Evolution
Problems identified:

- Culture of no-change (especially when the organization has 'critical mass'
  customers)
- Granularity of API changes (small, frequent changes vs. large, infrequent
  changes)
- Too high cost associated with maintaining multiple versions of the API
- Lack of documentation of deprecated APIs
- No access to application code that uses the APIs

State-of-the-practice and state-of-the-art:

- Deprecated APIs
- Wrappers
- Several levels for marking stability/instability of APIs
- Migration user guide manuals
- Record and replay of refactorings
- Automated detection of refactorings (e.g., see [2,8]

- Merging component and application refactorings (e.g., see [4])
- Automated generation of compatibility adapters

  What needs to be done next:

- Behavioral (not only structural) API changes
- Automated classification of API changes
- Automatic patching of bytecodes

Program Representation for Refactorings
Problems identified:

- Scalability
- Comments, annotations, layout, support for literate programming
- Hybrid of languages and embeddings
- Macro-processors

Suggesting Refactorings
Challenges identified:

- Agree on areas of bad design
- Need for common repository of test systems
- Need better integration with analysis tools
- In what form to present the suggestions to the user

Model-driven software refactoring
Challenges identified:

- What does 'behavior preservation' mean in the context of refactoring the models?
- How to define the model quality
- Generic refactorings for domain-specific modeling languages

Refactoring for non OO languages
Refactoring is similar for any language, but each language seems to require its own tools.

  Challenges:

- Building tools for each language
- Reusable infrastructure for building tools
- Refactoring systems built from several languages

3.4   Retrospective

At the end of the day, the audience unanimously agreed to organize another session in the future. Therefore, we concluded the workshop with a retrospective of the whole event. We wanted to learn what are the things that worked well and we should keep doing in the future, what are the things that did not work well and we should do differently in the future, what are the things that still puzzle us (things for which we do not have a good answer).

Things that worked well

- Many participants (both industry and academia)
- Posters
- Small group discussions on special themes
- Short 1-slide introductions
- Everybody liked the presentations from Eclipse and NetBeans
- The program was kept on schedule

Things to do differently next time

- More time for presentation slots
- Multiple, *non-overlapping* small groups
- Allocate time for demos of the tools
- Submission format should be a standard one (ACM templates)
- Need more time for the industry refactoring engines
- Ask industry refactoring developers to give tutorials
- 1-slide intros need headshots

Things that still puzzle us

- Should this be a one- or two-day event?
- Should we organize this as a separate refactoring conference?
- Is the poster session really useful?

4   Concluding Remarks

Refactoring is still a young field. Most work on refactoring has been done for one language (Java). Some programmers are enthusiastic users of refactoring tools, others ignore them. Even enthusiastic users see many ways to improve the tools. Refactoring tools are needed for every language. They need to be easier to use, more powerful, and easier to develop. Refactoring tools will improve for many years, so this is probably only the first in a long line of workshops.

The webpage [9] contains the slides, the proceedings, and the schedule of the workshop. This webpage might change in the future, but it will be always accessible from http://refactoring.info

References

1. Demeyer, S., Van Rysselberghe, F., Gîrba, T., Ratzinger, J., Marinescu, R., Mens, T., Du Bois, B., Janssens, D., Ducasse, S., Lanza, M., Rieger, M., Gall, H., El-Ramly, M.: The LAN-simulation: A Refactoring Teaching Example. In: Proceedings of International Workshop on Principles of Software Evolution, pp. 123–134. IEEE Computer Society Press, Los Alamitos (2005)
2. Dig, D., Comertoglu, C., Marinov, D., Johnson, R.: Automatic detection of refactorings in evolving components. In: Thomas, D. (ed.) ECOOP 2006. LNCS, vol. 4067, pp. 404–428. Springer, Heidelberg (2006)

3. Dig, D., Cebulla, M. (eds.): 1st workshop on refactoring tools (wrt 2007). Technical Report ISSN 1436-9915, Technical University of Berlin (July 2007)
4. Dig, D., Manzoor, K., Johnson, R., Nguyen, T.N.: Refactoring-aware Configuration Management for Object-Oriented Programs. In: Proceedings of International Conference on Software Engineering, pp. 427–436. IEEE Computer Society Press, Los Alamitos (2007)
5. Fowler, M., Beck, K., Brant, J., Opdyke, W., Roberts, D.: Refactoring: Improving the Design of Existing Code. Adison-Wesley, London (1999)
6. Tip, F.: Refactoring using type constraints. In: Riis Nielson, H., Filé, G. (eds.) SAS 2007. LNCS, vol. 4634, pp. 1–17. Springer, Heidelberg (2007)
7. Tip, F., Kiezun, A., Bauemer, D.: Refactoring for generalization using type constraints. In: OOPSLA 2003. Proceedings of Object-oriented programing, systems, languages, and applications, pp. 13–26. ACM Press, New York (2003)
8. Weissgerber, P., Diehl, S.: Identifying refactorings from source-code changes. In: ASE 2006. Proceedings of the 21st IEEE/ACM International Conference on Automated Software Engineering, pp. 231–240. IEEE Computer Society Press, Los Alamitos (2006)
9. WRT 2007 homepage, http://netfiles.uiuc.edu/dig/RefactoringWorkshop

Author Index

Lecture Notes in Computer Science

Sublibrary 2: Programming and Software Engineering

For information about Vols. 1– 4279
please contact your bookseller or Springer